THE ENCYCLOPEDIA OF SAUCES FOR YOUR FOOD

Publisher: Marcus Kimberly Publishing

Copy Editor: Joan Packard
Cover Design: Lisa Bacchini
Illustrations: Kimberly L. Bellissimo
Typography: Kathie Nute, Western Type

ISBN 1-879743-02-7

Library of Congress Catalogue in Publication Number: 96-09814
Author: Charles A. Bellissino
THE ENCYCLOPEDIA OF SAUCES FOR YOUR FOOD ·
Includes indices.

Ist Printing, May 1997

Other Books By Charles A. Bellissino:
THE ENCYCLOPEDIA OF SAUCES FOR YOUR PASTA

DEDICATION

To Chef John, my first tutor, who in 1961 answered my question "What must I learn to become a great cook?", with a single word…, Sauces.

ACKNOWLEDGMENTS

Over the past thirty-five years I have received wonderful recipes from a variety of sources, including but not limited to the following: Chefs I have known and worked with who willingly shared their recipes; Restaurateurs; The National Pork Producers Council, Des Moines, Iowa; The National Dairy Board; The National Cattlemen's Beef Association, Chicago, Illinois; Foster Farms, Livingston, California; The Agricultural Extension Services of the University of California at Davis; Sunkist Growers, Inc.; The Onion Growers of Texas, Washington and California; The Italian Trade Commission, NY, NY; The Spanish Institute for Foreign Trade.

Additional support and encouragement to write the book came from friends, customers and family. I am particularly grateful for the encouragement from Frank Jakubka, tasting room manager for the Kunde Winery, Sonoma Valley, Kenwood, California; Charley Spinetta, vintner and owner of the Charles Spinetta Winery, Amador County, Plymouth, California and especially my daughter Kimberly, who's gentle prodding brought to the fire the need for the book and who believes her Dad can do anything.

I wish to express my gratitude to the people whose genuine efforts turned my ideas into hard copy. While writing the book I have had marvelous input from friends and family who had the opportunity to eat the foods and sauces I prepared. A great deal of help and encouragement came from my children, Marcus and Kimberly. Whenever they sampled a new sauce I had made, they would say, "Keep this one Dad", or the phrase I never really wanted to hear, "Lose that recipe Dad". To Megan Myron, who suffered a burglary of her home in which she lost not only many of her household possessions, but her computer and all her discs, which included most of this book. In spite of that, she managed to format the book on a borrowed computer from my archaic floppies to an acceptable conditions for my typographer, Kathie Nute of Western Type. And a special THANK YOU, goes to my wonderful editor, Joan Packard, who while maintaining a full-time private practice, part-time involvement in a volunteer organization and remodeling her home, put in many, many hours editing the manuscript. In spite of the fact that she discarded many of my best lines and funniest comments, she is my companion and greatest friend.

INTRODUCTION

Chef John's suggestion that I learn to master sauces was a good one. Thirty years later, (I don't rush into things) further encouragement came from the owner of an upscale kitchen supply store, who was doing an outstanding job of selling my first book "The Encyclopedia of Sauces for Your Pasta". His customers frequently requested a book that dealt with sauces in general. He passed that information on to me and therein lies the reason for writing this book.

My grandmother was the first person to school me in the mysteries of making marvelous pasta sauces. I was twelve years old. No one, not even my American-Hungarian mother (who was a wonderful cook) could make pasta sauce the way my grandmother could. So on Sundays, I hopped on a bus and traveled the fifteen miles to my grandmothers house. Not exactly "over the river and through the woods", but close. Well it didn't take me very long to realize that I needed to learn how to do it myself, or permanently give up my weekends. That was when I got her wonderful pasta sauce recipes in writing, which then became the basis of my lifetime interest in collecting and cooking recipes, particularly sauce recipes.

My commercial involvement with food started with the past-time jobs I held while attending Primary and Junior High school (work permits were not required back in the 40's). Early in the morning, around 4:00 A.M., I would rise and shine (I'm not so sure about the shine part) hop on my bike and make a bee-line down to a large bakery in my neighborhood. Drivers busy with paperwork and routing would pay eager youngsters, like me, a buck or so to load their delivery trucks with cakes, pies, rolls, cupcakes and bread(this was during the days of door to door delivery).

On Saturdays a driver would often take me along to be his "runner" (one loaf of white bread, four cupcakes and an apple pie for Mrs. Smith) and away I ran…, all day long. In return I got breakfast, lunch and several dollars pay for my efforts. I thought it was great! I did similar loading and legwork for a nearby dairy when I tired of loading the bread. I also worked in a bakery after school, where I learned a great deal about cleanliness in the kitchen, I worked for an old German baker who would say to me, often, "Sharly, make schure you use lots of hot und zoapy vater und scrub zem sheet pans schparkling clean!" That was before I scraped, swept and mopped the kitchen floor! This education in food service led me to realize that while it may be a labor of love for many, is also hard work and long hours for some.

Not one to let experience deter me, I re-entered the food industry shortly after my discharge from the Marine Corps in 1954. My first job was as a salesman for a food broker in Cleveland where I sold Stokley-Van Camp products. From there I joined up with Beechnut Products, selling their baby food line. In early 1960 I decided I need a change, so I moved from Ohio to California. It was a good move, but not the right time. 1960 in California, was a period of high unemployment. I tried selling air-time for a rock and roll AM station in Sacramento while simultaneously holding a part-time disc jockey position at an FM radio station and going to college at night. The AM station was sold, the new owners fired everybody, including me.

That's when I entered civil service work, the most frustrating and unproductive period of my work life. The government has an interesting term they use when they end a major project and let everyone go. They call it a "reduction in force". I, and about five hundred others, was "RIF-ted" out. It was then that food service work began looking good. So I got a job as an assistant

transport. When the horsemen became hungry, they only needed to reconstitute the meat in a little hot water, or pulverize it and eat on the run.

As stews of meats and vegetables gave way other forms of preparation (spit cooking broiling and grilling) that developed a desire to flavor food differently — voila — the development of more complex sauces! So in addition to the major role of sauces as stated above, their specific role is to dress up your food, dazzle the taste buds and make the dish more pleasing to the eye. The Encyclopedia of Sauces for Your Food lets you do all those things and more. The preparation of food involves your creativeness and your feelings and the purpose is to create a series of highlights in the lives of those you feed. It not only creates a comfort zone that we can fall back upon at any moment in time, but also creates experiences that we can and do cherish throughout our lives. What you prepare in the kitchen is in reality an expression of your love. Buono Appetito!

manager of a large restaurant chain. Their policy required me to spend my first six weeks working in the kitchen with the chef, who also became my first tutor, Chef John. That job led to a substantial portion of the recipes in my collection that make up the body of the book. I spent ten years in food service, as a restaurateur and independent food broker and over fifty years collecting and developing recipes.

In writing the book I have drawn extensively from my Italian-Hungarian heritage. I feel very fortunate to have had grandparents who came from two countries recognized throughout much of the world for their outstanding cuisine. In addition I benefited greatly from the background of so many of my friends who had foreign born parents. After the close of World War II, my high school staged a folk pageant annually where students representing 28 ethnic groups dressed in their native costumes, presented dances and the music of their heritage. The point of this story is that when I had the opportunity to eat at friend's home there was a world of tastes and flavors for me to sample. They were experiences that not only broadened my outlook on food, but exposed me to a great variety of sauces. Other sources of recipes and information, especially those from Texas and Louisiana, are from neighbors and people that I have worked with during the ten years I spent in radio and television broadcasting.

I use my love of history and etymology (the study of words) to embellish the explanations accompanying many of the recipes. So in addition to the ingredients, you'll find history and language trivia sprinkled liberally throughout the text.

Cooks have used sauce to improve the food they've prepared for at least several thousand years. In fact one of the worlds first major recipe collections lists over 175 sauces. It was written by a wealthy Roman gourmet named Apicius, during the first century A.D. (And by the way, an updated version of his book is available today.) One of the likely reasons sauces came about was to add interest to their bland diets. There is a bit of kitchen wisdom that says: "No matter how good something may be, if you only know one way to prepare it, it becomes very tiresome". That's as true as anything ever said. So simple sauce took on a major role in food preparation very early on, when nomads settled in one place and became farmers. That allowed them to eat foods that had not been available to them while constantly on the move. Wild game was slowly replaced by domesticated animals and a stable source of grains, fruits, nuts and vegetables became the basis of their cooking and that encouraged the development of sauces.

I read a story sometime ago that the Magyars, tribes of marauding, pillaging, hard riding, fast moving, well structured and disciplined horsemen, would sometimes wrap freshly butchered and salted meat in sheep skin and then put it on, or under their saddle, to be tenderized by the days journey. If they had more time, they would cook the meat until it was quite dry. Then it was placed on a sheepskin, or a fur coat (skins side up) in the sun light for several days until it was completely dried (an early version of jerky). Then it was packaged in sheep stomachs for

Contents

Chapter 4

Sauces And Gravies For Beef

Chapter 5

Sauces And Gravies For Pork

Chapter 6

Sauces And Gravies For Veal

Chapter 7

Sauces And Gravies For Lamb Or Mutton

Chapter 8

Sauces For Game And Game Birds

Chapter 17

Sauces For Invertebrates

Chapter 18

Sauces For Variety Meats

Chapter 19

Barbecue Sauces (aka: BBQ)

Chapter 20

Sauces For Egg Dishes

Chapter 21

Sauces For Sandwich Fillings

CHAPTER 26

DRESSINGS AND SAUCES TO BE SERVED OVER OR WITH SALADS

CHAPTER 27

SAUCES FOR CREPES AND OTHER PANCAKES

CHAPTER 28

FLAVORED BUTTERS

CHAPTER 29

SAUCES FOR HOT OR COLD VEGETABLE DISHES

Chapter 30

Relish Type Sauces To Be Used As Dips

Chapter 31

Sauces For Fruit

Chapter 32

Sauces To Be Served Over / Under Or With Desserts

Chapter 33

Dry Mixes And Wet Sauces

SAUCES FOR YOUR FOOD

SAUCES AND THE THINGS THEY DO!

Sauces add such a wonderful touch to so many of the foods you eat and it is early impossible to cook without knowing how to prepare a selection of them. More importantly for the novice, or the experienced cook who has goofed, they provide a great cover-up for your mistakes.

Perhaps you have a sauce or two committed to memory. One you can whip up to pour on something or other. But in the world of cookery, there are hundreds upon hundreds of sauces that are used. Consider the number of dressings you've had on a salad, or the number of times you've reached for a sauce like mayonnaise, ketchup or mustard. There is a very impressive assortment of sauces that you eat during any given day. I'm sure that on more than one occasion you've scrambled to find the right sauce to serve with something. In "The Encyclopedia of Sauces for Your Food" you now have them all at your fingertips.

Well almost all, there is one exception to this list - - - pasta sauces. Those you'll find in my best-selling book, "The Encyclopedia of Sauces for Your Pasta".

The method of listing a sauce in most cookbooks is usually:

1) Alphabetically, - Aioli Sauce to White Sauce . 2) By ingredient, - butter sauces, cream sauces or 3) By genre, - warm sauces, compound sauces, leading sauces, small sauces, simple sauces. But that doesn't help you if you are an amateur cook. When you search for a sauce to go with a dish, your hunt through existing cookbooks requires you to read through the entire category of sauces to find right one.

Well I've come to your rescue! In "The Encyclopedia of Sauces for Your Food", the sauces are listed under the name of the food you'll serve them on. Hooray for me! Now you can go directly to the type of food you want to enhance, and discover one or more available sauces to compliment or hide (if you messed up) your dish. The right sauce on the right dish will be outstanding. In fact there is an old cooks expression that you should hang somewhere on your kitchen wall; "The sauce makes the meal". I couldn't have said it better myself!

A WHO?

If you want to sound erudite, you refer to the sauce maker as "saucier" (sos-yea). Sauces are so important in European and American cookery, that in commercial kitchens, the sauce maker is a specialist.

Compound Sauces

This is a large group of sauces that are very involved multi-step preparation recipes. Actual time required to prepare these sauces can run several hours or more. They are much too time consuming for todays home cook. I've included several compound sauces in the book, but unless you are a very dedicated cook, chef or saucier, I suggest you avoid them.

What Have I Got?

You think you've just made a gravy, but what you really wanted was a sauce! How do you know what you've got? Good question and I've got the answer for you.

Gravy Is Made From The Drippings Of Cooked Meat! Sauce Is A Flavored Liquid Or Relish.

WOW, that leaves a lot of room for creativity. Sauces can be made from a single item or they can be as complex as you want. Your sauce can be as simple as melted butter, pureed ripe fruit, pureed vegetables, or whipped soft cheeses. It can also be a blend of ingredients, cooked or uncooked, smooth or chunky. The choice is yours. Now that you know that, I can move along.

Substitutions:

In any sauce that calls for butter or lard, you can successfully substitute extra light olive oil. If your decision to substitute the fat is based on a dietary consideration, you need to know that "Extra Light Olive Oil" has a neutral flavor and adds no taste to the sauce. It also has no cholesterol.

However, if the fat is an important part of the flavor of the sauce (like in a butter sauce) you may not want to switch.

A Stock Is A Soup, Right! Is It? If Its Not, What's The Difference? Soup Is A Liquid Food Prepared From Stock.

There are several terms cooks use to define various meat, poultry, fish or vegetable flavored liquids. They are listed as follows in an increasing percentage of liquid reduction:

Stock(s):

Stocks are a flavored liquid. Usually the liquid is water, but sometimes wine or milk is used. One or more of the following ingredients are added to the liquid to extract all their flavor: bones, fat scraps, meat scraps, meat, fish, poultry, vegetables, herbs, spices and seasoning. After several hours of simmering, the stock is generally clarified by straining and then chilled to allow easy fat removal. The solid ingredients are discarded and the clear strained liquid is used as the flavor base for gravies, sauces or soups.

It is easier for you not to have your refrigerator stuffed with bottles of broth, but to just buy what you need. The most readily available (and most often used) stocks are broth, bouillon and consume. They are available in liquid or dry form, and they come in the following flavors; chicken, beef, vegetable, fish and clam. Except for an occasional brand of canned chicken broth, most of them are very salty. Stocks you have to make are; veal, pork and fish.

Stocks play an important role in cookery by providing the basic flavoring for a large number of soups, sauces and gravies. If it is your intention to be a great saucier, then it is important for you to be knowledgeable about stocks and how to make them. On the other hand, if being a saucier is not in your future job description, learn them anyway because during your lifetime there will be many occasions when you will want to have a good stock to make a gravy, sauce or soup.

Broth:

A liquid in which meats, poultry, fish or vegetables have been cooked and then discarded: (Generally clear, but sometimes containing bits of the items cooked.)

Bouillon:

Concentrated brown stock made from beef. Also served as a clear soup.

Consomme:

Clarified and concentrated (generally double strength bouillon) brown stock.

Glaze:

Clarified and very concentrated beef stock reduced by 90% (give or take a little).

Sauce Thickeners:

In most gravies and some sauces, you'll use a roux as your thickening and/or coloring agent. They are very simple to make. Use the following guide for:

Thick gravy: 3 tablespoons roux to 1 cup liquid

Medium gravy: 2 tablespoons roux to 1 cup liquid

Thin gravy: 1 tablespoon roux to 1 cup liquid

Cooks Alert: The above formula applies only to wheat flour. All other flours and starches have about twice the thickening capacity of wheat flour. Therefore, when using a non-wheat flour, double the amount of liquid. Or, reduce the amount of your non-wheat ingredient(s) by one-half.

Roux: A roux is made from flour and oil or fat, (the choice is yours). The fat determines the taste of your gravy. You can use butter, margarine, shortening, vegetable oil, bacon oil, lard, sausage oil, rendered ham fat, rendered chicken fat, turkey fat or any other fat drippings you have.

To make a roux, place equal amounts of flour and oil/fat into a pan. Whisk them together for several minutes over medium low heat. Brown the roux only if you do not use a separate coloring agent for your sauce/gravy.

Arrowroot: It adds gloss and luster to your sauce. And when you want to show off, it's a dream. It has a very short life-span and it cannot be reheated since it doesn't require cooking. It must be prepared at the moment of serving. Add 1 scant tablespoon to 1 cup of sauce to thicken. Arrowroot is ideal for egg sauces.

Blood: Probably not available unless you're a farmer or hunter. Blood is used as a thickener in a sauce made for the meat of the animal it came from. It can be kept refrigerated for several days if a tablespoon or two of vinegar is added to it. To use, strain the blood and whisk it into the sauce during the last 2-3 minutes of cooking. Do not allow it to boil.

Blood is used to make a number of sausage products, i.e., Hurka; a blood and rice sausage favored by Hungarians and other east Europeans.

4

BREAD CRUMBS:	Toss $^1/_4$ cupful into your sauce and cook for a minute. If you want a smooth sauce, strain before serving.
BROWNED FLOUR:	Using 1 cup all purpose flour, place it in a skillet over medium heat and cook until browned. Cool and set aside in a well sealed container. Use as directed in a recipe.
	Browned flour loses its thickening ability compared to white flour. It's a trade off. You get a nuttier taste from the browned flour, but you generally will use twice as much of it to thicken a sauce.
BUTTER SWIRLS:	More decoration than thickener. It is the finisher, or final touch in a sauce and its all done with the wrist. Drop small pieces of butter into your sauce pan, then move the pan in a circular motion to get a swirled effect. Don't stir! Pour the sauce over or under your preparation and serve.
CORN STARCH:	It's quick and it will give your sauce/gravy a translucent look. To make approximately 2 cups of sauce, dissolve a tablespoon of corn starch into a little cold water. Then slowly pour and whisk the mixture into your sauce and serve.
EGG YOLKS:	Egg yolks thicken and enrich any sauce they are added to. They are also temperamental and require a light delicate hand. Two to three yolks are required to thicken 1 cup of liquid. Mix them with a little liquid first, then thin further with some hot liquid from your sauce. Drizzle the mixture slowly into your sauce and whisk until blended. Cook in a double boiler or over a heat diffuser. If your liquid or heat is too hot, kiss the sauce good-by because it will curdle. It might be salvaged if you pour some cold whipping cream into the sauce and place the pan in cold water and whisk together. If you get lucky it will re-form into the smooth sauce it was supposed to be.
FILE:	Dried and ground Sassafras leaves. Used largely in Creole and some Cajun cookery. It is added just prior to serving and does not reheat. It can be replaced with Tapioca Flour.
FLOUR PASTE:	Whisk 2 tablespoons of flour and $^1/_4$ cup cold water together until smooth, or place the ingredients into a small jar with a lid, and shake the daylights out of it until the contents are well blended. Whisk the paste into 1 cup of milk or other liquid and bring the mixture to a boil.

Reduce the heat to simmer and cook for several minutes until thickened.

GRATED POTATO:
Any variety of potato will do. Grate the potato, or whirl it through your blender/food processor. Add $^1/_3$ cup of grated potato to 2 cups of sauce. You'll need a minimum of 10 minutes cooking time for this to work.

KNEADED BUTTER:
(AKA BEURRE MANIE)
Knead together the flour and butter, with a ratio of 2 parts flour to 1 part butter. Roll, or pinch and roll, into small pea sized balls. Drop them into the sauce as the recipe directs.

POTATO STARCH:
A favorite thickener for cooks who like delicate sauces. It has no staying power and will thin out if overheated or left for any length of time. An advantage it has over wheat flour, is that it takes less time to cook. To use, dissolve $^1/_2$ tablespoon of potato starch in a little water and whisk it into 1 cup of sauce. Simmer for several minutes.

REDUCTION:
A process to evaporate liquid from a sauce which intensifies the flavors and thickens the sauce without adding anything to it. One method requires very long and very slow simmering until the sauce has the thickness you want. If you want to try this method, follow this caveat; DO NOT SEASON THE LIQUID UNTIL READY TO SERVE.

A second method used for reduction is rapid evaporation, where you reduce the liquid over high heat by half or more and thereby intensify the flavor. This method will not thicken the pan juices.

TOMATO PASTE:
Can be used as is to thicken sauces, or with water added it can also be the sauce. Canned tomato sauce can also be used in this dual fashion. Either allows you to reduce the cooking time of a sauce made from fresh or canned tomatoes (packed in water or their own juices).

TAPIOCA FLOUR:
Typically used in deserts and clear glazes. It is tricky to handle and will go stringy if overheated. This flour, as with all non-wheat flours, has twice the thickening capacity of wheat flour. Use 1/2 tablespoon of tapioca flour to 1 cup liquid.

THE BEST PAN FOR YOUR SAUCE

Normally you make a sauce in the pan in which you've cooked your entree. However, if it is a delicate sauce or a multiple sauce recipe, that won't do.

What you need then is a double boiler, or at the very least, a device to keep your pan up off the burner while still over the heat. A pan directly on the burner can ruin some delicate sauces. Therefore if a double boiler is recommended, it is probably a safe bet that anything else is hazardous to your sauce.

INGREDIENTS

ANCHOVY:
Small fry (baby fish) from several fishes, although normally from one family of Herring-like fish. Smoked and heavily salted, it always dissolves when added to hot liquids or mashed when sauted. That's why it is used as a seasoning and not as a fish.

BOUQUET GARNI:
A flavoring packet for soups and stocks made up of parsley, bay leaf, fresh thyme, leek and cloves. Tied in cheese cloth or bundled and tied in celery ribs, or if you're going to strain your stock, just chuck 'em in.

BUTTER:
Churned from cream, it is almost pure animal fat and is available salted or unsalted. Unsalted butter is often marketed as Sweet Butter. In British recipes, salted butter is called Irish butter.

As of this writing, there are low-fat butters on the market which actually have less fat than most real margarines. The fat is displaced with jellied skim milk and water. That means one pound of butter is now two pounds of low fat or light butter. It is not suitable for cooking or baking, but it does make a nice spread.

CAPERS:
Pickled buds of the Caper bush. The best are the small, round, Nonesuch variety. They are used as both a seasoning and a condiment.

CAVIAR:
Fish eggs (roe). Available from a wide array of fish and they are heavily salted. The very best are from the sturgeon and even then there are varieties with differing qualities.

CELERY:
A term that causes confusion to cooks and some cookbook writers. Celery is sold in stalks, and a stalk is made up of ribs.

CURRY POWDER:
A mixture of the full spectrum, or partial selections, of dried herbs and spices, ground to a powder. A starter list for curry might include; tumeric, coriander and cumin. Generally used in South East Asian and

East Indian sauces or relishes, for use on rice, meats, fish and salads. Temperaments run from mild to very hot.

DEMI-GLAZE: Equal amounts of Glaze and wine or other strong flavored liquid.

FINES HERBES: Can be a mixture of herbs for seasoning, stuffing or garnish. Including but not limited to; parsley, chervil, tarragon, chives and possibly mushrooms. Can also be limited to a single item. The choice is yours. Also see Bouquet Garni and Herb Bouquet.

GARLIC: A member of the lily family used extensively in cookery throughout the world. In the U.S. it has taken on a life of its own, following the realization that it has beneficial health effects for humans, particularly against heart disease. Fresh garlic comes in bulbs and the bulbs are divided into cloves. Like anything else in the world of cookery; if a little is good, a lot is not necessarily better. Excessive garlic in any recipe becomes the dominant taste. Even if you love it, don't inflict that love on others (at least not without their consent).

GELATIN: When unflavored, it is used as a thickening agent in some broths and a bonding agent in aspics and as a sealant for small loafs, such as pate. It is also used as a clear glaze for cold meat and fish preparations.

HERBS: When using fresh herbs, realize that how you cut, mince or tear the leaves largely determines their potency.

Finely chopped herbs yield the most intense flavor.

A very good rule of thumb for measuring fresh to dry herbs is a ratio of 3 to 1; 1 tablespoon chopped fresh = to 1 teaspoon dry.

In most sauces flavoring can be maximized by adding the herbs during the last few minutes of cooking. Or immediately after cooking, just before serving.

HERB BOUQUET: Interchangeable term with Bouquet Garni.

HORSERADISH: A root, grated and combined with vinegar or lemon juice.

It can also be creamed with sour cream, yogurt, or assorted thickening and flavoring agents. Use sparingly since fresh, strong horseradish will clear your sinuses in a heartbeat.

PAPRIKA: Hungarian word for pepper. Specifically, dried and finely ground red peppers. Temperaments run from sweet to hot.

PEPPERCORN: The dried berry of the pepper plant, generally black. But now available in a variety of colors.

PIMENTO: Spanish sweet red peppers. Occasionally available in some grocery stores in their fresh state. This pepper is also dried and ground to make Spanish Paprika.

TOMATOES: I am limiting my comments here to the differences in canned tomato products, which is basically the amount of liquid remaining in the product. From the most amount of liquid to the least they are:
  1. Peeled whole tomatoes (includes; crushed, ground or diced).
  2. Tomato sauce.
  3. Tomato puree.
  4. Tomato paste.

One additional note is that European and English terms do not correspond to American terms, i.e., tomato puree can mean tomato paste.

VINEGAR: All vinegars are mild forms of acid. Their acid content rarely measures above 6% percent and seldom below 4% percent.

Cider vinegar is made from fermented apple juice.

Distilled white vinegar is made from re-fermented distilled and diluted alcohol.

Malt vinegars are made from cider vinegars re-fermented with barley malt or other cereals whose starch has been converted by malt.

Wine vinegar is made from refermented wine.

Balsamic vinegar is a wine vinegar that has naturally condensed, through evaporation, while in the barrel. This "angel share" reduction yields a sweet vinegar. Ages are between 2 years old to well over 100 years and priced accordingly.

HERB VINEGARS:	These are made from any of the above vinegars by steeping one or several of the following in the vinegar:
	Fresh or dried herbs, garlic, peppers, spices, fruits or nuts. Steep them for a period of two to four weeks before filtering and bottling.
WINE:	In the United States there are hundreds of wine varieties, while across the world there are thousands. In Italy alone there are over 2,000 varieties. Luckily for us vines and wines can be divided into a few categories: red, white, blush, dessert, sparkling, aperitif/appetizer. Between the vineyard and the winery (they're not always in the same place), the vintners art comes into play. With great skill and sometimes serendipity, they convert grape juice into outstanding wine varietals and hundreds of marvelous blends. The list of wines available to you is positively overwhelming. So, I'm only going to provide you with a short list of wines generally used in cookery. (Not cooking wines, which are salted. Salting good wine was a method used by landed gentry of England to keep the household staff from sipping away the sherries.)
MY CAVEAT TO YOU:	Add wine to your food with a specific intent, i.e., you want the flavor of the wine to be an integral part of your sauce. That means you should cook with a good wine. Do not damage a sauce with a wine you wouldn't drink. An outstanding French chef is credited with the saying; the better the wine, the better the sauce. Sounds right to me.
	Wines and spirits most frequently used in American cookery are: Sherry, Madeira, Marsala, Muscato and Port, notwithstanding the non-descript dry whites or reds frequently called for in many recipes. Also used extensively are distilled wine products, such as Cognac and its immediate cousin, Brandy. Cognac is an exclusive product of the Charente area of France, while brandy is everyone else's version of Cognac.
	These in turn are followed by liqueurs: They are distilled from an astounding array of edibles and non-edibles: including fruits, nuts, pips, beans, seeds, weeds, herbs, spices, berries, cherries, oranges, grapefruit and left over grape squeezings (marc). And I'm not sure I've covered them all!

INGREDIENT EQUIVALENTS

There are times when you don't have a fresh lemon in the house, but you do have one those cute little bottles filled with juice and no pouring guidelines, so how do you know how much lemon juice to pour out for a recipe that calls for the juice of one-half lemon? The answer is below along with a group of equivalent measurements. They are not exact, but approximations.

ITEM:	QUANTITY USED:	YIELD:
BREAD:		
Bread crumbs:	1 slice fresh bread	$^1/_2$ to $^3/_4$ cup of soft crumbs
Bread crumbs:	1 slice dry bread	$^1/_4$ cup fine crumbs
CITRUS:		
Lemon juice:	1 medium lemon	3 tablespoons juice
Lemon zest:	1 medium lemon	2 teaspoons shredded peel
Lime juice:	1 medium lime	2 tablespoons juice
Lime zest:	1 medium lime	1 $^1/_2$ teaspoons shredded peel
Orange juice:	1 medium orange	$^1/_3$ cup juice
Orange zest:	1 medium orange	4 teaspoons shredded peel
EGGS:		
Large:	2	$^1/_2$ cup
Medium:	3	$^1/_2$ cup
HERBS:		
Any fresh herb:	1 tablespoon chopped =	1 teaspoon dried
VEGETABLES:		
Celery:	1 medium stalk	4 $^1/_2$ cups chopped
Green bell peppers:	1 large	1 cup chopped
Mushrooms:	1 pound	2 cups sliced and cooked
Onions:	1 medium	$^1/_2$ cup chopped

Tomatoes:	1 medium	$^1/_2$ cup cooked

DAIRY PRODUCTS:

Cheese:	4 ounces	1 cup shredded
Whipping cream:	1 cup liquid	2 cups whipped

"THE RULE OF FAT CONTENT"

If knowing the percentage of fat in your food is important to you, a "grams of fat" multiplier is very useful. Keep in mind that there are 9 calories in each gram of fat. The following formula calculates the percentage of fat in your food.

$$\frac{\text{Grams of fat} \times 9}{\text{Total calories per serving}} = \text{Percentage of fat per serving.}$$

Example: There are 150 calories with 8 grams of fat in something you want to eat. Multiply the fat grams 8, by 9 (the number of calories in a gram of fat) the answer is 72. Divide the answer, 72, by 150 and that equals 48%. Therefore 48% (almost one-half) of the 150 calories are fat calories.

ESSENTIAL METHODS
OR
THINGS YOU ALWAYS WANTED TO KNOW HOW TO DO!

BUTTERED BREAD CRUMBS: Use 2 tablespoons of butter, to each 1/2 cup bread crumbs. Melt the butter, add the bread crumbs and stir until the crumbs are well coated and lightly toasted. If using soft bread crumbs, double the quantity.

CARAMELIZED SUGAR: Caramelized sugar has a number of cooking uses, but here we're only interested in its ability to act as a coloring agent. It's easy to make, but if you are new at this, PLEASE follow the directions.

Place 1 cup of sugar in a glass, stainless steel or heavy aluminum pan. Over low heat, stir the sugar constantly until it has changed color. You want a light to medium amber color. (This is a critical stage. If it gets too dark it will have a scorched taste. In that case, throw it out and start over.) Remove from the heat and let cool.

When the sugar has cooled, add 1 cup hot water, slowly, while stirring. Return the pan to the heat and stir until all the sugar has dissolved and you have a dark syrup.

Store the caramelized sugar on a shelf in your pantry or cupboard in a lidded container. It keeps indefinitely.

COAT:

You coat a food by dredging (dragging) it through flour, or toss the food in a bag with the coating ingredients. Coating some foods, particularly meat, fish and vegetables, allows for easier browning and seals in the foods natural juices. The coatings most often used are; flour, very fine bread crumbs, or occasionally grated nut meats.

DEGLAZING:

To scrape up all the particles of meat and juices that have stuck to your cooking pan.

After you have drawn off the juices from your pan, throw in a splash of liquid and with a little quick whisking you'll "deglaze" your pan. At this point you can add the contents of the deglazing to your defatted pan juices. Or reduce the pan juices to an intensified sauce by evaporating more of the liquid.

FLAMING:

French; flambe There are two products and two methods generally used on a variety of meat, fowl, cheese, seafood, thin pancakes, sauces, coffees, punches and desserts They are:

1. Brandy. When using brandy, the safest method is to place a ladle or large metal spoon in very hot to boiling water for a moment or two. Shake the water from the ladle, then pour a measure of brandy or other liqueur into the hot ladle. This action warms the brandy and allows for easier ignition. Light the brandy with a match or other lighter and immediately pour the flaming brandy over your food. When the flame dies it is ready to serve.

To add a little pizzazz, dim the lights and have your food on the table when you set it aflame.

2. Sugar cube. To flame a sugar cube, dip the cube (or splash it) with a little extract of lemon, orange or any flavor you choose. Place the wet cube on your food, such as ice cream, and light it.

13

SOURING FRESH MILK:	Occasionally a sauce recipe will call for buttermilk or sour milk. If you don't have any handy, this method does the job. Add 1 tablespoon white vinegar to 1 cup fresh milk or diluted evaporated milk (2 parts water to 1 part evaporated milk).

GLOSSARY:

A DICTIONARY OF COOKING TERMS EVERY HOME COOK SHOULD KNOW.

ABSORBENT:	Any paper that absorbs moisture. In this context it is used to lift water or oil from food. Absorbent paper towels are especially useful when removing oil from a hot broth and you don't have a separator, or the time to chill it before removing the oil.
ACIDULATED WATER:	Water that is acidified with vinegar or a citrus juice. It is used as a soak for fresh vegetables prior to cooking. The formula is 1 tablespoon of acid to 1 quart water.
Á LA:	In the manner of.
Á LA CARTE:	According to the bill of fare. Translation: a separate price for each item on the menu. Although in many restaurants in the United States a meat may be served with one added item, such as a vegetable or a potato.
Á LA DIABLE:	A French term meaning deviled, spicy or highly seasoned. To use Spanish, call it Diablo. To use Italian call it (Fra) Diavolo or al Divolicchio. Italians seldom use the word devil or deviled to describe food. Their choice is "angry" as in Pasta Arrabbiata. Also "purgatory" as in Uova 'mpriatorio (Eggs in Purgatory)
Á LA GRECQUE:	A French term meaning "in the Greek style". It refers to vegetables cooked in a blend of oil and vinegar.
Á LA KING:	An entree served in a rich white sauce, and can include mushrooms, colorful vegetables and/or variously colored sweet peppers.
Á LA NEWBURG:	Typically a crustacean served up in a rich sauce of butter, cream, egg yolk and wine. Not for dieters.

14

Á LA MODE:	According to the style of, or fashion of.
ASPIC:	When gelatin is used to hold a mixture of ingredients together such as meat, fish, tomatoes, fruits, or as a sealant for small loaves, such as pate.
AU GRATIN:	To make a crust of bread crumbs or cheese. It is generally used to cover baked macaroni, potatoes, vegetables or fruit pie and some roasted meats, such as "steak in a bag".
	Au Gratin can also mean (although incorrectly) "with cheese". That is, the cheese is blended as an ingredient throughout the dish.
AU JUS:	The natural unthickened juices from roasted or braised meat. It means that the meat is served in its own juices, especially roast beef and Prime Rib Roast. It is also used a dip for sandwiches (French Dip).
BAKE:	To cook by dry heat, in an oven. Generally, foods made from flour products are referred to as "baked", while meats cooked in the same manner are referred to as roasted.
BARBECUE:	Originally this referred to spit-roasted meat basted with a seasoned sauce. Now it refers to just about anything, whether spit-roasted, broiled or grilled, over or under a flame or charcoal, indoors or out... and served with a sauce.
BASTE:	To re-moisturize meat during the cooking process by spooning liquid over it. The liquid can be juices from the meat, melted butter, wine or a seasoned sauce.
BEAT:	To cream or incorporate air into a food, by hand with a whip or spoon, or an egg beater.
BISQUE:	Soups made from cream and shellfish.
BLANCH:	A first step to removing skins from certain foods. It means to briefly bathe the food in boiling water (30 seconds or more), then drop it into cold water (iced is better) which stops the cooking process before peeling.
BLEND:	To combine two or more ingredients into a single mixture.
BOUCHEE:	From the French, meaning a small pastry shell filled with a fish or meat mixture. Akin to Scottish and English meat pies.

BOUILLABAISSE:	A chowder made from two or more types of seafood. The original meaning of bouillabaisse is: Stop the boiling. Translation is: it's done. So saith Larousse Gastronomique.
BRAISE:	To cook by browning in a small amount of oil or fat, then keeping a small amount of liquid in the pan while the meat cooks to the desired tenderness. It is important that meats cooked in this way are never covered with liquid or be allowed to dry out.
BREAD:	To coat food with eggs or milk and then with seasoned bread crumbs.
BROCHETTE:	French term for skewer, as in "En Brochette". Kabobs are cooked in this fashion.
BROIL:	To cook by direct heat. The heat source can be above the food as in a conventional oven, or on a grill with the heat below the food.
BROWN(ING):	To cause food to brown by sauteing, frying, toasting, broiling or baking.
CANAPE:	Appetizer; generally made from crackers or small pieces of toasted bread covered with cheese, vegetables, spreads, meats or seafood.
CAPON:	A castrated rooster.
CARAMELIZE:	To cook sugar until browned.
CELERIAC:	Root of the celery stalk.
CELERY:	Sold in stalks and the individual pieces that make up a stalk are called ribs.
CHOP:	To cut foods into irregular small pieces.
CHOWDER:	Thick vegetable, seafood or meat soup. Generally made with milk, diced vegetables (especially potatoes), and seasoned with salt pork, or occasionally, bacon.
CLARIFY:	To remove the solids from a fat (butter) or stocks to make them clear. Melted butter is chilled to solidify it, then the solids (mostly salt) are removed and discarded. What remains is clarified butter. Stocks should be filtered and then chilled to solidify the fat. The hard fat is then peeled off the surface and discarded.

CREAM(ED):	A soup that is usually vegetable based and made with one or more of the following: cream, butter, cereal or eggs.
CROQUETTE:	French term for a meat ball dipped in egg and rolled in toasted bread crumbs before frying. It has a crusty outside, with a soft inside. Generally made from beef or lamb and onion. The meat and onion are ground together.
CROUTONS:	Originally small cubes or very thin slices of bread either toasted or sauted in butter/oil. Now they are available with a variety of flavorings or seasonings.
CURRY:	The individual cooks choice. A mixture of (or part of) the full spectrum of dried herbs and spices, ground to a powder. Generally used in South East Asian and East Indian sauces and salads. Temperaments run from mild to very hot.
DASH:	10 drops or $1/_8$ teaspoon
DICE:	To cut into small pieces that are uniform and cubical in size and shape.
DREDGE:	Specifically it means to coat with flour, or very fine bread crumbs, by dragging or rolling the food through the flour. It can also be also done by shaking the food in a bag containing the flour or bread crumbs.
EMULSION:	The result of emulsifying two liquids that have no natural ability to join together, such as oil and vinegar. It requires a third ingredient, the emulsifier to hold them together.
(E)SCALLOPED:	As in scalloped potatoes. To bake food, usually in a white sauce, topped with bread crumbs and/or cheese.
FILLET:	A boneless piece of fish or lean meat. Pronounced; "fill-it", (although it is usually said as fil-lay). Also when fillet is used as a verb, it means to bone or slice a cut of meat or fish.
FILE:	Ground or powdered leaves of sassafras and used to thicken soups and stews. Pronounced "fil-lay".
FILET MIGNON:	A small, very choice, tender cut of beef from the short loin. Pronounced; "fil-lay min-yoan".

FINNAN HADDIE:	Smoked haddock.
FLAKE:	Not necessarily someone from California. It means to separate into small pieces with a fork, such as cooked fish.
FONDUE:	Melted cheese, thinned with wine and used as a dipping sauce for dry bread cubes. It is important that the bread cubes be fairly dry. Fresh bread can fall off the fork with the added weight of the cheese. Beer and milk are often used instead of wine where a different taste is desired. It is often called Welsh Rarebit and is served over toast or warmed crackers or grilled tomato slices. Welsh Rarebit uses a variety of seasonings, such as butter, paprika, saffron, worcestershire, dry mustard, cayenne, white pepper, salt and possibly an egg yolk or two.
FORCEMEAT:	You won't see this word often unless you read French cookbooks. It is chopped or ground meat, seasoned and used as a stuffing. As in stuffed double-cut pork chops or stuffed lamb breasts.
FRUIT SOUP:	Soups made from cooked, fresh or frozen fruits and often pureed. They can be used as a soup, a dessert, or as a palate cleanser when served before the entree. Sorbet's are frequently used for this purpose. These soups are popular in many parts of Europe.
FRICASSEE:	Poultry, and occasionally veal or lamb, cut up, stewed and served in their own gravy.
FRY:	To prepare food in a small amount of fat/oil. As opposed to deep-fat frying, where the fat/oil is deep enough to completely cover the food being cooked.
GARLIC:	Sold in bulbs. The individual pieces that make up a bulb, are called cloves.
GARNISH:	To decorate food with parsley or other vegetables that create color contrast and eye appeal.
GEE:	The clear oil from clarified butter after removing all impurities. It keeps indefinitely.
GLAZE:	As a noun; to cover certain foods, i.e., ham, with a shiny coating. As a verb; to apply a glaze, with or without heat.

GOULASH:	From Hungarian cookery. In the U.S. it has been transformed from a beef and onion soup (Hungarian; Gulyas) to a stew featuring beef or veal with vegetables and seasoned with paprika.
GRATE:	To reduce a food to small particles by rubbing it across a grater. Also grind or shred food by rubbing on a grater.
GRIBICHE:	A dressing made from hard cooked eggs, cucumbers, capers, vinegar, oil and your choice of seasonings. Can be used to dress cold fish, meat and/or vegetable dishes.
GRILL:	a) Started out as a verb, meaning to broil meats on a gridiron. b) It can also be a noun when referring to the a wide, broad and flat cooking surface found in many restaurants. c) It sometimes becomes part of the name of food prepared on such a surface, as in Grilled Cheese Sandwich.
GRIND:	To put food through a food chopper.
GUMBO:	A thick meat and/or vegetable soup featuring Okra.
HERBS:	There are several schools of thought on how to define herbs and spices. The one I prefer maintains that herbs are highly flavorful leaves or seeds that grow within the temperate zones of the world. While spices, either leaves or seeds, grow within the tropical zones.
JELLIED SOUPS:	Differing from Aspics in that they are made from meats and bones that are gelatinous, such as; ham or beef knuckle bones. They can also be made from vegetables and gelatinized with packaged gelatin. They're clarified and served cold.
JERK:	Not necessarily anyone you know or want to know, but a very hot sauce that originated in Jamaica.
JERKY:	Can be any of several types of meat that are very lean, thinly sliced, or ground and formed, seasoned and dried by heat or sunlight. Old timey term was "jerked beef".
LARD:	As a verb it means to wrap, cover or insert fat on or into lean meat or fish. As a noun it refers to the rendered fat from pork.

19

LIQUOR:	A preferred term in parts of the country to describe the liquid in which some foods and fruits are packed. It does not mean packed with alcohol. A second type of food liquor, called by some cooks, "pot liquor", which refers to the juices left in the pan following cooking.
LUKEWARM:	A temperature for liquids of 100° F. to 110° F.
MARGARINE:	A very old butter substitute, that may have roots that go back as far as the 1700's (when food canned in tins was developed to meet the need of feeding Napoleon's fast moving army). It is made largely from solidified oil.
	Today there are dozens of variations and many use water and/or skim milk to displace some of the oil. These variations are not suitable for baking or most cooking uses. Also, there are a large number of oil/fat free margarines that are made from water, skim milk and a host of chemicals. They are suitable only as a spread on bread or toast. They spoil within a few weeks of opening.
MAYONNAISE:	A sauce made from egg yolks, vinegar, salt, cayenne and oil. It is used as a base for many well known sauces such as; Remoulade, Tartare, Mustard Sauce, Ravigote, Sauce Verte, Thousand Island, Green Goddess, Russian Dressing, Tyrolean, et cetera, et cetera.
MARINADE:	A mixture containing one or more acidic liquids; vinegar, tomato juice, lemon juice, lime juice, orange juice, pineapple juice, plus water and/or wine and seasonings.
MARINATE:	The act of soaking food in a marinade.
MASK:	To cover food completely with a thick sauce, mayonnaise or jelly.
MELT:	To dissolve by heat.
MINCE:	To chop into very fine pieces.
PANBROIL:	To cook meat in a preheated skillet over high heat, removing fat as it accumulates in the pan.
PANFRY:	To cook food in a skillet with a small amount of fat.
PARBOIL:	Dropping food into rapidly boiling water and allowing it to cook until partially done.

PARE / PEEL:	Interchangeable terms for the removal of skin and/or rind from fruits and vegetables.
PATE:	Chopped and formed food served up as small paste loafs, rolls or mounds and very spreadable. In France it can also be a pie.
PATE DE FOIE GRAS:	Quite specifically it means a paste made from goose or duck livers.
PIECE DE RESISTANCE:	The main dish in a meal. (Or, with tongue in cheek, someone who won't date you.)
PILAF:	Of middle eastern origin, this rice dish is cooked with one of the following; meat, poultry, fish and spices. Not dissimilar from rice dishes in Europe, Asia and the Americas, i.e., Spanish Paella, Chinese Fried Rice, Cajun Jambalaya.
PLANK:	Not for walking on, but rather a board made specifically to broil meat/fish and to serve as a platter.
POACH:	To cook food slowly in simmering water. Eggs and fish can be cooked in this fashion. As a verb; the act of cooking food in a container over simmering water.
Pot-au-feu:	A French term meaning pot-on-the-fire. Translation is; beef stew with vegetables.
PREHEAT:	To bring your oven or skillet to a desired temperature before adding the food to be cooked.
PRIX FIXE:	Means "fixed price". If you are going to eat in a restaurant with "prix fixe" pricing, each and every person in your party pays the same price for selections from the menu. This method is often used in New Orleans, especially at such outstanding houses as Brennan's and Antoine's. "Table d'hote" has a similar meaning. The table is set family style and everyone at the table pays the same price. You can eat from all the dishes on the table. It is quite popular in many Italian and Basque restaurants.
PUREE:	As a noun; a smooth sauce. As a verb; the action of making it that way. Also a type of soup, generally made from vegetables and/or Legumes, with or without added cream.

RAGOUT:	A French word meaning a thick, highly seasoned stew.
RAGU:	An Italian word for a meat-laden pasta sauce with tomatoes and possibly other vegetables.
REMOULADE:	A sauce for cold meats, fish and crustaceans, made from a base of Mayonnaise and several additional ingredients.
RENDER:	To melt the fat from meat trimmings by heating at a low temperature.
RISSOLE:	Pronounced ree-sole. A type of meatball made from either, meat, poultry or fish, wrapped in pastry dough and deep fried.
ROAST:	To cook by dry heat.
ROUX:	A paste of melted fat/oil and flour. Basic to cream sauces and gravies.
SAUTE:	To pan fry foods in a small amount of fat/oil while turning or stirring frequently.
SCALD:	To bring a liquid to the simmering point. If using a thermometer it's about 180 F. hot, but below 212 F., the boiling point at sea level.
SCALLION:	Americans have two names for this onion. In the East scallion is the preferred word, while in the interior and West the choice is green onion. Also mistakenly called chive in some localities. In French cookery, green onion may refer to shallots.
SCANT:	As a measurement it means just a smidgen less than the amount called for, i.e., a tablespoon should be less than level and never greater than level.
SCORE:	When not related to human interaction or sports, it refers to cutting narrow gashes into the surface of meats. Most notably hams are scored for visual effect, often with a criss-cross pattern.
SEAR:	To brown the surface of meat very quickly over high heat thereby sealing the meats surface. This prevents the loss of its juices during further cooking.
SHRED:	To render into narrow strips.
SHUCK:	To remove the outer layer of something, such as corn, clams, oysters, et cetera.

SIMMER:	To cook very gently just below the boiling point.
SKEWER:	To pierce or fasten meat or vegetables on long metal pins that hold the food in position during cooking.
SOUP:	Made from stock(s). They come in a variety of viscosities and flavors. All fit into the following categories: bouillon, consomme, broth, jellied, vegetable, puree, cream(ed) and bisque. Non stock soups are: chowders and fruit.
SPICE:	There are several schools of thought on how to define spice and herb. The one I prefer maintains that spices are highly flavorful leaves or seeds that grow within the tropical zones of the world. While herbs, either leaves or seeds, grow within the temperate zones.
SPIT:	A thin rod or bar used to skewer food during cooking over a fire.
SQUAB:	Young pigeon. Probably nothing you will ever prepare, but more likely a dish you'll find in older cookbooks. A squab is close in size and taste to quail. Surprisingly, quail is readily available at the Tudor or Renaissance Faires being staged across the country.
SQUISHED:	My term for using your hand to crush whole canned tomatoes prior to cooking. Grab a tomato and squish it!
STEAM:	A method of using the steam from boiling liquid to cook food.
STEEP:	To soak in liquid, hot or cold, to extract the flavor.
STERILIZE:	To kill micro-organisms by intense heat.
STEW:	As a verb it means to cook by simmering. As a noun, the name of a finished dish, generally made from meat and vegetables.
STIR:	To mix foods with a circular motion in order to blend them for uniform consistency.
STOCK:	The liquid in which meats, fish and/or vegetables have been cooked.
SUET:	The hard fat from beef. Little used in American cookery, unless you're into making English-style plum puddings or old fashioned minced pie.

SWEETBREAD:	One of several calf innards used as food: the pancreas (for stomach sweetbread) and the thymus (neck or throat sweetbread). The Creole definition of sweetbread is that it is only the thymus found in the throat of a suckling calf. Once the calf begins to feed on grass, the gland withers away.
TOAST:	To brown by direct heat.
TOSS:	To mix lightly, as in preparing a salad.
TRIPE:	The stomach(s) from calves or older cows.
TRUFFLE:	Not the confection, but a very expensive mushroom that grows underground.
TRUSS:	To tie-up or skewer poultry wings and legs before cooking.
VEGETABLE SOUP(S):	Made solely from vegetables, or a vegetable dominant soup prepared from a base of meat, poultry or fish stock.
WELSH RAREBIT OR WELSH RABBIT:	Melted cheese thinned with beer or ale and served on crackers or toast (also see Fondue). When made for children the alcohol is replaced with milk.
WIENER SCHNITZEL:	Austrian/German term for a breaded veal cutlet.
WURST:	German term for sausage.
YORKSHIRE PUDDING:	An egg and flour mixture baked in the drippings of a roast. In early American kitchens (and some English ones, particularly in Yorkshire), the egg and flour mixture was placed in the pan and then put under the spit or rack of the roasting meat to collect the drippings. Todays' cook makes a Yorkshire Pudding by adding the roast juices to an egg/flour mixture and then baking it while the roast is resting.

An English peculiarity about this pudding it that since it is from Yorkshire, some Englishmen won't eat it and even disparage it. But then again I've known Englishmen who wouldn't eat corn-on-the-cob either, because from their point of view, it is a food fed only to pigs. Their loss!

CHAPTER 1

GLAZES AND STOCKS

Glazes and stocks are basic to soups, gravies and sauces. Glaze is the foundation for many excellent sauces and the process of making a glaze usually requires a quality piece of meat. Whereas stock is made from inferior cuts of meat or fish or fowl scraps, along with bones and vegetables, herbs and seasonings for additional flavor. The primary reason to use inferior cuts of meat when making stock, is that the cooking process removes everything of value from the meat and what remains is devoid of both nutrients and taste and should be thrown away. However, many people cannot in clear conscience, throw out a piece of meat even if it has simmered for hours. So for that reason I have included many sauces to use on "boiled" meats.

"Reduction" is a key word in preparing a stock and it refers to the process of simmering or boiling the liquid. Whenever a liquid is evaporated through cooking the flavor of the remaining liquid becomes very concentrated and potent. Some stocks are reduced by as much as 90% (as are glazes) and are basically an essence. For most home cooking you needn't reduce your stock to an essence. Let the pro's do that, then eat at their place.

When making a stock, cut everything up into chunks, or first cut the larger pieces so that they fit into your pot. Bones can either be sawn into small rings or splintered by using a hammer. The object is to expose the marrow so it becomes part of the stock. Some meats need to be browned prior to adding the liquid. Bones can be roasted, or in some fashion seared, then simmered in water with or without a little wine. In most cases, browned meats included, I recommend simmering the meats, bones, fish or fowl for about 20 to 30 minutes and skimming the scum off prior to adding any other ingredients.

VEAL STOCK

This recipe can easily be upgraded to become a "Jus de Veal Lie", by adding 1 medium leek, 1 clove, 1 small piece of blanched bacon rind and 3 tablespoons arrowroot. Swap the white wine for $^1/_2$ cup Madeira and double everything else.

Add the arrowroot and the Madeira at the end of the cooking time and remove from the heat. Freeze the portion not immediately used in cup sized containers for future use.

INGREDIENTS:		
	1	TABLESPOON BUTTER
	2	POUNDS VEAL SHANK, VEAL SCRAPS AND/OR BONES
	1	CARROT, CHOPPED
	1	MEDIUM ONION, CHOPPED
	4	CHIVES, CHOPPED
	$1^1/_2$	CUPS WINE (DRY WHITE OR YOUR CHOICE)
	3	QUARTS WATER
	1	TEASPOON SALT
	PINCH	DRIED THYME
	4	SPRIGS PARSLEY
	1	BAY LEAF

METHOD:

1. Slowly brown the veal, carrot, onion and chives in the butter. Add $^1/_2$ cup wine and cook until the wine is reduced and the pan is nearly dry. Repeat with a second $^1/_2$ cup wine and again with a third $^1/_2$ cup wine.

2. Now add the water and the remaining ingredients. Bring the stock to a boil and reduce the heat to hold the stock at a simmer. Cook for 2 hours or more.

3. At this time, strain and reserve the stock and discard the solids. Chill the stock. When the fat has congealed remove and discard it. Use the stock as directed by your recipe.

USE: As a veal demi-glaze and as a base for sauces or gravy.

YIELD: 3 Cups.

GLAZE

To prepare a glaze, choose one of two routes. Make the following recipe, or go to the next page and prepare the brown stock. If you choose the brown stock, you need to reduce the liquid until it coats your cooking spoon. Strain and refrigerate the remaining stock and it will solidify into a thick jell. Use this jell sparingly in other sauces.

Making this glaze is an expensive preparation for a home cook. You start with a 6 pound rump roast and 6 pounds of beef bones. I remember when bones used to be give-a-ways at the store, but now I find some butchers charging for "soup" or "dog" bones. Oh well, everything changes sooner or later.

INGREDIENTS:	6	LB RUMP ROAST
	6	LBS BEEF BONES
	1	CELERY RIB
	4	CARROTS
	2	GALLONS OF WATER
	1	BOUQUET GARNI: TIE UP THE FOLLOWING IN A DOUBLE WRAP OF CHEESE CLOTH:
	6	SPRIGS OF PARSLEY
	2	CLOVES GARLIC
	8	BLACK WHOLE PEPPERCORNS
	1	BAY LEAF
	1	TEASPOON DRY THYME OR A TABLESPOON IF FRESH

METHOD:

1. Preheat the oven to 500° F and roast the beef rump for 20 minutes to sear the outer surface. Remove the meat and cut into 2" chunks. Deglaze the roasting pan with some water, then transfer the beef and deglazed juices into a stock pot along with 2 gallons of water.

2. Place all the remaining ingredients into the stock pot and bring to a boil. Reduce the heat to a simmer and skim off the scum as it rises. Cook until the liquid has been reduced to about 1 quart.

3.   Season, if desired, with salt and pepper just prior to removing the stock from heat.

4.   Strain the contents and discard all the solids. Cool, then refrigerate. The glaze will jell.

USE: As a demi-glaze by mixing equal amounts of glaze and wine. (i.e., 1 tablespoon glaze and 1 tablespoon sherry or Madeira.) In this fashion it can be used as a sauce on sweetbreads or filet mignon.

As the thickener for light sauces or a terrific flavor addition to a Brown Sauce (Espagnole) or a Madeira Sauce.

YIELD: 4 cups.

BROWN STOCK

Brown stock is the foundation of one of the three mother sauces. Some chefs never use brown stock as a sauce on its own because of its versatility as an excellent base for many other sauces. The brown stock is easy to make, (although time consuming) and can be frozen. Those are big pluses to a busy cook.

Let me qualify that last sentence. It's easy to make if I assume that roasting the ingredients, deglazing the roasting pan and then simmering the stock for several hours to reduce the liquid, doesn't interfere with other things happening in your life. If that's the case, then follow this recipe.

A comparison of this recipe against brown stock recipes in other cookbooks shows that the only consistent ingredient is water. Everything else seems to be a personal choice by the chef, or limited to what's on hand. This sauce has a vociferous, if divided group of admirers. Those who maintain that this is a foundation stock, that it is never salted and only used as a base for sauces. And those who believe that it can be used as a sauce by itself by merely seasoning and thickening it to serve. You decide. Personally, I use it both ways.

Read the recipe first, (you may not want to make this one). If you have the time and look forward to simmering a pot on the stove all day, do it. If you don't, buy dehydrated beef stock at your market, reconstitute and thicken it, and bypass the following procedure.

INGREDIENTS:	5	POUNDS MEATY VEAL AND BEEF BONES. (IF YOU BUY FRESH OR CURED PICNIC HAM OR SLAB BACON, USE THE BLANCHED RIND FROM ANY OF THEM.)
	3	CARROTS (GREEN TOPS ARE OK)
	2	CELERY RIBS, TOPS INCLUDED
	1	ONION
	2 OR 3	GARLIC CLOVES
	3	TOMATOES, HALVED
	1	GALLON WATER
	$^1/_2$	CUP FLOUR
	2	TABLESPOONS LARD, BUTTER OR OIL

$^1/_2$	TEASPOON DRIED THYME (1 SMALL SPRIG IF FRESH)
$^1/_2$	TEASPOON PEPPERCORNS
1	BAY LEAF
2 OR 3	PARSLEY SPRIGS

METHOD:

1. Roast the bones and meat in a pan for 30 to 45 minutes in a 450° F oven. Add the vegetables and continue roasting for another 30 minutes. Transfer all the ingredients to a stock pot, then deglaze the roasting pan. Add the deglazed juices to the stock pot, along with 1 gallon of water.

Or, bypass step one and go directly to the option.

OPTION:

Place those same six ingredients into a stock pot, with 1 gallon of water. Bring it to a boil and lower the heat to simmer. Cook and skim for about six hours to reduce the liquid by 50%. Remove the meat, cut into cubes or chunks and roll the meat in the flour. Brown the floured meat in your choice of fat, then deglaze the pan.

2. Transfer all the ingredients, cooked and uncooked, into a second stock pot and add water to bring the liquid level to about 3 quarts. Bring the mixture to a boil and reduce the heat to a simmer. Simmer and skim as needed, until reduced to 2 quarts or less. Strain, cool and refrigerate or freeze. Use as called for in the sauce recipes.

USE: As a base for sauces or soups.

YIELD: 8 cups.

FISH STOCK

(AKA: FUMET)

INGREDIENTS:	1	POUND FISH HEADS, BONES AND TAILS
	1	SMALL ONION
	3	SPRIGS PARSLEY
	1	BAY LEAF
	PINCH	DRIED THYME
		SALT AND PEPPER AS DESIRED
	2	CUPS WATER
	$^1/_2$	CUP WINE (YOUR CHOICE)

METHOD: Place all the ingredients into a sauce pan and bring the mixture to a boil. Reduce the heat to a simmer and cook for 30 minutes. Skim the stock several times while cooking. When cooked, strain and reserve the stock. Discard all solids and use as directed by your recipe.

USE: As a base for sauces and some seafood soups.

YIELD: 1 $^1/_2$ Cups.

PORK BROTH

Why is this a broth and not a stock? Good question. Stock is a liquid sometimes flavored by a meat, with a selection of added ingredients. Broth is a liquid flavored from a single ingredient, with or without salt. The latter is what we have here. Admittedly pork broth has very limited uses. Its most frequent application is when used as a gravy for a pork roast. However, if you want extra gravy to cover mashed potatoes, stove-top stuffing or hot pork sandwiches, then take the time to make this broth.

INGREDIENTS:		CRACKED PORK BONES (NOT FROM HAM OR SMOKED MEATS)
	2	CUPS WATER PER POUND OF BONES
	$1/_4$	TEASPOON SALT PER CUP OF WATER

METHOD: Bring the ingredients to a boil and lower the heat to simmer. Cover and cook for 1 hour. Remove the fat and scum while simmering. Strain the broth and discard the solids.

USE: As a base for pork gravy.

YIELD: 2 Cups.

VEGETABLE STOCK

INGREDIENTS:

$1/4$	CUP DRIED BEANS (WHITE ARE PREFERRED)
$1/4$	CUP DRIED SPLIT PEAS (GREEN ARE PREFERRED)
1	MEDIUM ONION
1	CARROT
1	CELERY RIB
1	BUNCH PARSLEY
$1/2$	TEASPOON THYME (2 SPRIGS FRESH)
1	BAY LEAF
3	WHOLE CLOVES
PINCH	MACE
2	QUARTS WATER

METHOD: Place all the ingredients into a pot and bring them to a boil. Reduce the heat to simmer and cook for at least 3 hours. Occasionally skim the stock of any scum. Strain the stock and discard all solids. Use the stock as directed by your recipe.

USE: As a base for soups and sauces.

YIELD: 2 Cups.

VEGETABLE STOCK II

INGREDIENTS:

2	QUARTS WATER
1	POUND POTATOES, PEELED
2	ONIONS, HALVED
1	CELERY RIB
3	CARROTS, PEELED
3	TOMATOES, HALVED
3	SPRIGS PARSLEY
$1/_2$	TEASPOON DRIED THYME (2 SPRIGS IF FRESH)
1	BAY LEAF
1	TEASPOON SALT
$1/_4$	CUP OLIVE OIL

METHOD: Place all the ingredients into a stock pot, bring the mixture to a boil and reduce the heat to simmer. Cook for $1^1/_2$ hours. Strain the stock, and discard the solids.

USE: As a base for soups and sauces.

YIELD: 3 Cups.

"This page is blank by Design"

CHAPTER 2

VERSATILE MULTI-PURPOSE SAUCES AND GRAVIES

Some sauces defy categorization, while others are simply basic and versatile enough to be used on a variety of foods. I have heard at one time or another, that sauces in France could always be reliably reproduced. That is, they are "exact and true to the recipe". Well if that's so, it's true only in the mind of the person who coined the phrase. My bubble of naivete was punctured when I realized that sauce recipes - especially French sauces - are never reliably reproduced. When I look up two French sauce recipes, with the same name (like Espangole) in two different cookbooks, it's easy to see that sauce names travel but ingredients don't. Because the ingredients are usually different from recipe to recipe and yet it's called by the same name.

MAYONNAISE

Mayonnaise is a major component in several dozen well known and extensively used sauces and is probably the number one packaged sauce in America. It's right up there with ketchup and mustard. When freshly prepared it ranks along side white sauce. In smaller quantities, such as this recipe provides, it can be made in a shallow soup bowl. For larger quantities use a whip or egg beater and a medium sized bowl. It can also be made with a hand held blender in a large jar or iced tea glass and of course in a regular sized blender. Failure of the egg and oil to homogenize is generally the result of adding the oil too quickly. With this instruction permanently etched in your mind, go for it!

There are two conditions that must be met:

1.   All the ingredients must be at room temperature.

2.   The oil must be d-r-i-p-p-e-d into the egg mixture. Increase the flow to a drizzle after the mixture begins to thicken.

INGREDIENTS:	1	EGG YOLK
	$1/2$	TEASPOON SALT
	$1/4$	TEASPOON DRY MUSTARD
	1	CUP LIGHT OLIVE OIL
	2	TABLESPOONS OR LESS OF THE FOLLOWING, INDIVIDUALLY OR COMBINED:
		DISTILLED WHITE VINEGAR
		WHITE WINE VINEGAR
		LEMON JUICE

OPTIONS:	ADD ONE OR ALL OF THE FOLLOWING:	
	$1/2$	TEASPOON PAPRIKA
	PINCH	CAYENNE PEPPER
	1	TEASPOON SUGAR

METHOD: Beat the egg yolk, salt and dry mustard together until light and creamy.

Add the oil a few drops at a time until the mixture begins to thicken. Slowly increase the oil drops to a drizzle until all the oil has been fully blended and the mixture is fairly stiff. Add the vinegar to taste (and to thin the mixture).

USE ON: Sandwiches, cold meats, cold fish or vegetables.

YIELD: $1\frac{1}{4}$ cups.

MULTIPLIER: For a larger batch, double or triple the ingredients.

NUTRITIONAL FACTS:			
Serving Size: 1 T	Total Fat: 12 g	Sodium: 65 mg	Sugar: 0 g
Calories Per Serving: 110	Sat Fat: 1.5 g	Total Carbs: 0 g	Protein: 0 g
Fat Calories: 110	Cholest: 10 mg	Fiber: 0 g	

WHITE SAUCE

(BECHAMEL)

White Sauce (Bechamel) is one of a trinity of sauces called "Sauces Meres", meaning Mother Sauces. The other two parts of the trinity are; "Sauce Espagnole" meaning Brown Sauce (although Espagnole is the French spelling for the word "Spanish"), and "Glace" (French) or "Glaze" meaning the jell derived from roasted meats and bones, which are then simmered, reduced, seasoned, chilled and used sparingly in other sauces.

White Sauce is probably the basic cooking sauce of the western world and America in particular. In certain areas of Europe it is generally known as "Bechamel" and it is a name that has a variety of spellings. In Italian cookery it is called "Besciamella" or "Balsamella". Same sauce, different dialects. In the United States it's just called White Sauce. In the Creole/Cajun country of the gulf states it can also be called "Sauce Allemande" (Allemande is a French word that translated means "German"). Since so many sauces use a white sauce as a base and the fact that it is used in a very large list of recipes is what makes white sauce so incredibly versatile.

Peeking into the kitchens of America, you're apt to find a white sauce made from any fat or oil to which a little flour and milk has been added. That's a home cooks version of the white sauce. Elsewhere in culinary circles, an arbitrary selection of a fat in a white sauce sets the purist cook off into a snit. From their standpoint, a Bechamel sauce can only be made by using butter. That is not bad advice though, since a white sauce with one or several simple additions then become other famous sauces, i.e., "Mornay", "Florentine", "Dijonnaise", et cetera, et cetera, et cetera. In the group I hang out with, that's called "a bigga buncha."

However, since you're the one who'll be eating it, make it from what ever fat you like. Use butter, margarine, lard, bacon fat, sausage oil, rendered ham fat, rendered chicken fat or vegetable oil. It must be obvious to even the most inexperienced cook, that the fat you use becomes the dominant flavor of your sauce.

One additional point. Some recipes for Bechamel Sauce call for several ingredients to be stewed in the sauce and then strained just prior to serving. The following additions are used together, not individually: ham, mushrooms, onions, celery, carrots, sweet herbs, cloves, allspice and mace. You can also substitute the milk with heavy whipping cream and add a cup of Veloute sauce.

If the preceding sounds good to you, feel free to use it.

INGREDIENTS: 2   TABLESPOONS BUTTER (OR YOUR CHOICE OF FAT)
                  2   TABLESPOONS FLOUR
                  1   CUP MILK
                           SEASON TO TASTE WITH;
                           SALT, WHITE PEPPER OR FRESHLY GROUND BLACK PEPPER

METHOD: Melt the butter over low heat. Add the flour and whisk for about 3 minutes. Remove the pan from the heat. Whisk while you slowly add the milk. When the sauce is very smooth, return it to the heat and bring it to a low boil. Stop. It's done. Remove the sauce from the heat.

EMBELLISHMENTS: You may add the following ingredients to your sauce in any combination you wish, using just one addition to all of them:

                  PINCH   NUTMEG (FRESHLY GRATED IF POSSIBLE)
                  $^1/_4$ TEASPOON CELERY SEED
                  $^1/_4$ TEASPOON ONION POWDER
                  1   TEASPOON LEMON JUICE
                  1   TEASPOON SHERRY OR MARSALA WINE
                  $^1/_2$ TEASPOON WORCESTERSHIRE
                  1   TABLESPOON CHOPPED PARSLEY
                  1   TEASPOON DRIED/FRESH DILL WEED
                  2   TABLESPOONS CHOPPED CHIVES
                  PINCH   GARLIC POWDER
                  1 OR 2   HARD-COOKED EGG(S), CHOPPED
                  1   TABLESPOON CAPERS
                  1   TABLESPOON PICKLE RELISH

USE ON: 1. Chicken or turkey as in "ala King".
                  2. Biscuits - for biscuits and gravy.
                  3. Toast - as in creamed beef on toast.
                  4. Cooked ground beef (the military version of "S.O.S.").
                  5. 4 ounces of dried chipped beef or shaved luncheon meats.
                  6. Pasta (for a passably good and cheap "Alfredo" sauce, add grated Parmesan cheese).
                  7. Baked macaroni (melt in a little shredded yellow cheese).

8. Poached fish and other seafood.
9. Egg dishes.
10. Vegetables.

YIELD: 1 cup.

NUTRITIONAL FACTS:			
Serving Size: 1/4 cup	Total Fat: 7 g	Sodium: 75 mg	Sugar: 2 g
Calories Per Serving: 90	Sat Fat: 4 g	Total Carbs: 5 g	Protein: 2 g
Fat Calories: 60	Cholest: 20 mg	Fiber: 0 g	

MORNAY SAUCE

Although the sauce is named after its creator, Philippe de Mornay, to me the name Mornay, sounds too much like the name of a mean and ugly eel. If I hadn't already enjoyed the taste of the sauce, the name would keep me from wanting to try it. However, this reaction must be mine alone, everyone else seems to love this sauce. It is very likely the second most popular sauce for egg dishes, right behind Hollandaise.

If you have a double boiler, use it to prepare the sauce (not a requirement).

INGREDIENTS:		
	1	CUP WHITE SAUCE
	1	EGG YOLK
	2	TABLESPOONS CREAM
		USE ONE OR A MIXTURE OF THE FOLLOWING CHEESES;
	2	TABLESPOONS FRESHLY GRATED PARMESAN CHEESE
	2	TABLESPOONS GRATED SWISS OR GRUYERE CHEESE
	$1/4$	TEASPOON ONION POWDER OR,
	$1/2$	TEASPOON ONION JUICE OR,
	1	TEASPOON GRATED SHALLOTS

METHOD: Blend the egg yolk and cream with the white sauce. Place these ingredients into a sauce pan and bring the contents slowly to a low boil. Whisk in the cheese(s). Remove the sauce from the heat and season to taste with salt and/or a few grains of cayenne pepper.

USE ON:
1. Poached eggs, souffles, or on omelets.
2. Fish, when poached, broiled or steamed.
3. Vegetable dishes.

YIELD: $1^{1}/_{4}$ cups.

NUTRITIONAL FACTS:			
Serving Size: 1/4 cup	Total Fat: 8 g	Sodium: 90 mg	Sugar: 2 g
Calories Per Serving: 100	Sat Fat: 4.5 g	Total Carbs: 5 g	Protein: 3 g
Fat Calories: 70	Cholest: 45 mg	Fiber: 0 g	

MORNAY SAUCE TOO

This sauce is close to the preceding Mornay with some variance, but equally as rich.

A double boiler is the best choice for this sauce. If you don't have one, and you have a gas stove, keep the flame well below the pan. If you have an electric stove, use a diffuser or other device to keep your pan up off the heating surface.

INGREDIENTS:

2	TABLESPOONS CHOPPED ONION
6	TABLESPOONS BUTTER
$^1/_2$	CUP FLOUR
2	CUPS MILK
3	EGG YOLKS, BEATEN
1	TABLESPOON HEAVY CREAM
2	TABLESPOONS FRESHLY GRATED PARMESAN CHEESE

METHOD:

1. Beat the egg yolks with the cream and set aside.

2. Saute the onion in 4 tablespoons of the butter until soft.

3. Whisk the flour into the butter and onion and when thoroughly blended, whisk in the milk. Cook until the mixture thickens.

4. At this point, you'll need to strain the onion out of the sauce. After you do so, return the sauce to the heat, whisk in the egg yolk mixture and cook for several minutes. Whisk in the Parmesan cheese and the remaining 2 tablespoons of butter.

USE ON:

1. Poached eggs, souffles, omelets.
2. Fish (when poached, broiled or steamed).
3. Vegetable dishes.

YIELD: 3 cups.

NUTRITIONAL FACTS:			
Serving Size: 1/4 cup	Total Fat: 9 g	Sodium: 95 mg	Sugar: 2 g
Calories Per Serving: 120	Sat Fat: 5 g	Total Carbs: 6 g	Protein: 3 g
Fat Calories: 80	Cholest: 75 mg	Fiber: 0 g	

WHITE ONION SAUCE

(SOUBISE)

This delicately onion-flavored sauce has wide application. Any dish you want to give an onion flavor to, will benefit from this recipe.

Start by making a Veloute sauce (unless you just happen to have some in the refrigerator).

INGREDIENTS:	$1^1/_2$	CUPS VELOUTE SAUCE
	2	MEDIUM ONIONS CHOPPED
	2	TABLESPOONS BUTTER
	2	TABLESPOONS WHIPPING CREAM
		SALT AND PEPPER

METHOD:

1. Saute the onions in the butter until transparent. Add the Veloute sauce to the onions and bring the sauce to a boil. Reduce the heat to a simmer and cook for 30 minutes.

2. At this point puree the sauce in a blender, or press it through a sieve. This will give you a smooth sauce. Add the whipping cream and then season to taste.

USE ON: Poultry, fish or vegetables.

YIELD: $1^3/_4$ cups.

NUTRITIONAL FACTS:			
Serving Size: 1/4 cup	Total Fat: 4 g	Sodium: 115 mg	Sugar: 2 g
Calories Per Serving: 50	Sat Fat: 2.5 g	Total Carbs: 3 g	Protein: 1 g
Fat Calories: 35	Cholest: 10 mg	Fiber: 1 g	

HUNGARIAN PAPRIKA SAUCE

I love this sauce and make it quite often. Not only is it good on a variety of meats, but it is particularly good on home made dumplings. The Hungarians call these little egg dumplings, tarhonya. The Germans and the Austrians call it spatzle. My mother (nee: Nagy) taught me how to whip up these light, tasty dumplings to go with her chicken paprika. And I can do it as quick as a cat can wink it's eye.

The standard cooking fat in Hungary is lard and if you have it, use it. You can also use bacon fat or butter. If you wish to forgo the animal fat, use vegetable oil or extra light olive oil.

Paprika makes a difference and I recommend the sweet, bright red, Hungarian kind. The most readily available brand in America is from Szeged and called by the same name. It is available in several intensities from sweet to hot.

Pepper types; you use one sweet bell-type pepper (not green they are overpowering in this sauce). Instead use a red, orange or yellow pepper, as they are milder. Occasionally you may find whole pimento peppers in your market and they are quite sweet and similar to the Hungarian sweet red pepper.

INGREDIENTS:	2	TABLESPOONS FAT
	2	MEDIUM ONIONS, CHOPPED
	1	LARGE TOMATO, PEELED AND CHOPPED
	2	TABLESPOONS PAPRIKA
	1	TEASPOON SALT
	1	SWEET PEPPER, CHOPPED
	$^1/_2$	CUP SOUR CREAM

ALTERNATE: You can replace a tablespoon or two of sour cream with whipping cream.

METHOD: Saute the onions in the fat until they are quite soft, then add the tomato, paprika, salt and bell pepper. Continue cooking the sauce for an additional 20 minutes. Remove from the heat and stir in the sour cream.

USE ON: Chicken, fish, veal, dumplings or noodles.

YIELD: 2 ¹/₂ cups.

WE TRIED THIS SAUCE ... AND

SUPREME SAUCE

Another expansion of a basic Veloute sauce. It is white in color and delicate in taste.

INGREDIENTS:

1 $^1/_2$ CUPS VELOUTE SAUCE (MADE WITH CHICKEN STOCK)
1 CUP CHICKEN STOCK
$^1/_4$ CUP CHOPPED MUSHROOM STEMS/PIECES
$^1/_2$ CUP WHIPPING CREAM
1 TABLESPOON BUTTER
SALT AND PEPPER TO TASTE

METHOD:

1. Bring the Veloute sauce, chicken stock and mushrooms to a boil and reduce the heat to a simmer. Cook the sauce uncovered until reduced by 25% to approximately 1-1/2 half cups.

2. Remove the sauce from the heat and strain to remove the mushrooms. Thoroughly blend in the whipping cream, and add the butter and seasoning.

USE ON:

Eggs, poultry and fish.

Yield:

2 $^1/_2$ cups.

NUTRITIONAL FACTS:

Serving Size: 3 T	Total Fat: 3..5 g	Sodium: 110 mg	Sugar: 1 g
Calories Per Serving: 45	Sat Fat: 2 g	Total Carbs: 2 g	Protein: 1 g
Fat Calories: 35	Cholest: 10 mg	Fiber: 0 g	

CELERY SAUCE

Celery has a flavor that sometimes I can smell and taste in my mind. I think it is absolutely wonderful. This sauce, when used on the foods recommended below, are a pairing that is outstanding.

INGREDIENTS:	$1/4$	CUP BUTTER
	$3/4$	CUP FINELY CHOPPED CELERY
	$1/4$	CUP FLOUR
	2	CUPS MILK
		SALT AND PEPPER TO TASTE

METHOD: Saute the celery in the the butter for 5 minutes. Slowly add the flour, while continuously stirring, until the mixture is lump free and smooth. Continue stirring while you add the milk. Cook until the sauce thickens, stirring constantly. Remove from the heat and season to taste.

USE ON: Meat loaves, fish, eggs and meat croquettes.

YIELD: 2 $1/2$ cups.

NUTRITIONAL FACTS:

Serving Size: 1/4 cup	Total Fat: 6 g	Sodium: 70 mg	Sugar: 2 g
Calories Per Serving: 80	Sat Fat: 3.5 g	Total Carbs: 4 g	Protein: 2 g
Fat Calories: 50	Cholest: 15 mg	Fiber: 0 g	

CURRY SAUCE

When you get a taste for curry, this sauce is a great one to satisfy it.

Curry is the seasoning of India and much of Southeast Asia. A little of it goes a long way, so use it sparingly. Also bear in mind that it has a very interesting quality. The regular daily or weekly use of curry will cause the spices to permeate your body and vent through your pores. If that doesn't create a social problem for you, then eat it to your hearts content.

As a point of information, the ingredients in curry powders are the cooks choice. They are made from a variety of dried herbs and spices which are ground into a powder. The range of flavor intensity runs from mild to hot. There is no standard recipe.

INGREDIENTS:

$^1/_4$	CUP BUTTER
$^1/_4$	MINCED ONION
2	TABLESPOONS FLOUR
1	TEASPOON CURRY POWDER (+/- ACCORDING TO YOUR TASTE)
PINCH	CRUMBLED SAFFRON
1	CUP CHICKEN BROTH
1	CUP CREAM
$^1/_2$	TEASPOON FRESH LEMON ZEST

OPTIONS TO TASTE:

Hot pepper sauce
Cayenne
Ground or grated ginger
Sherry
Chutney (minced)
Sweet pickle relish

METHOD: Saute the onion in the butter until soft, then blend in the flour, curry powder and saffron. Cook for a moment or two before adding the chicken broth, cream and lemon zest. Bring your sauce to a boil. Reduce the heat to a simmer and add your chosen options. Cook the sauce for an additional 10 minutes, then remove from the heat. Strain if you want a smooth sauce.

Use On: Chicken, fish or vegetables.

Yield: 2 $\frac{1}{2}$ cups.

NUTRITIONAL FACTS:

Serving Size: 1/4 cup	Total Fat: 12 g	Sodium: 130 mg	Sugar: 1 g
Calories Per Serving: 120	Sat Fat: 7 g	Total Carbs: 3 g	Protein: 1 g
Fat Calories: 110	Cholest: 40 mg	Fiber: 0 g	

BROWN BUTTER SAUCE

(SAUCE AUX BEURRE NOISETTE)

In making this sauce you can choose how much preparation time you are willing to devote to it. The sauce is simplicity itself, since the time you invest is simply to clarify the butter. There are two schools of thought on this subject. One calls for the butter to be clarified before cooking. Presumably this step avoids the possibility of burning the the non-fat sediment found in butter. The other ignores that step and uses the butter straight from the package. You decide what method you prefer.

INGREDIENTS: $^1/_4$ POUND BUTTER, CLARIFIED OR NOT

METHOD: Melt the butter over medium heat until it begins to brown. Remove from heat.

USE ON: Shrimp, Crawfish, Brains, Asparagus And Broccoli.

YIELD: $^1/_2$ cup.

NUTRITIONAL FACTS:

Serving Size: 1 T	Total Fat: 12 g	Sodium: 125 mg	Sugar: 0 g
Calories Per Serving: 110	Sat Fat: 8 g	Total Carbs: 0 g	Protein: 0 g
Fat Calories: 110	Cholest: 35 mg	Fiber: 0 g	

BLACK BUTTER

(BEURRE NOIR)

If you're the type who routinely burns the butter, this is your sauce! Well, maybe..., however, if you don't want to risk burning the butter while browning it, you can use clarified butter, because you'll be cooking the butter until is is quite brown. Actually clarified butter won't brown, but you can get it hot enough to influence the flavor.

INGREDIENTS:	$^1/_4$	POUND BUTTER
	2	TABLESPOONS PARSLEY, FINELY CHOPPED
	3	TABLESPOONS LEMON JUICE, OR VINEGAR
		SALT AND PEPPER TO TASTE

METHOD: Melt the butter over medium heat until it begins to brown, stir in the parsley and cook 30 seconds before adding the lemon juice. Simmer the sauce for 2 additional minutes, then season to taste.

USE ON: Crawfish, fish, eggs, sweetbreads, calves brains and vegetables.

YIELD: $^3/_4$ cup.

NUTRITIONAL FACTS:			
Serving Size: 1 T	Total Fat: 8 g	Sodium: 85 mg	Sugar: 0 g
Calories Per Serving: 70	Sat Fat: 5 g	Total Carbs: 0 g	Protein: 0 g
Fat Calories: 70	Cholest: 20 mg	Fiber: 0 g	

CAULIFLOWER SAUCE

Here is another wonderful use for a white sauce. As a cook, you may not think of cauliflower as having the best flavor for a sauce, but there are dishes to which it adds just the right touch. The ones that benefit from a mildly flavored sauce. It also helps you get rid of leftover cauliflower.

INGREDIENTS:	1	CUP WHITE SAUCE
	$^1/_2$	CUP COOKED AND MINCED CAULIFLOWER

METHOD: Heat and serve.

USE ON: Boiled fish, sauted veal, cooked cauliflower.

YIELD: 1 $^1/_2$ cups.

NUTRITIONAL FACTS:

Serving Size: 1/4 cup	Total Fat: 5 g	Sodium: 90 mg	Sugar: 2 g
Calories Per Serving: 70	Sat Fat: 3.5 g	Total Carbs: 4 g	Protein: 2 g
Fat Calories: 50	Cholest: 15 mg	Fiber: 0 g	

DRAWN BUTTER

(CLARIFIED BUTTER)

As a youngster going to the movies was a marvelous event. Especially the part where we stopped at the candy store next door to the theatre, to buy freshly popped corn and have it drenched with clarified butter. M-m-m-m-m! It was so good. I miss it. Aside from pouring it all over popcorn, drawn butter is used in many sauces, particularly seafood sauces.

By the way, don't confuse this with the Drawn Butter Sauce in Chapter Two.

INGREDIENTS:	1	POUND BUTTER

METHOD:

1. Melt the butter in a microwave oven, or small pan. When completely melted, allow it to sit at room temperature while the milk solids and salt settle to the bottom.

2. Chill the butter and when solid, remove it from your container. Turn it upside down, then remove and discard the light colored solids.

3. To use, reheat the chilled clarified butter.

USE ON: Recipes calling for clarified butter such as a dip for lobster and shrimp. And if your doctor allows, on popcorn.

YIELD: 1 $^3/_4$ cups.

NUTRITIONAL FACTS:

Serving Size: 1 T	Total Fat: 12 g	Sodium: 125 mg	Sugar: 0 g
Calories Per Serving: 110	Sat Fat: 8 g	Total Carbs: 0 g	Protein: 0 g
Fat Calories: 110	Cholest: 35mg	Fiber: 0 g	

ASPIC

Aspic itself is very basic and there are a number of flavors you can use in making it. Many sauciers make aspic from bouillon. That's fine, if you have the time to make a bouillon, but it's quicker to make it from packaged, dehydrated soup base or from bouillon granules or cubes. However convenience comes with a draw back, because salt is the major ingredient of these products. Thus is a serious consideration for people who must restrict salt in their diet. In that case you'd be better off following the recipe.

If you are new at this, always serve aspic cold.

INGREDIENTS:	1	PACKAGE UNFLAVORED GELATIN
	1	CUP MEAT OR VEGETABLE STOCK OR WATER

METHOD: Bring the stock or water to a boil. Whisk or stir while adding the unflavored gelatin to the liquid. Allow the liquid to cool slightly and pour the gelatin over your food. Allow the mixture to cool to room temperature before refrigerating. Chill for several hours.

FLAVORING OPTIONS YOU CAN ADD TO THE ASPIC:

$^{1}/_{2}$	CUP COINTREAU IS GOOD ON DUCK.
$^{1}/_{2}$	CUP WHITE WINE
1	TEASPOON WORCESTERSHIRE SAUCE AND POSSIBLY A PINCH OF CAYENNE IF IT IS TO BE USED ON COLD ROAST BEEF SLICES.

OPTIONS: To decorate the jelled food you can use: Olives (whole, stuffed or sliced), orange sections or slices, cucumber slices, water cress, parsley, whole fresh basil leaves, or slices of bell pepper.

USE ON: Beef, chicken, duck, fish, tomatoes, pate.

YIELD: 1 cup.

NUTRITIONAL FACTS:

Serving Size: 1 T	Total Fat: 0 g	Sodium: 50 mg	Sugar: 0 g
Calories Per Serving: 0	Sat Fat: 0 g	Total Carbs: 0 g	Protein: 1 g
Fat Calories: 0	Cholest: 0 mg	Fiber: 0 g	

KETCHUP

Ketchup... Catsup... Catch-Up. These words and possibly other variants are used in the United States to define this sweet tomato sauce. Certainly one of America's favorite sauces, ketchup is a nearly indispensable condiment to French Fries.

To keep your life uncomplicated, buy it! However, should you chose to make your own. In this recipe you'll be using canned tomatoes. To add more freshness, replace the canned tomatoes with 2 pounds of fresh tomatoes. Wash, quarter and cook them until slightly reduced. Add salt to taste, then continue by following the recipe.

INGREDIENTS:		
	1-28	OUNCE CAN WHOLE TOMATOES, SQUISHED.
	1	ONION, COARSELY CHOPPED
	$1/_2$	CLOVE GARLIC
	$1/_2$	BELL PEPPER, SEEDED
	2	TABLESPOONS SUGAR (BROWN SUGAR IS OK)
	$1/_4$	TEASPOON CELERY SEED
	$1/_4$	TEASPOON ALLSPICE
	PINCH	CRUSHED RED PEPPER
	1	STICK CINNAMON
	$1/_2$	CUP VINEGAR

METHOD: Place all the ingredients, except the vinegar, into a sauce pan and bring the mixture to a boil. Reduce the heat to a simmer and cook the sauce for 15 minutes. Add the vinegar and continue cooking for 10 more minutes. Check for thickness. You may wish to cook it down for several additional minutes. Strain the sauce and cool before using.

USE ON: French fries, hot dogs, hamburgers, meat loaf. Or as a base for other sauces, such as barbecue, shrimp cocktail, sloppy joe's or chili sauce.

YIELD: 4 cups.

NUTRITIONAL FACTS:			
Serving Size: 2 T	Total Fat: 0 g	Sodium: 40 mg	Sugar: 2 g
Calories Per Serving: 15	Sat Fat: 0 g	Total Carbs: 3 g	Protein: 0 g
Fat Calories: 0	Cholest: 0 mg	Fiber: 1 g	

MUSTARD

Somewhere in the middle 80's mustard seems to have developed a life of it's own. That's when Americans became aware of the many varieties of mustards, and they were welcomed voraciously. During that time most of the mustards entering the general marketplace were the older European or Asian varieties. Today the variety of mustards available from creative American entrepreneurs ranges between bewildering and staggering. Here I'm giving you only the basic starter, dry mustard and liquid.

Be creative and select your liquid from water, white wine vinegar, distilled vinegar, lemon juice, lime juice, beer or champagne (either singly or in combination). To give texture to the mustard, add any of the following in small amounts: whole or crushed mustard seed, garlic, sugar, honey, horseradish, flavored syrups, cinnamon, nutmeg, mace, cloves and/or rubbed herbs such as thyme, sage, marjoram, tarragon, chervil, parsley, mint, tumeric (for color), lemon peel, ginger, capers, chives, shallots, leeks, green onion or minced onion.

Use a cold liquid and blend it with the ground dry mustard. It is easy and uncomplicated. One grade above the cold mix is the cooked version, where hot liquids are blended with the dry mustard and then cooked in a double boiler for about 15 minutes. You can either drain off the liquid, or whisk in a little flour (or a small amount of bread crumbs reduced to flour) and continue to cook until all the liquid is absorbed.

INGREDIENTS: $1/2$ CUP DRY MUSTARD
                 $1/3$ CUP VINEGAR
                 PINCH   GROUND TUMERIC

METHOD: Whisk the mustard and tumeric into the vinegar.

USE ON: Hot dogs, hamburgers, grilled sausages, roast chicken, barbecued ribs, cold meats, cheese sauces and anything else that comes to mind.

YIELD: $1/2$ cup.

NUTRITIONAL FACTS:

Serving Size: 1 T	Total Fat: 0 g	Sodium: 0 mg	Sugar: 0 g
Calories Per Serving: 20	Sat Fat: 0 g	Total Carbs: 2 g	Protein: 2 g
Fat Calories: 5	Cholest: 0 mg	Fiber: 0 g	

AIOLI SAUCE

Aioli, (pronounced ee-o-lee), is a French word for garlic-laden mayonnaise. It also has a second name in France, well at least in Paris, where it is called Provence Butter. It is a sauce for people who take to garlic like a duck takes to water. If your dinner companion loves the sauce and you don't ..., keep a pocketful of breath mints handy to offer to them to keep their breath as sweet as yours.

INGREDIENTS:	8	CLOVES GARLIC, SMASHED, MASHED OR PRESSED
	3	EGG YOLKS
	$1\frac{1}{2}$	TABLESPOONS LEMON JUICE
	$\frac{1}{2}$	TEASPOON SALT
	1	CUP OLIVE OIL (YOUR CHOICE; EXTRA LIGHT, EXTRA VIRGIN, REGULAR)

METHOD:

1. Place all the ingredients, except the olive oil, into a bowl and whisk until thoroughly blended.

2. If you have an electric mixer with wire beaters, use them during this next step, or continue with the whisk.

3. While beating constantly, add the oil a few drops at a time. Slowly increase the flow to a light drizzle until you've used all the oil and the sauce has thickened. Allow the sauce to meld at room temperature for several hours before using.

USE: As a sauce or dip for a whole host of cooked and raw vegetables, greens, hard cooked eggs and seafood. As an appetizer spread for bread.

YIELD: $1\frac{1}{2}$ cups.

NUTRITIONAL FACTS:

Serving Size: 1 T	Total Fat: 11 g	Sodium: 55 mg	Sugar: 0 g
Calories Per Serving: 100	Sat Fat: 1.5 g	Total Carbs: 1 g	Protein: 0 g
Fat Calories: 100	Cholest: 30 mg	Fiber: 0 g	

TERIYAKI SAUCE

This recipe makes about five cups of Teriyaki sauce. If that is more than you'll use in this lifetime, reduce the recipe by half or more. Do your own math.

The sauce will keep indefinitely and actually improve during storage as a result of the melding of flavors.

INGREDIENTS:	1	CUP SOY SAUCE
	1	QUART UNSWEETENED PINEAPPLE JUICE
	1	TABLESPOON GARLIC POWDER
	1	TABLESPOON GROUND GINGER
	1	TABLESPOON DRY MUSTARD
	1	TEASPOON WHITE PEPPER
	$^{1}/_{2}$	CUP BROWN SUGAR

METHOD: Place all the ingredients into a blender and let 'er rip for several minutes. Store in the refrigerator.

USE ON: Rice, chicken, fish and Japanese dishes, hamburgers and as a marinade for steak.

YIELD: 5 cups.

NUTRITIONAL FACTS:

Serving Size: 1 Tsp.	Total Fat: 0 g	Sodium: 120 mg	Sugar: 1 g
Calories Per Serving: 5	Sat Fat: 0 g	Total Carbs: 2 g	Protein: 0 g
Fat Calories: 0	Cholest: 0 mg	Fiber: 0 g	

CAPERS SAUCE

This sauce has a built-in versatility, because you choose the type of bouillon for the sauce. A meat bouillon makes this sauce great with veal or poultry. A fish bouillon (fumet) is terrific on fish. You'll need a roux and if you have some ready, get it out. If not, follow the recipe.

INGREDIENTS:	3	TABLESPOONS BUTTER
	3	TABLESPOONS FLOUR
	$1\frac{1}{2}$	CUPS BOUILLON (YOUR CHOICE)
	$\frac{1}{2}$	CUP HALF AND HALF
	2	TABLESPOONS CAPERS, DRAINED BUT NOT RINSED
	SALT AND PEPPER TO TASTE	

METHOD:

1. Melt the butter over medium heat.

2. Whisk the flour into the hot butter and continue cooking for 2 to 3 minutes.

3. Whisk the bouillon into the roux, cook until the sauce begins to thicken. Whisk in the cream and continue cooking until the sauce thickens again.

4. Remove the sauce from the heat, add the capers and seasoning.

USE ON: Veal, poultry or fish.

YIELD: 2 cups.

NUTRITIONAL FACTS:			
Serving Size: 2 T	Total Fat: 3 g	Sodium: 85 mg	Sugar: 0 g
Calories Per Serving: 35	Sat Fat: 1.5 g	Total Carbs: 1 g	Protein: 1 g
Fat Calories: 25	Cholest: 5 mg	Fiber: 0 g	

WE TRIED THIS SAUCE ... AND

LOVED IT ( )
HATED IT ( )
MAYBE WE'LL TRY IT AGAIN ( )
WE'LL USE IT FOR UNWELCOME GUESTS ( )

DILL SAUCE

This sauce is a part of my childhood and is also more versatile than other dill sauces (at least it has more uses). You'll need a little roux for this and if you have it on hand, use it. If not, follow the recipe.

INGREDIENTS:	2	TABLESPOONS FLOUR
	2	TABLESPOONS BUTTER
	2	CUPS CHICKEN BROTH
	2	TABLESPOONS BUTTER
	1	ONION, FINELY CHOPPED
	$^{1}/_{2}$	CUP SOUR CREAM
	2	TABLESPOONS FRESH DILL WEED
		OR
	2	TEASPOONS DRIED DILL WEED

METHOD:

1. In a sauce pan, melt the butter, whisk in the flour and continue to cook for several minutes. Remove the roux from the heat and whisk the chicken broth into the roux. Set it aside.

2. In a skillet, saute the onion in the butter until a few onion edges begin to brown. Transfer the sauteed onion to the sauce pan and stir in the lemon juice.

3. Return the sauce pan to the stove and bring the mixture to a boil. Cook until the sauce begins to thicken. Remove the sauce from the heat and whisk in sour the cream and dill weed.

USE ON: Poached, baked or broiled fish, assorted vegetables (such as asparagus, carrots or green beans), cold roast pork, or veal and roasted beef hot off the spit.

YIELD: 3 cups.

NUTRITIONAL FACTS:

Serving Size: 3 T	Total Fat: 4 g	Sodium: 115 mg	Sugar: 1 g
Calories Per Serving: 45	Sat Fat: 2.5 g	Total Carbs: 2 g	Protein: 1 g
Fat Calories: 35	Cholest: 10 mg	Fiber: 0 g	

YOGURT SAUCE

INGREDIENTS:	2	CLOVES GARLIC, SMASHED AND MASHED WITH A PINCH OF SALT
	2	TABLESPOONS BUTTER
	1	TEASPOON PAPRIKA
	2	TABLESPOONS FLOUR
	2	TABLESPOONS FRESH DILL WEED
	$^1/_4$	CUP BEEF OR CHICKEN BOUILLON
	2	CUPS PLAIN YOGURT

METHOD:

1. Thoroughly blend the first 5 ingredients together and set aside.

2. In a sauce pan, blend the bouillon and yogurt together. Slowly bring the mixture to scalding and whisk in the remaining ingredients. Cook for about 2 minutes until the sauce begins to bubble. Remove from the heat and serve.

USE ON: Assorted vegetables or poached fish.

YIELD: 2 $^1/_2$ cups.

NUTRITIONAL FACTS:

Serving Size: 1/4 cup	Total Fat: 4 g	Sodium: 70 mg	Sugar: 2 g
Calories Per Serving: 60	Sat Fat: 2.5 g	Total Carbs: 4 g	Protein: 2 g
Fat Calories: 35	Cholest: 15 mg	Fiber: 0 g	

WE TRIED THIS SAUCE ... AND

MARCHAND DE VIN SAUCE

(WINE MERCHANTS SAUCE)

This version of Marchand de Vin is a very rich sauce. The best way to use it, is to chill the finished sauce and when it has solidified, spread it like butter over your meat. Or, roll it into balls, as you would roll butter balls, and place a ball on each piece of cooked hot meat. It melts and flows over the meat to flavor and season it.

INGREDIENTS:		
	1	POUND BUTTER AT ROOM TEMPERATURE
	2	CUPS OF A DEEP RED WINE: BURGUNDY, ZINFANDEL, MERLOT, PETIT SIRAH OR PINOT NOIR
	$^1/_2$	CUP MINCED SHALLOTS
	$^1/_2$	CUP PARSLEY, FINELY CHOPPED
	$^1/_2$	TEASPOON FRESHLY GROUND BLACK PEPPER

OPTIONS:
1. REPLACE THE SHALLOTS WITH GREEN ONIONS.
2. ADD 1/2 CUP COOKED MUSHROOMS.
3. REPLACE 1 CUP WINE WITH AN EQUAL AMOUNT OF BROWN SAUCE.
4. ADD 2 TABLESPOONS LEMON JUICE.

METHOD:
1. Place the wine, shallots, parsley and black pepper into a sauce pan. Bring this mixture to a fast boil and continue cooking until the liquid is reduced by half.

2. Remove the sauce from the heat and allow it to cool. When lukewarm, thoroughly blend in the softened butter. You can use the sauce as is, or chill it before using as I have suggested above.

USE ON: Broiled steaks, broiled or barbecued chicken, shrimp.

YIELD: 2 cups.

NUTRITIONAL FACTS:			
Serving Size: 3 T	Total Fat: 16 g	Sodium: 170 mg	Sugar: 0 g
Calories Per Serving: 160	Sat Fat: 10 g	Total Carbs: 1 g	Protein: 0 g
Fat Calories: 140	Cholest: 45 mg	Fiber: 0 g	

Sauce Robert

Sauce Robert is a well known and widely used sauce, both in restaurants specializing in French style foods, and in American Steak and Chop Houses.

INGREDIENTS:		
	1	ONION, CHOPPED
	2	TABLESPOONS BUTTER
	$^3/_4$	CUP WHITE WINE
	1	CUP BROWN SAUCE OR DEMI-GLAZE
	1	TEASPOON DRY MUSTARD
	PINCH	POWDERED SUGAR

METHOD:

1. Saute the onion in the butter until it wilts. add the wine and bring the sauce to a boil. Cook until reduced by $^1/_3$.

2. Add the brown sauce, then reduce the heat to a simmer and continue cooking the sauce for 20 minutes more.

3. Before removing the sauce from the heat, stir in the dry mustard and powdered sugar.

USE ON: Pork steaks, pork loin medallions, slices from a pork roast, grilled or broiled steak, veal or chicken.

Sauce Robert can also be used on fish, but you'll need to add a tablespoon of capers for piquancy.

YIELD: $2^1/_2$ cups.

NUTRITIONAL FACTS:			
Serving Size: 3 T	Total Fat: 3 g	Sodium: 70 mg	Sugar: 1 g
Calories Per Serving: 50	Sat Fat: 2 g	Total Carbs: 3 g	Protein: 1 g
Fat Calories: 25	Cholest: 10 mg	Fiber: 0 g	

CREOLE SAUCE

For group entertaining, Creole sauce served over croquettes or unseasoned meatballs provides a nice change to the usual Swedish meatballs or cocktail franks.

INGREDIENTS:		
	2	CUPS WATER
	1	SMALL CAN TOMATO PASTE
	$^1/_2$	CUP SUGAR
	$^1/_2$	CUP CIDER VINEGAR
	1 $^1/_2$	CUPS CHOPPED CELERY
	$^1/_2$	CUP CHOPPED ONION
	1	TEASPOON SALT
	PINCH	OREGANO

METHOD:

1. Place all the ingredients into a sauce pan and bring the mixture to a boil. Reduce the heat to simmer, cover and cook for 2 hours.

2. At the end of the cooking time, check the sauce for thickness. If the sauce is thin, thicken it with 1/4 cup cornstarch dissolved in 1 cup of water.

USE ON: Beef or lamb croquettes, or other lightly seasoned meatballs.

YIELD: $3^1/_2$ cups.

NUTRITIONAL FACTS:

Serving Size: 1/4 cup	Total Fat: 0 g	Sodium: 200 mg	Sugar: 4 g
Calories Per Serving: 25	Sat Fat: 0 g	Total Carbs: 7 g	Protein: 0 g
Fat Calories: 0	Cholest: 0 mg	Fiber: 1 g	

CHAPTER 3

SAUCES AND GRAVIES FOR MEATS, FISH AND FOWL.

Gravies made from meat juices are sometimes called "pan gravy" and they are simple and quick to make. If you're the type of cook who keeps a little roux handy, start by placing one or more tablespoons of the roux into a sauce pan or skillet. Heat the roux, then add the defatted pan juices it (while whisking) to get a smooth, lump-free thickened sauce. Four tablespoons of roux to 2 cups of fat free liquid, gives a medium thick gravy. If you're like most cooks and don't have a roux on hand, follow the recipe.

PAN GRAVY

Pan gravy is a thin gravy made from the drippings and juice of meats that have been roasted, browned, sauteed, broiled or braised. When braising you get a liquid some cooks call "pot liquor". If you've roasted the beef, the unthickened juices in the pan plus a little water gives you "Au Jus". Similarly when you've seared a ham steak and then deglazed the pan with a little strong black coffee or water, you have what many Southerners call "Red Eye Gravy".

INGREDIENTS: 2   TABLESPOONS OF FAT FROM THE PAN DRIPPINGS
                  2   TABLESPOONS FLOUR

                  1   CUP LIQUID, (SELECT YOUR CHOICE OF LIQUID FROM THE FOLLOWING):

DEFATTED PAN JUICES, STOCK, BROTH, WATER, WINE, COFFEE, BEER, MILK, HALF N' HALF AND CREAM. USE FRUIT JUICE IF YOU ARE COOKING PORK OR HAM.

SEASON TO TASTE:

SELECT 1, OR SEVERAL OF THE FOLLOWING:
SALT
PEPPER (BLACK, WHITE, CAYENNE OR PAPRIKA)
HERBS (MINCED IF FRESH, CRUMBLED IF DRY)
GRATED LEMON RIND (TRY ORANGE OR LIME RIND W/PORK)

OPTIONAL: Sliced mushrooms, uncooked or precooked. If uncooked, you will need to simmer them in your gravy for 5 to 6 minutes.

COLOR: For beef cuts use a coloring agent such as Kitchen Bouquet, Gravy Master or caramelized sugar. Beef gravies are normally darker than gravies for pork or veal. Use cream or milk when coloring chicken or turkey gravy.

METHOD:

1. Make a roux by first separating the hot fat from the pan juices. Add the flour and cook them together for several minutes.

2. Remove the roux* from the heat.

3. Add your liquid to the roux and whisk 'til smooth. Return the pan to the heat and cook the gravy on low heat until it thickens. Season to taste and add mushrooms and/or color.

4. To double your recipe, double the first three ingredients.

* You can color your roux by cooking until it turns a light to medium shade of brown. This step colors your gravy and no additional coloring is needed.

USE ON: Meats or poultry that have been roasted, fried or braised.

YIELD: 1 $^1/_2$ cups.

NUTRITIONAL FACTS:			
Serving Size: 1/4 cup	Total Fat: 6 g	Sodium: 160 mg	Sugar: 0 g
Calories Per Serving: 70	Sat Fat: 3 g	Total Carbs: 3 g	Protein: 1 g
Fat Calories: 50	Cholest: 5 mg	Fiber: 0 g	

SOUTHWESTERN RAISIN SAUCE

INGREDIENTS:

2	TABLESPOONS BUTTER
$1/_3$	CUP CHOPPED ONION
$1/_3$	CUP CHOPPED BELL PEPPER
1	CLOVE GARLIC, MINCED
1	8 OZ CAN TOMATO SAUCE
1	CUP WATER
$2/_3$	CUP SLICED, PITTED RIPE OLIVES
$1/_2$	CUP DARK RAISINS
1	TABLESPOON SHERRY
$1 \, 1/_2$	TEASPOONS CHILI POWDER
1	TEASPOON SUGAR
$1/_2$	TEASPOON SALT
2	SHAKES OF BOTTLED HOT SAUCE (YOUR CHOICE)

METHOD:

1. In a sauce pan, saute the onion, bell pepper and garlic in the butter for 3 to 4 minutes.

2. Place all the remaining ingredients in the same pan and bring to a boil. Reduce the heat and simmer for 10 minutes. Use warm, or move to step 3.

3. Chill 24 hours for a better melding of the flavors.

USE ON: Beef, pork, chicken and lamb.

YIELD: 3 cups.

NUTRITIONAL FACTS:

Serving Size: 3 T	Total Fat: 2 g	Sodium: 210mg	Sugar: 3 g
Calories Per Serving: 40	Sat Fat: 1 g	Total Carbs: 5 g	Protein: 0 g
Fat Calories: 20	Cholest: 5 mg	Fiber: 1 g	

CARROT SAUCE

If you prefer a sauce over your meat loaf instead of a gravy, this is one you can try. You can also use it over fried liver as an alternative to onions.

INGREDIENTS:	1	TABLESPOON FLOUR
	$1/_2$	CUP WATER
	1	CUP CHICKEN BROTH
	1	CUP GRATED CARROTS
	$1/_2$	CUP KETCHUP

METHOD:

1. Mix the water and flour into a paste and set aside.

2. Cook the carrots in the broth for 5 minutes at a low boil. Whisk in the ketchup and flour paste, stirring constantly until the sauce returns to a boil, then remove it from the heat.

USE ON: Meat or vegetable loafs, fried liver.

YIELD: $2 \, 1/_2$ cups.

NUTRITIONAL FACTS:

Serving Size: 3 T	Total Fat: 0 g	Sodium: 220 mg	Sugar: 1 g
Calories Per Serving: 20	Sat Fat: 0 g	Total Carbs: 4 g	Protein: 1 g
Fat Calories: 0	Cholest: 0 mg	Fiber: 0 g	

BEARNAISE SAUCE

Bearnaise is another well known versatile sauce. Even if you've never tasted a Bearnaise, you've probably heard of it. It goes well with several kinds of meat, fowl and fish. If you just happen to have a small amount of glaze on hand, add 1 tablespoon of it, along with the yolk, in step 2.

INGREDIENTS:		
	1	TABLESPOON FLOUR
	1	TABLESPOON BUTTER
	1	CUP WHITE WINE
	1	CUP CONSOMME
	2	SHALLOTS, CHOPPED
	$1/_2$	CLOVE GARLIC, MINCED
	$1/_2$	CUP WHITE VINEGAR
	$1/_2$	TEASPOON GRATED NUTMEG
	2	TABLESPOONS LEMON JUICE
	4	EGG YOLKS, BEATEN
		SALT AND PEPPER TO TASTE

METHOD:

1. Mix the flour and butter together and place all the ingredients (except egg yolks, salt and pepper) into a sauce pan. Whisk constantly while bringing the sauce to a low boil. Reduce the heat and cook until slightly thickened.

2. Remove the pan from the heat and whisk in the egg yolks until the sauce thickens, then season to taste.

USE ON: Broiled steaks, chops and fish.

YIELD: 3 cups.

NUTRITIONAL FACTS:			
Serving Size: 3 T	Total Fat: 2 g	Sodium: 210 mg	Sugar: 0 g
Calories Per Serving: 40	Sat Fat: 1 g	Total Carbs: 2 g	Protein: 1 g
Fat Calories: 20	Cholest: 55 mg	Fiber: 0 g	

BORDELAISE SAUCE

(FRENCH VERSION)

There are several versions of this sauce. I'll give you two, the French and an American version, in that order. If you want additional variations of this sauce, be creative and do it on your own.

INGREDIENTS:	2	SHALLOTS, MINCED
	$1/_2$	CUP CLARET OR OTHER DRY RED WINE
	$1 \, 1/_2$	CUPS OF BROWN SAUCE (ESPAGNOLE)
	PINCH	CAYENNE PEPPER

OPTION: Several cooked and sliced chestnuts.

METHOD: Place the shallots and claret into a sauce pan, bring to a boil to reduce the liquid by $1/_2$. Add the brown sauce and cayenne. Cook on low heat an additional 15 to 20 minutes.

USE ON: Steaks, chops and roasts.

YIELD: $1 \, 3/_4$ cups.

NUTRITIONAL FACTS:			
Serving Size: 3 T	Total Fat: 2 g	Sodium: 95 mg	Sugar: 0 g
Calories Per Serving: 40	Sat Fat: 1.5 g	Total Carbs: 3 g	Protein: 1 g
Fat Calories: 20	Cholest: 10 mg	Fiber: 0 g	

BROWN SAUCE

(ESPAGNOLE)

This version is probably more in keeping with what the average person considers to be a "Brown Sauce".

INGREDIENTS:	1	QUART BROWN STOCK OR BEEF BROTH
	$1/4$	CUP TOMATO PUREE, OR
	1	TOMATO, HALVED
	$1/4$	POUND BUTTER
	$1/2$	CUP DICED VEAL AND AND HAM
	1	ONION, CHOPPED
	$1/4$	CUP FLOUR
		SALT AND PEPPER TO TASTE

OPTIONS:	4	SLICED MUSHROOMS, FRESH OR CANNED (WHEN YOU ADD THE MUSHROOMS IS DETERMINED BY WHETHER YOU WANT THEM TO BE PART OF THE SAUCE OR ONLY FOR FLAVOR).
	1	BAY LEAF

METHOD:

1. Blend the stock and tomato puree in a sauce pan and bring it to a boil to reduce by 10%.

2. Melt the butter in a skillet, add the meat, onion (add fresh mushrooms now for flavor and/or the bay leaf). Saute the mixture until the meat is browned and the onion is wilted.

3. Whisk the flour into the meat and onion mixture and cook for a minute or two. Remove the mixture from the heat and slowly whisk in the reduced stock. Return the sauce to the heat and simmer for 30 minutes. Season, strain the sauce and discard all the solids.

4. If you want mushrooms (fresh or canned) in the sauce, add them now and cook for 6 more minutes.

USE ON: Any meat, fish or fowl.

YIELD: 5 cups.

NUTRITIONAL FACTS:			
Serving Size: 1/4 cup	Total Fat: 4.5 g	Sodium: 180 mg	Sugar: 1 g
Calories Per Serving: 60	Sat Fat: 2.5 g	Total Carbs: 4 g	Protein: 2 g
Fat Calories: 40	Cholest: 15 mg	Fiber: 0 g	

BORDELAISE SAUCE

(CREOLE AMERICAN VERSION)

This sauce is easy as pie when compared to the preceding French version. In fact, they are so different that if it didn't come into my collection with the name Bordelaise attached, I wouldn't consider it even remotely related to the French one.

Interestingly, this sauce can be converted into one version of the well known "Wine Merchants Sauce" (aka "Sauce Marchands de Vin") by the addition of some "Brown Sauce" (see Alternate below). To make it into a "Madeira Sauce", swap the red wine for Madeira. If you have no Madeira on hand, use Sherry.

INGREDIENTS:		
	1	ONION, MINCED, OR
	2	SHALLOTS, MINCED
	1	TABLESPOON OLIVE OIL
	2	TABLESPOONS RED WINE

METHOD: Saute the onion in the olive oil until translucent, then add the wine and cook 1 minute longer.

ALTERNATE:		
	1	CUP BROWN SAUCE
	$^1/_2$	TEASPOON LEMON JUICE. ADD TO ABOVE MIXTURE TO HEAT THROUGH.

USE ON: Steaks and chops.

YIELD: $^3/_4$ cup.

NUTRITIONAL FACTS:

Serving Size: 3 T	Total Fat: 2.5 g	Sodium: 0 mg	Sugar: 2 g
Calories Per Serving: 45	Sat Fat: 0 g	Total Carbs: 5 g	Protein: 0 g
Fat Calories: 26	Cholest: 0 mg	Fiber: 1 g	

BROWN SAUCE II

(ESPAGNOLE)

This version of Sauce Espagnole is preferred by the Creole and Cajun communities. Like the White Sauce, a Brown Sauce is one of the "Mother Sauces". It is a good foundation sauce and it has a built in multiplier. So if you want 2-1/2+ cups of sauce, double the ingredients.

INGREDIENTS:	2	TABLESPOONS BUTTER
	2	TABLESPOONS FLOUR
	1	TABLESPOON BROWN STOCK
	2	TABLESPOONS SHERRY WINE
	1	CUP WATER OR BEEF BROTH
		SALT AND PEPPER TO TASTE
OPTIONS:		SLICED MUSHROOMS OR TRUFFLES

METHOD: Make a white roux by cooking the flour in the butter for a minute or two. Then add the remaining ingredients. If using fresh mushrooms, add them now and bring the sauce to a boil to thicken.

USE ON: Any meat, fish or fowl.

YIELD: 1 $^1/_4$ cups.

NUTRITIONAL FACTS:

Serving Size: 3 T	Total Fat: 3.5 g	Sodium: 150mg	Sugar: 0 g
Calories Per Serving: 50	Sat Fat: 2 g	Total Carbs: 4g	Protein: 1 g
Fat Calories: 30	Cholest: 10 mg	Fiber: 0 g	

VELOUTE SAUCE

(KISSIN' KIN TO A WHITE SAUCE AND IT'S MADE WITH STOCK)

This sauce is as basic as the Bechamel. Be sure to use veal stock with veal, fish stock with fish and poultry stock with poultry. Failure to follow these guidelines may cause your family to think you've lost the use of your taste buds.

Traditionally, the mushroom peelings are used for the sauce. If peeling mushrooms is not an activity you're into, substitute chopped fresh stems and pieces for the peelings.

INGREDIENTS:		
	3	TABLESPOONS ROUX
	2	CUPS STOCK
	$^1/_2$	CUP MUSHROOM PEEL, OR
	$^1/_2$	CUP FRESH MUSHROOM STEMS AND PIECES
	PINCH	NUTMEG
		SALT AND PEPPER TO TASTE

Method: Whisk the stock into the roux to get a smooth mix and add the mushrooms. Bring the sauce to a low simmering boil and cook for 10 minutes. Strain to remove the mushrooms, add nutmeg, season to taste and serve.

Use On: Veal, fish or chicken.

Yield: 1 $^1/_2$ cups.

NUTRITIONAL FACTS:

Serving Size: 1/4 cup	Total Fat: 2 g	Sodium: 190 mg	Sugar: 0 g
Calories Per Serving: 30	Sat Fat: 1 g	Total Carbs: 1 g	Protein: 1 g
Fat Calories: 20	Cholest: 5 mg	Fiber: 0 g	

CHAMPAGNE SAUCE

American champagne is so inexpensive that you might buy a bottle just to make the sauce. However, you can also use any white sparkling wine as well. Whatever you choose, serve the champagne with your meal, because you'll only use one cup of it for the sauce.

INGREDIENTS:

1	CUP VELOUTE (MADE FROM FISH STOCK FOR FISH OR CHICKEN STOCK FOR CHICKEN)
1	CUP CHAMPAGNE
$^1/_2$	CUP MINCED SWEET ONIONS OR SHALLOTS
$^1/_2$	CUP BUTTER (CUT INTO PATS)
$1\,^1/_2$	TEASPOONS CHOPPED FRESH TARRAGON

METHOD:

1. Place the onions and champagne into a sauce pan, bring it to a low boil and cook until it is reduced by half.

2. While the champagne/onions are cooking, heat but do not boil the Veloute sauce.

3. Remove the champagne/onions from the heat and thoroughly stir in the Veloute and the tarragon.

4. Lightly swirl the butter into the sauce and when the butter is very soft but not melted, spoon over fish or chicken (the effect you want, is to have butter streaks on the sauce).

USE ON: Fish Fillets or chicken breasts.

YIELD: 2 $^1/_2$ cups.

NUTRITIONAL FACTS:

Serving Size: 3 T	Total Fat: 7 g	Sodium: 115 mg	Sugar: 0g
Calories Per Serving: 80	Sat Fat: 4.5 g	Total Carbs: 1 g	Protein: 0 g
Fat Calories: 60	Cholest: 20 mg	Fiber: 0 g	

OYSTER SAUCE

In making this sauce, look for the smallest oysters you can find. If you must use large ones, clean out the sac, then coarsely chop the oysters.

INGREDIENTS:

1	PINT OYSTERS
1	ONION, GRATED
2	TABLESPOONS BUTTER
2	TABLESPOONS FLOUR
$^1/_2$	CUP WHITE WINE
$^1/_2$	TEASPOON SALT
PINCH	WHITE PEPPER
2	TABLESPOONS LEMON JUICE

METHOD:

1. Drain the oysters and reserve the liquid. Set aside.

2. Briefly saute the onion in the butter for 1 to 2 minutes. Whisk in the flour, add the reserved oyster liquid, wine, salt, pepper and lemon juice. Whisk the entire mixture until thickened. Add oysters and cook until edges of the oysters begin to curl. Remove from the heat.

USE ON: Sliced turkey breasts or turkey rolls. Broiled fish.

YIELD: 3 cups.

NUTRITIONAL FACTS:

Serving Size: 3 T	Total Fat: 3 g	Sodium: 170 mg	Sugar: 1 g
Calories Per Serving: 70	Sat Fat: 1.5 g	Total Carbs: 5 g	Protein: 4 g
Fat Calories: 30	Cholest: 30 mg	Fiber: 0 g	

RAVIGOTE SAUCE

A Ravigote requires a cup of Veloute as one of it's ingredients. So make the Veloute first. You'll also need several fresh herbs. Dry herbs won't do.

INGREDIENTS:	2	SHALLOTS, MINCED
	1	TABLESPOON TARRAGON VINEGAR
	1	CUP VELOUTE SAUCE
		SEASON TO TASTE WITH SALT AND PEPPER
	1	TABLESPOON CHOPPED PARSLEY
	1	TABLESPOON CHOPPED CHERVIL
	1	TEASPOON CHOPPED CHIVES
	1	TEASPOON CHOPPED TARRAGON
	1	TABLESPOON CHOPPED CAPERS

METHOD:

1. Cook the shallots in the vinegar until it evaporates and the shallots are still moist. Add the Veloute sauce, season and simmer for about 10 minutes. Put the sauce aside to cool.

2. When lukewarm, stir in the fresh herbs and serve.

USE ON: Fish and poultry. Also on variety meats such as brains, tongue, sweetbreads, liver, kidney and even tripe.

YIELD: 1 cup.

NUTRITIONAL FACTS:

Serving Size: 3 T	Total Fat: 1.5 g	Sodium: 210 mg	Sugar: 0 g
Calories Per Serving: 25	Sat Fat: 1 g	Total Carbs: 2 g	Protein: 2 g
Fat Calories: 15	Cholest: 5 mg	Fiber: 0 g	

GENOESE SAUCE

Traditionally this sauce would use Claret wine, but that seems to be difficult to find today. Clarets appear to be losing shelf space to a whole group of dark reds such as Cabernet Sauvignon, Petite Sirah, Merlot, Pinot Noir and Zinfandel. Use any dry red you like.

INGREDIENTS:

1	TABLESPOON BUTTER
2	TABLESPOONS FLOUR
1	CUP DRY RED WINE
1	CUP WATER
$^1/_4$	TEASPOON SALT
PINCH	ALLSPICE
PINCH	NUTMEG
	CHOPPED PARSLEY FOR GARNISH

METHOD: Melt the butter, stir in the flour and cook for 2 to 3 minutes to make a roux. Add all the remaining ingredients except the parsley. Bring the sauce to a boil and reduce the heat. Cook until the sauce has thickened and reduced by at least one third to one half.

Garnish with parsley and serve.

USE ON: Broiled, boiled or baked fish and boiled meat or poultry.

YIELD: 1 to 1 $^1/_2$ cups.

NUTRITIONAL FACTS:

Serving Size: 3 T	Total Fat: 2 g	Sodium: 120 mg	Sugar: 0 g
Calories Per Serving: 60	Sat Fat: 1 g	Total Carbs: 3 g	Protein: 0 g
Fat Calories: 20	Cholest: 5 mg	Fiber: 0 g	

CHOPPED EGG SAUCE

(HARD-EGG SAUCE)

Chopped egg sauce is another variation of white sauce. If you wish to forego a white sauce you can exchange the flour and milk for two cups of chicken or fish Veloute.

INGREDIENTS:	3	HARD COOKED EGGS, CHOPPED
	2	TABLESPOONS BUTTER
	$1/_2$	CUP CHOPPED ONION
	2	TABLESPOONS FLOUR
	2	CUPS MILK
	$1/_2$	TEASPOON SALT
	PINCH	NUTMEG, OR FRESHLY GROUND BLACK PEPPER

METHOD:

1. Cook the eggs in boiling water for 10 minutes. Cool, chop and set aside.

2. Saute the onions in butter for 2 to 3 minutes, then whisk in the flour and cook 2 additional minutes. Add the milk and bring the sauce to a low boil, then add the chopped eggs and seasoning.

USE ON: Toast, boiled, broiled or baked fish or chicken.

YIELD: 3 cups.

NUTRITIONAL FACTS:			
Serving Size: 1/4 cup	Total Fat: 4.5 g	Sodium: 140 mg	Sugar: 2 g
Calories Per Serving: 70	Sat Fat: 2.5 g	Total Carbs: 4 g	Protein: 3 g
Fat Calories: 40	Cholest: 60 mg	Fiber: 0 g	

MADEIRA SAUCE

In making this sauce, use a stock or bouillon to match your meat selection.

INGREDIENTS:	4	TABLESPOONS BUTTER
	2	TABLESPOONS FLOUR
	1	ONION, CHOPPED
	1	CUP SLICED MUSHROOMS
	1	CUP MEAT STOCK
	$1/4$	CUP MADEIRA
	$1/2$	TEASPOON SALT

METHOD:
1. Make a roux with $1/2$ the butter and flour. Set aside.

2. In a second pan, saute the onion in the remaining butter. When the onion begins to wilt, add the mushrooms and cook until they release their liquid. Add the stock of your choice and the roux and stir well. Continue to cook until the sauce begins to thicken. Add Madeira wine and cook until the sauce returns to a boil. Remove from the heat.

USE ON: Beef or chicken.

YIELD: $2 1/2$ cups.

NUTRITIONAL FACTS:

Serving Size: 1/4 cup	Total Fat: 5 g	Sodium: 240 mg	Sugar: 1 g
Calories Per Serving: 60	Sat Fat: 3 g	Total Carbs: 3 g	Protein: 1 g
Fat Calories: 45	Cholest: 10 mg	Fiber: 0 g	

FRESH MUSHROOM SAUCE

INGREDIENTS:

2	TABLESPOONS FLOUR
1	CUP BROTH: VEGETABLE OR CHICKEN
1	ONION, CHOPPED
$^1/_4$	CUP BUTTER
8	OUNCES SLICED MUSHROOMS
1	TABLESPOON LEMON JUICE
1	CUP SOUR CREAM
2	TEASPOONS DRIED DILL WEED

METHOD:

1. Mix the flour with the broth and set aside.

2. Saute the onion in butter until wilted. Add the mushrooms and cook the mixture about 3 minutes. Add lemon juice and broth and cook for 5 minutes more or until the sauce begins to thicken. Remove the sauce from the heat.

3. Thoroughly blend in the sour cream and dill weed, then return the sauce to the stove just long enough to heat through.

USE ON: Cold or hot roast beef, broiled chicken or broiled fish.

YIELD: $3 \, ^1/_2$ cups.

NUTRITIONAL FACTS:

Serving Size: 1/4 cup	Total Fat: 6 g	Sodium: 140 mg	Sugar: 1 g
Calories Per Serving: 70	Sat Fat: 4 g	Total Carbs: 3 g	Protein: 1 g
Fat Calories: 60	Cholest: 15 mg	Fiber: 0 g	

SAUCE DIANE

(FOR FISH CHICKEN OR PORK)

"Sauce Diane" is a name that drives me crazy because it means whatever the chef wants it to mean. The chef can change the recipe..., but doesn't change the name. In most restaurants a "Diane" is a preparation for steak with the resulting juice, butter and alcohol being the sauce. "Steak Diane" is usually sirloin, but this version of Sauce Diane is for fish, chicken and pork and if you like, it could be served with a little showmanship, by flaming the dish when you serve it (see the Option).

When dining out you may have the chance to order a "Steak Diane". If you do, here is what you'll get; the steak would be sauteed in butter, cognac would be used for flaming, a splash of sherry added for taste and the steak would be topped with a dollop of creamed chive butter. If that sounds good to you, try it, the next paragraph gives you the preparation method.

The steak should be beaten quite flat, cooked quickly in the hot butter, then turned once and flamed. The butter creamed with chives can be added at this point, along with the Sherry. Transfer the steak to a plate and pour the sauce over it. Or, spread the chive butter on the steak and then pour the sauce over it.

INGREDIENTS:	2	TABLESPOONS BUTTER
	6	TABLESPOONS LEMON JUICE
	1	TABLESPOON WORCESTERSHIRE SAUCE
	1	TEASPOON DIJON MUSTARD
		CHOPPED PARSLEY TO GARNISH

OPTION: For a little razzle-dazzle make it a "Flambe" by replacing the lemon juice with 2 tablespoons of lemon extract. Remove the sauce from the heat before adding the extract. Blend in thoroughly, then ignite the sauce and pour it over your meat.

METHOD: Melt the butter and when it begins to foam, add the remaining ingredients and blend thoroughly. Pour the sauce over your meat, garnish and serve.

Use On: 1.   Cold water white bodied fish fillets.

　　　　　　 2.   Pork medallions. Or

　　　　　　 3.   Boneless chicken breasts pounded or pressed flat

　　　　　　　　 (try adding 1 teaspoons lemon zest and 1 teaspoon freshly ground black pepper sprinkled on the meat while flattening).

Yield: $^1/_2$ cup.

NUTRITIONAL FACTS:			
Serving Size: 2 T	Total Fat: 5 g	Sodium: 115 mg	Sugar: 0 g
Calories Per Serving: 50	Sat Fat: 3 g	Total Carbs: 2 g	Protein: 0 g
Fat Calories: 45	Cholest: 15 mg	Fiber: 0 g	

Authors Meat Sauce

(Charley's Sauce)

To me there is something about the taste of a slowly simmered hunk of meat in a good tomato sauce that is unique. The meat absorbs the juice from the tomato and becomes very moist and tender and the meat juices give a marvelous flavor to the sauce. There are no short cuts in preparing this sauce because the exchange must occur during the slow simmer.

I serve the meat as an entree accompanied with steamed vegetables. Some of the cuts I use are:

1) pork ribs (including the chime),

2) country style ribs,

3) a small pork roast from the shoulder or butt,

4) beef chuck roast,

5) round steak, seasoned, filled, rolled and tied,

6) flank steak, seasoned, filled, rolled and tied,

7) Italian sausage (my favorite).

These meats singly, or as a mixture, are slowly simmered in the tomatoes for hours until the meat falls away from the bone. You can also use this recipe to simmer "meat balls a'blanc" when you would like to use them as an entree. Any leftover sauce can be used on pasta.

Ingredients:	2		POUNDS MEAT (YOUR CHOICE FROM THE ABOVE LIST)
	1	·	28 OUNCE CAN OF ITALIAN STYLE TOMATOES. USE ONLY WHOLE (SQUISHED) OR DICED
	1		CUP WATER
	2		CLOVES GARLIC, HALVED
	$^1/_2$		ONION COARSELY CHOPPED
	$^1/_2$		TEASPOON WHOLE FENNEL SEED, CRUSHED (USE WITH PORK)
	2		SPRIGS PARSLEY
	2-3		WHOLE PEPPERCORNS

METHOD: Put the meat into a large sauce pan, place all the ingredients over the meat and bring the sauce to a boil. Reduce the heat to simmer, cover and cook for 3 to 4 hours or more. Occasionally remove the rising fat.

USE ON: Serve the sauce with your selected meat(s).

YIELD: 3 cups.

NUTRITIONAL FACTS:

Serving Size: 1/3 cup	Total Fat: 11 g	Sodium: 320 mg	Sugar: 2 g
Calories Per Serving: 130	Sat Fat: 4 g	Total Carbs: 3 g	Protein: 5 g
Fat Calories: 90	Cholest: 25 mg	Fiber: 1 g	

CHERRY SAUCE

When I was a youngster, my Hungarian grandmother made a tomato sauce that she put on boiled beef. I didn't like the sauce then and I still don't like it. Generally when you boil a piece of meat, you render it devoid of taste and nutrients. But, for cooks who ascribe to the theory, "waste not, want not" I have included sauces for boiled meats to add some flavor to the dish, and this Cherry Sauce is one of them.

INGREDIENTS:	1	POUND FRESH UNPITTED CHERRIES (YOUR CHOICE)
	$^1/_2$	LEMON, PEEL ONLY - NO PITH (THAT'S THE WHITE PART)
	1	TABLESPOON LEMON JUICE
	$^1/_2$	CUP WATER
		SUGAR TO TASTE

METHOD:

1. Put the cherries, lemon peel, lemon juice and water into a sauce pan and bring it to a boil. Reduce the heat to simmer. Cover and cook for 1 hour.

2. Strain the cooked cherries through a colander and discard the pits. Add sugar to taste and return the sauce to the heat. Cook 5 more minutes to dissolve the sugar.

USE ON: Boiled meats such as chicken, ham or beef.

YIELD: 1 cup.

NUTRITIONAL FACTS:			
Serving Size: 3 T	Total Fat: 0 g	Sodium: 0 mg	Sugar: 5 g
Calories Per Serving: 25	Sat Fat: 0 g	Total Carbs: 6 g	Protein: 0 g
Fat Calories: 0	Cholest: 0 mg	Fiber: 1 g	

DILLED SOUR CREAM SAUCE

As an entree or party hors d'oeuvres little meatballs are always a favorite. They can be made from any single ground meat, or a mixture of meats, plus a wide assortment of additions, like onions, garlic, herbs, fruit, nuts and many vegetables. You can also include eggs, milk or cheese. The addition of bread crumbs or crushed crackers gives you a softer meatball. There's more, but you get the point, meatballs are your personal taste preference.

The sour cream and dill in this sauce lends itself more to meatballs made from ground beef, or a mixture of beef with veal, turkey, chicken or fish.

INGREDIENTS:		
	$^1/_4$	CUP PAN DRIPPINGS FROM THE COOKED MEATBALLS
	$^1/_4$	CUP FLOUR
	1	CUP WATER
	2	CUPS SOUR CREAM
	1	TABLESPOON DRIED DILL WEED
	$^1/_2$	TEASPOON SALT

METHOD:

1. Thoroughly whisk the flour into the pan drippings and cook for 3 minutes. Add the water and whisk until the mixture is smooth and begins to thicken. Then whisk in the sour cream and dill. Bring the sauce to a simmer.

2. To serve, place the meatballs into a chafing dish and pour the sauce over the them. Or serve over patties.

USE ON: Meatballs, Burger Patties, Fish Patties (Especially Salmon).

YIELD: 3 $^1/_2$ cups.

NUTRITIONAL FACTS:			
Serving Size: 3 T	Total Fat: 8 g	Sodium: 80 mg	Sugar: 1 g
Calories Per Serving: 90	Sat Fat: 5 g	Total Carbs: 3 g	Protein: 1 g
Fat Calories: 80	Cholest: 15 mg	Fiber: 0 g	

FRESH TANGERINE SAUCE

The tangerine family includes mandarins, temple oranges and tangelos. While they have slight taste differences, they are interchangeable in this sauce. If tangerines are not available, don't make the sauce. Frozen tangerine juice doesn't qualify, because it is a combination of fruit juices plus a little tangerine juice for color. It tastes like pineapple, and that is not what you want (if you want a pineapple sauce for your entree or meatball hors d'oeuvres, see my Pineapple Sauce in Chapter 4).

Pork and chicken have an affinity with sweet sauces that beef and turkey do not. I suggest that you use pork or chicken for the meatballs.

INGREDIENTS:

1	TABLESPOON CORN STARCH
1	TABLESPOON SUGAR
2	TEASPOONS GRATED TANGERINE RIND
1	CUP FRESH TANGERINE JUICE
1	TABLESPOON LEMON JUICE
$^1/_4$	CUP BROTH

Method: Place all the ingredients into a sauce pan and whisk until well blended. Bring the sauce to a boil, reduce the heat and cook for 3 minutes or until the sauce has thickened. Serve at this time or add your prepared meatballs or patties to the sauce for a final few minutes of cooking before serving.

Use On: Cooked meatballs or patties.

Yield: $1^1/_4$ cups.

NUTRITIONAL FACTS:

Serving Size: 3 T	Total Fat: 0 g	Sodium: 30 mg	Sugar: 1 g
Calories Per Serving: 25	Sat Fat: 0 g	Total Carbs: 6 g	Protein: 0 g
Fat Calories: 0	Cholest: 0 mg	Fiber: 0 g	

CHAPTER 4

SAUCES AND GRAVIES MADE FOR BEEF

MUSHROOM SAUCE

If you serve grilled or broiled ground beef patties frequently at your house, then on occasion you probably want to make them more attractive. Well, here's a sauce that does it. If you make this sauce often, exchange the half-and-half for beef or chicken broth for a change of pace.

INGREDIENTS:		
	3	TABLESPOONS EXTRA LIGHT OLIVE OIL OR BUTTER
	1	CUP SLICED MUSHROOMS
	2	TABLESPOONS MINCED ONION
	3	TABLESPOONS FLOUR
	2	CUPS HALF-AND-HALF, OR MILK
		SALT AND PEPPER TO TASTE

METHOD: Saute the mushrooms and onion in the olive oil for 3 minutes. Whisk in the flour, continue cooking for 2 additional minutes. Slowly whisk in the half-and-half and cook until thickened. Season before serving.

OPTION: This sauce is very light in color. So if you prefer a darker color, add several drops of a commercial coloring agent.

USE ON: Ground beef patties, Salisbury steak, meat loaf and meatballs.

YIELD: 3 cups.

NUTRITIONAL FACTS:			
Serving Size: 1/4 cup	Total Fat: 7 g	Sodium: 20 mg	Sugar: 2 g
Calories Per Serving: 90	Sat Fat: 2.5 g	Total Carbs: 4 g	Protein: 2 g
Fat Calories: 60	Cholest: 10 mg	Fiber: 0 g	

HORSERADISH SAUCE

With this sauce you have some latitude with the whipping cream. You can whip the cream and get a thick sauce that won't flow, or don't whip the cream and get a thinner more flowing sauce.

INGREDIENTS:
1	CUP WHIPPING CREAM
$^1/_4$	CUP HORSERADISH
1	TEASPOON SALT

Method: Whip the cream and salt together until stiff, then fold in the horseradish and serve.

Use On: Cold beef or beef tongue.

Yield: 1 $^1/_4$ cups.

NUTRITIONAL FACTS:

Serving Size: 2 T	Total Fat: 7 g	Sodium: 240 mg	Sugar: 1 g
Calories Per Serving: 70	Sat Fat: 4.5 g	Total Carbs: 1 g	Protein: 1 g
Fat Calories: 70	Cholest: 25 mg	Fiber: 0 g	

WE TRIED THIS SAUCE ... AND

HORSERADISH SAUCE II

(SAUCE ALBERT)

You need to make a white sauce first. If you have one handy in the refrigerator, use it.

INGREDIENTS:
1	CUP WHITE SAUCE
3	TABLESPOONS PREPARED HORSERADISH
2	TABLESPOONS WHIPPING CREAM
1	TEASPOON SUGAR
1	TEASPOON DRY MUSTARD
1	TABLESPOON VINEGAR

METHOD: Bring the white sauce to a low boil, then add all the remaining ingredients. Remove from the heat and serve.

USE ON: Corned beef, pastrami, boiled beef.

YIELD: 1 ¼ cups.

NUTRITIONAL FACTS:
Serving Size: 2 T	Total Fat: 3 g	Sodium: 30 mg	Sugar: 1 g
Calories Per Serving: 45	Sat Fat: 2 g	Total Carbs: 3 g	Protein: 1 g
Fat Calories: 30	Cholest: 10 mg	Fiber: 0 g	

BRANDY STEAK SAUCE

I've never believed that you could improve a filet mignon or a porterhouse with steak sauce, but this one comes close.

INGREDIENTS:		
	$^1/_2$	CUP OLIVE OIL
	$^1/_2$	CUP FINELY CHOPPED MUSHROOMS
	6	ANCHOVY FILLETS
		OR
	2	TEASPOONS ANCHOVY PASTE
	1 OR 2	GARLIC CLOVE(S), MINCED
	$1^1/_2$	CUPS RED WINE
	$^1/_4$	CUP PARSLEY, FINELY CHOPPED
	$^1/_2$	TEASPOON FRESHLY GROUND BLACK PEPPER
	$^1/_4$	CUP BRANDY

METHOD: Saute the mushrooms, anchovy fillets and garlic in the olive oil for about 5 minutes. Add the remaining ingredients, except the brandy, bring the sauce to a boil and let 'er roll along for 10 minutes. Add the brandy and cook for 1 additional minute. Serve.

USE ON: Steak cuts such as T-bone, sirloin, New York Strip, rib eye, coloutte, skirt, cubed and round. Also hamburger patties and Salisbury steaks.

YIELD: 2 cups.

NUTRITIONAL FACTS:			
Serving Size: 3 T	Total Fat: 7 g	Sodium: 10 mg	Sugar: 0 g
Calories Per Serving: 90	Sat Fat: 1 g	Total Carbs: 2 g	Protein: 1 g
Fat Calories: 60	Cholest: 0 mg	Fiber: 0 g	

GARLIC SAUCE

As an option, you can modify the flavor of this sauce by adding one or both of the following; several drops of Tabasco sauce and / or a pinch of cayenne pepper. On the surface it doesn't sound like much, but each of these ingredients brings a distinctive quality to the sauce. They are all hot, but not uniformly so and each has its own unique taste.

INGREDIENTS:	2	CLOVES GARLIC
	1	TEASPOON SALT
	$1/2$	CUP OLIVE OIL
	$1/2$	CUP TOMATO JUICE
	$1/2$	CUP RED WINE VINEGAR
	$1/2$	CUP BEEF BOUILLON
	$1/4$	CUP CHOPPED BELL PEPPER
	2	TABLESPOONS MINCED ONION
	$1/4$	TEASPOON CRUSHED RED PEPPER

METHOD: Crush the garlic and sprinkle the salt on it, then smash both into a paste. Place all the ingredients into a sauce pan and bring them to a boil. Reduce the heat and cook for 15 minutes.

USE ON: Beef dishes that have been braised or broiled, roasted or fried, including meat balls.

YIELD: 2 $1/4$ cups.

NUTRITIONAL FACTS:

Serving Size: 3 T	Total Fat: 9 g	Sodium: 230 mg	Sugar: 1 g
Calories Per Serving: 90	Sat Fat: 1 g	Total Carbs: 2 g	Protein: 0 g
Fat Calories: 80	Cholest: 0 mg	Fiber: 0 g	

MEXICAN FILLING SAUCE

This is a sauce that is mixed with cooked or crumbled ground beef to fill tacos, taquitos and burritos, or cover your tostadas.

INGREDIENTS:		
	2	TABLESPOONS EXTRA LIGHT OLIVE OIL
	1	ONION, CHOPPED
	1	CLOVE GARLIC, MINCED
	1	TOMATO, CHOPPED
	1	ANAHEIM, OR JALAPENO, CHOPPED
	1	TEASPOON SALT
	1	TABLESPOON CHILI POWDER
	$^1/_4$	TEASPOON CUMIN
	PINCH	OREGANO
		DASH OR 2 OF HOT SAUCE

METHOD: Saute the onion and garlic in the olive oil for a few minutes. Then add the remaining ingredients and continue cooking for about 10 minutes.

USE ON: Cooked, crumbled and drained ground beef.

YIELD: 1 cup.

NUTRITIONAL FACTS:			
Serving Size: 2 T	Total Fat: 2.5 g	Sodium: 220 mg	Sugar: 1 g
Calories Per Serving: 30	Sat Fat: 0 g	Total Carbs: 2 g	Protein: 0 g
Fat Calories: 25	Cholest: 0 mg	Fiber: 1 g	

BERCY BUTTER SAUCE

This sauce differs from the Marchand de Vin Sauce by several ingredients. Specifically, the type of wine (red to white) and the addition of beef bone marrow. Escoffier didn't consider this a sauce, but rather a compound butter.

INGREDIENTS:	2	TABLESPOONS BEEF MARROW
	$1/_2$	POUND BUTTER
	1	CUP WHITE WINE
	1	SHALLOT, MINCED
	2	TEASPOONS CHOPPED PARSLEY
	$1/_2$	TEASPOON LEMON JUICE
		SALT AND PEPPER TO TASTE

METHOD:

1. Poach the beef bone in a small amount of salted water until the marrow is soft. Cool, scoop out the marrow and set aside.

2. Let the butter warm to room temperature.

3. Place the wine and shallot into a small sauce pan. Bring to a boil and cook to reduce by half or more Remove from the heat and allow to cool until it is lukewarm.

4. Thoroughly blend into the wine, the butter, beef marrow, parsley and lemon juice. Season to taste and serve. Or chill to use as a butter.

USE ON: Spread as a butter on broiled or grilled steak.

YIELD: 2 cups.

NUTRITIONAL FACTS:			
Serving Size: 1 T	Total Fat: 6 g	Sodium: 60 mg	Sugar: 0 g
Calories Per Serving: 60	Sat Fat: 3.5 g	Total Carbs: 0 g	Protein: 0 g
Fat Calories: 50	Cholest: 15 mg	Fiber: 0 g	

STEAK SAUCE

You may find this sauce to be the one that persuades you to stop using store bought brands.

INGREDIENTS:		
	1	CUP BEEF BROTH OR BOUILLON
	2	TABLESPOONS CORN STARCH
	$^1/_4$	CUP BUTTER OR LIGHT OLIVE OIL
	2	TABLESPOONS TOMATO PASTE
	$^1/_4$	TEASPOON DRIED THYME, RUBBED
	1	CLOVE GARLIC, MINCED
	1	TEASPOON SALT
	$^1/_2$	CUP FINELY CHOPPED CHIVES
	1	CUP WHITE ZINFANDEL OR BLUSH WINE

METHOD: Blend the corn starch and beef broth until smooth, then add all the ingredients, except the wine. Bring the sauce to a boil, reduce the heat and simmer for 15 minutes. Remove from the heat and blend in the wine. Cool and serve.

USE ON: Any cut of steak, beef rounds, tri-tips and burgers.

YIELD: 2 $^1/_2$ cups.

NUTRITIONAL FACTS:

Serving Size: 2 T	Total Fat: 4.5 g	Sodium: 360 mg	Sugar: 0 g
Calories Per Serving: 70	Sat Fat: 3 g	Total Carbs: 4 g	Protein: 1 g
Fat Calories: 40	Cholest: 10 mg	Fiber: 0 g	

DEVILS SAUCE

(SAUCE DIABLE)

If you guessed that this sauce is hot, you've guessed right. There is some real pepper zip to this one. I suggest you try it once as written, so that you'll know what it is supposed to taste like, before you begin adjusting the pepper.

INGREDIENTS:

2	TABLESPOONS BUTTER
$^1/_2$	ONION, CHOPPED
3	CUPS CHOPPED CELERY (ABOUT 1 WHOLE STALK)
1	CLOVE GARLIC, SMASHED
2	WHOLE CLOVES
3	CUPS WHOLE OR CHOPPED TOMATOES
1	SMALL CAN TOMATO PASTE
2	TABLESPOONS CAYENNE PEPPER
	OR
2	TABLESPOONS TABASCO SAUCE

METHOD: Saute the onion, celery and garlic in the butter for 5 minutes. Add the cloves, tomatoes, tomato paste and pepper and bring the sauce to a boil. Cook on high, to medium high for 10 minutes. Then strain before serving.

USE ON: Skirt steaks, culotte steaks, spit roasted or barbecued cubes of beef steak or tenderloin.

YIELD: 4 cups.

NUTRITIONAL FACTS:			
Serving Size: 1/4 cup	Total Fat: 0.5 g	Sodium: 50 mg	Sugar: 1 g
Calories Per Serving: 15	Sat Fat: 0 g	Total Carbs: 2 g	Protein: 0 g
Fat Calories: 5	Cholest: 0 mg	Fiber: 1 g	

WE TRIED THIS SAUCE ... AND

LOVED IT (   )
HATED IT (   )
MAYBE WE'LL TRY IT AGAIN (   )
WE'LL USE IT FOR UNWELCOME GUESTS (   )

SUKIYAKI SAUCE

This Japanese style sauce is generally served over thinly sliced beef sauteed in a skillet or stir fried in a wok. Then it is cooked with an assortment of vegetables, including tofu and bean sprouts. Ideally the vegetables should be cooked and still crisp.

I have dined in Japanese restaurants where this dish is considered to be a soup. If you hold to that thinking, then what you have here is a stock and not a sauce. You decide.

INGREDIENTS:	$^1/_2$	CUP JAPANESE SOY SAUCE OR THE SWEETER TERIYAKI SAUCE
	$^1/_2$	CUP BEEF STOCK OR CONSOMME
	2	TEASPOONS SUGAR
	2	TABLESPOONS SAKI OR SHERRY

METHOD: Place all the ingredients into a sauce pan and bring the sauce to a boil. Reduce the heat to medium and cook for 5 minutes. The sauce will be thin.

USE ON: Thinly sliced beef. Or if thickened slightly with 1 teaspoon of corn starch, it can be used on boneless chicken breast or chicken thighs.

YIELD: 1 cup.

NUTRITIONAL FACTS:
Serving Size: 2 T	Total Fat: 0 g	Sodium: 860 mg	Sugar: 1 g
Calories Per Serving: 15	Sat Fat: 0 g	Total Carbs: 2 g	Protein: 1 g
Fat Calories: 0	Cholest: 0 mg	Fiber: 0 g	

Pizzaioli Steak Sauce

This Italian style steak sauce can be used in two ways. As a steak sauce, or as a finishing sauce. That is, when your grilled or broiled steak is almost ready to serve, finish cooking it in the sauce.

Ingredients:	2	TABLESPOONS OLIVE OIL
	4	CLOVES GARLIC, CRUSHED
	6	ITALIAN STYLE TOMATOES, PEELED, SEEDED AND DICED
	1	TEASPOON DRIED OREGANO LEAF
		SALT TO TASTE

Method: Saute the garlic in the olive oil until lightly golden. Add the tomatoes, oregano and salt and cook for 8 minutes. Serve.

Use On: Sirloin, rib eye, culotte, skirt or cubed steaks.

Yield: 2 cups.

NUTRITIONAL FACTS:

Serving Size: 1/4 cup	Total Fat: 2 g	Sodium: 0 mg	Sugar: 2 g
Calories Per Serving: 30	Sat Fat: 0 g	Total Carbs: 3 g	Protein: 0 g
Fat Calories: 20	Cholest: 0 mg	Fiber: 0 g	

PINEAPPLE SAUCE

Beef is a little more difficult to serve up in a sweet sauce than pork, chicken or ham. But occasionally that combination will sound good and you'll want to try it. This is a good one for beef.

COOKS ALERT: Unless the label on your can of pineapple states that it is packed in its own juice, the liquid is a sugar syrup. DO NOT USE IT. It will over sweeten the sauce.

INGREDIENTS:	2	TABLESPOONS CORN STARCH
	$1/4$	CUP VINEGAR
	1	CUP PINEAPPLE JUICE
	1	TEASPOON SOY SAUCE
	$1/2$	CUP WATER
	$1/2$	CUP SUGAR
	$1/2$	CUP CHUNK PINEAPPLE (1/4 CUP IF CRUSHED)
	1	RED, YELLOW OR ORANGE BELL PEPPER, CUT INTO STRIPS

METHOD:

1. Blend the corn starch and vinegar together and set aside.

2. Place the pineapple juice into a sauce pan, bring it to a boil and reduce by half.

3. Add the vinegar mix, soy sauce, water and sugar and bring the sauce to a boil again. Add the remaining ingredients, cook over a low heat for 6 to 8 minutes and serve.

COOKS ALERT: If you are using meatballs, add them along with the pineapple and bell pepper.

USE ON: Salisbury steak, hamburger patties or meatballs.

YIELD: $2 1/4$ cups.

NUTRITIONAL FACTS:			
Serving Size: 1/4 cup	Total Fat: 0 g	Sodium: 35 mg	Sugar: 10 g
Calories Per Serving: 50	Sat Fat: 0 g	Total Carbs: 12 g	Protein: 0 g
Fat Calories: 0	Cholest: 0 mg	Fiber: 0 g	

SAUCE FOR SWEDISH MEATBALLS

The three Scandinavian countries, Norway, Sweden and Denmark, each have their own style of meatball for a Smorgasbord. In America Swedish Meatballs have gained greater popularity as an hors d'oeuvres or light buffet dish. They all basically use a mixture of ground pork, ground beef and onion. The Swedes like mashed potatoes added to the meat, the Norwegians seem to prefer bread crumbs and the Danes like flour. All of them throw in an egg and some milk.

The primary differences between Swedish, Norwegian and Danish meatballs are the spices they use. The Swedes use the largest number of spices; nutmeg, cloves, ginger, allspice, white pepper and brown sugar. The Norwegians seem to limit their choices to nutmeg and allspice. The Danes are happy with salt and pepper.

Now comes the sauce. To start with, the Danes like their meatballs just as they come out of the pan, no sauce. The Swedes like a equal mixture of cream and broth. The Norwegians prefer theirs served up in a white sauce made from equal amounts of cream and water. You can also use a mixture of milk and water. If you would like to avoid a cream sauce, replace it with a Veloute. In either case, add the cooked meatballs to the sauce and serve at once.

So as not to offend any Scandinavian who buys this book, I'll add this caveat. No recipe is inviolable, so add or discard ingredients according to your family's usage, and that might include a small measure of sugar or paprika or mushrooms.

INGREDIENTS:	3	TABLESPOONS ROUX
		OR
	3	TABLESPOONS FLOUR
	3	TABLESPOONS BUTTER
	$1/2$	TEASPOON SALT
	$1/4$	TEASPOON WHITE PEPPER
	1	CUP WHIPPING CREAM
	1	CUP BEEF BROTH

METHOD: Cook the flour and butter for 3 minutes, then add the remaining ingredients and cook until thickened.

USE ON: Any of the options in the opening paragraphs.

YIELD: 2 $\frac{1}{2}$ cups.

NUTRITIONAL FACTS:

Serving Size: 2 T	Total Fat: 6 g	Sodium: 130mg	Sugar: 0 g
Calories Per Serving: 60	Sat Fat: 3.5 g	Total Carbs: 2 g	Protein: 1 g
Fat Calories: 50	Cholest: 20 mg	Fiber: 0 g	

PIQUANT SAUCE

INGREDIENTS:

1	TABLESPOON BUTTER
2	ONIONS, MINCED
2	CLOVES GARLIC, MINCED
2	TABLESPOONS WATER
1	TEASPOON CIDER VINEGAR
1	TEASPOON THYME
1	TABLESPOON PARSLEY
2	CORNICHON GERKINS OR SMALL DILL PICKLE, SLICED INTO 1/8" ROUNDS
	SALT AND FRESHLY GROUND PEPPER TO TASTE
PINCH	CAYENNE PEPPER

METHOD: Saute the onions and garlic in the butter for 5 minutes. Add the remaining ingredients, then cover the pan and simmer for 10 minutes. Serve.

USE ON: Boiled beef tongue, boiled pork tongue, boiled beef or boiled veal.

YIELD: 2 $\frac{1}{4}$ cups.

NUTRITIONAL FACTS:

Serving Size: 1/4 cup	Total Fat: 2 g	Sodium: 20 mg	Sugar: 3 g
Calories Per Serving: 40	Sat Fat: 1 g	Total Carbs: 6 g	Protein: 0 g
Fat Calories: 20	Cholest: 5 mg	Fiber: 1 g	

CHAPTER 5

SAUCES AND GRAVIES MADE FOR PORK

This chapter covers the entire pork family, including ham and all sausages made with pork.

DIJONNAISE SAUCE

The base of this dijonnaise is a white sauce. The Dijon mustard is a very small addition to the sauce, but it packs a wollop. In fact Dijon mustard lends itself so well to so many sauces that it could probably have a chapter of its own. You'll be using several pans at once to make the sauce (you can do it by using one pan, it just takes a little longer).

INGREDIENTS:		
	2	CUPS CHICKEN BROTH (OR 1 CAN)
	1	CUP DRAINED, DICED CANNED TOMATOES
	2	TABLESPOONS BUTTER
	$1/_3$	CUP MINCED ONIONS
	1	CUP WHITE SAUCE
	$1/_4$	TEASPOON THYME
	$1/_4$	TEASPOON MINCED GARLIC
	1	TEASPOON BASIL
	1	TABLESPOON PREPARED DIJON MUSTARD
	2	TABLESPOONS SHERRY OR MADEIRA WINE

METHOD:

1. Place the chicken broth and the tomatoes into a sauce pan. Bring the broth to a rolling boil and keep it there until the liquid is reduced by half.

2. Saute the onions in the butter until they are translucent.

3. When the onions are cooked, blend in the thyme, garlic and basil. Combine with the white sauce and the chicken/tomato mixture. Bring the sauce to a low boil and remove it from the heat. At this point sieve the sauce if you want it to be very smooth. Stir in the Dijon mustard and the wine. Serve.

USE ON: Baked or boiled ham.

YIELD: 3 cups.

NUTRITIONAL FACTS:			
Serving Size: 1/3 cup	Total Fat: 3.5 g	Sodium: 250 mg	Sugar: 2 g
Calories Per Serving: 50	Sat Fat: 2 g	Total Carbs: 3 g	Protein: 1 g
Fat Calories: 30	Cholest: 10 mg	Fiber: 0 g	

BASTING SAUCE FOR HAM

Ham lends itself so well to sweet sauces. This one is very simple, with just enough sweetness to accent the meat.

INGREDIENTS:	2	TABLESPOONS HONEY
	2	TABLESPOONS CATSUP OR CHILI SAUCE
	1	TEASPOON LEMON JUICE

METHOD: Blend all the ingredients and use.

USE ON: Baked or broiled ham, ham steaks, ham loaf or smoked pork chops.

YIELD: $\frac{1}{3}$ cup.

NUTRITIONAL FACTS:

Serving Size: 1 T	Total Fat: 0 g	Sodium: 85 mg	Sugar: 6 g
Calories Per Serving: 30	Sat Fat: 0 g	Total Carbs: 8 g	Protein: 0 g
Fat Calories: 0	Cholest: 0 mg	Fiber: 0 g	

RED (EYE) GRAVY

This ham gravy is well loved in different areas of the South and Southwest. If it's new to you, try it. This is a coffee drinkers gravy, or possibly not. You choose.

INGREDIENTS: $^1/_2$ CUP WATER
                          OR
                 1   CUP COFFEE

METHOD: 1.   Fry your ham steak over medium heat until browned then remove it from the pan.

            2.   Deglaze the pan by placing your liquid in the pan and whisking and scraping 'til all the crusty particles have been loosened from the bottom of the pan. Boil for a moment to reduce the liquid slightly, then pour the gravy over your ham steak and serve.

USE ON: Ham steaks ($^1/_4$ inch thick or better).

YIELD: $^1/_2$ to 1 cup.

NUTRITIONAL FACTS:

Serving Size: 2 T	Total Fat: 0 g	Sodium: 0 mg	Sugar: 0 g
Calories Per Serving: 0	Sat Fat: 0 g	Total Carbs: 0 g	Protein: 0 g
Fat Calories: 0	Cholest: 0 mg	Fiber: 0 g	

CIDER RAISIN SAUCE

INGREDIENTS:

2	TABLESPOONS BROWN SUGAR
2	TABLESPOONS CORN STARCH
$1\,^1/_2$	CUPS APPLE CIDER
$^1/_4$	CUP RAISINS

METHOD: In a sauce pan, blend the sugar and corn starch and whisk in the apple cider. Bring the mixture to a boil while whisking constantly. Add the raisins and reduce the heat to simmer. Cook for an additional 5 minutes.

USE ON: Ham.

YIELD: 2 cups.

NUTRITIONAL FACTS:

Serving Size: 3 T	Total Fat: 0 g	Sodium: 0 mg	Sugar: 8 g
Calories Per Serving: 40	Sat Fat: 0 g	Total Carbs: 11 g	Protein: 0 g
Fat Calories: 0	Cholest: 0 mg	Fiber: 0 g	

APPLE SAUCE

Apple sauce is enjoyed by many Americans as a dessert, or as a condiment with roast pork and grilled or barbecued pork chops. If you like tart sauce, use a tart variety of apple. If you prefer more sweetness, select sweet apples.

INGREDIENTS:	6	LARGE APPLES (THE VARIETY IS YOUR CHOICE)
	$1/_4$	TEASPOON GROUND CLOVES
	$1/_2$	TEASPOON GROUND CINNAMON
	2	TABLESPOONS BUTTER
		SUGAR TO TASTE

METHOD: Peel and slice the apples and place them, with the cloves and cinnamon, into a sauce pan. Cook over low heat, stirring and mashing until they collapse. Continue cooking until the sauce has a thick consistency, then add the butter and sugar and cook 5 minutes more.

USE ON: Roast pork, pork loin, pork steaks, pork chops and if you ever roast a Christmas goose, it's good on that too!

YIELD: $1 \, 1/_2$ cups.

NUTRITIONAL FACTS:

Serving Size: 1/4 cup	Total Fat: 1.5 g	Sodium: 15 mg	Sugar: 8 g
Calories Per Serving: 45	Sat Fat: 1 g	Total Carbs: 9 g	Protein: 0 g
Fat Calories: 15	Cholest: 5 mg	Fiber: 1 g	

SAUCE FOR PORK CUTS

If you're not sure what I mean by pork cuts, think of chops, cutlets and steaks. Ah, now it's familiar. This sauce is one step removed from a simple pork gravy. It's made from the fat and juices of the sauteed meat, plus a broth and a hint of fruit.

INGREDIENTS:	2	TABLESPOONS OIL FROM THE FRIED OR SAUTEED PORK
	2	TABLESPOONS CHOPPED ONION
	2	TABLESPOONS FLOUR
	1 $^1/_2$	CUPS VEGETABLE BROTH OR WATER
	$^1/_2$	CUP WHITE WINE
	1	TABLESPOON OF YOUR FAVORITE TART JAM OR JELLY

METHOD: Drain and discard any remaining oil. Saute the onion in the 2 tablespoons of oil and when the edges begin to brown, whisk in the flour and cook the mixture for 2 minutes. Add the vegetable stock and whisk to deglaze any particles from the pan bottom. Add the wine and jelly and cook until the sauce has Thickened.

USE ON: Pork chops, pork steaks, blade cuts, pork cutlets.

YIELD: 1 $^1/_4$ cups.

NUTRITIONAL FACTS:			
Serving Size: 3 T	Total Fat: 2.5 g	Sodium: 100 mg	Sugar: 1 g
Calories Per Serving: 45	Sat Fat: 0 g	Total Carbs: 4 g	Protein: 1 g
Fat Calories: 20	Cholest: 0 mg	Fiber: 0 g	

CUCUMBER SAUCE

The cucumber is one of the most versatile vegetables on the market. It is a prime ingredient in several cold soups and salads, as well as being the featured ingredient in sandwiches and several salad dressings. When peeled it can be eaten out of hand and with a light sprinkling of salt, it becomes a cool, crunchy snack. It can be served with an interesting variety of dressings like sour cream or sugar and vinegar. In short, the cucumber is wonderful. In this recipe it is used to create a light, very flavorful sauce for meat and it requires a white sauce base.

INGREDIENTS:	2	CUPS WHITE SAUCE MADE WITH BUTTER
	1	TABLESPOON BUTTER
	2	SHALLOTS, MINCED
	$\frac{1}{2}$	CUP FINELY CHOPPED CUCUMBER

METHOD: Saute the shallots in butter until soft then add the cucumber. Cook for 3 minutes then add the white sauce and bring to a scald.

USE ON: Pork cutlets, chops or steaks.

YIELD: 2 $\frac{1}{2}$ cups.

NUTRITIONAL FACTS:

Serving Size: 1/4 cup	Total Fat: 7 g	Sodium: 75 mg	Sugar: 2 g
Calories Per Serving: 90	Sat Fat: 4 g	Total Carbs: 5 g	Protein: 2 g
Fat Calories: 60	Cholest: 20 mg	Fiber: 0 g	

PORK SAGE SAUCE

As with the preceding cucumber sauce you need a white sauce as your base.

INGREDIENTS:
- 2 CUPS WHITE SAUCE MADE WITH BUTTER.
- 2 TABLESPOONS EXTRA LIGHT OLIVE OIL
- 1/2 CUP CHOPPED ONION
- 1/2 TEASPOON GROUND SAGE
- 1/2 TEASPOON FRESHLY GROUND BLACK PEPPER

METHOD: Saute the onion in the olive oil until the edges begin to brown, then whisk in the white sauce. Add the sage and black pepper and bring the sauce to a low boil.

USE ON: Pork cuts, grilled, broiled or fried.

YIELD: 2 1/4 cups.

NUTRITIONAL FACTS:

Serving Size: 3 T	Total Fat: 6 g	Sodium: 45 mg	Sugar: 2 g
Calories Per Serving: 80	Sat Fat: 3 g	Total Carbs: 4 g	Protein: 1 g
Fat Calories: 60	Cholest: 10 mg	Fiber: 0 g	

APPLE-CRANBERRY SAUCE

This is pretty enough to be a Christmas dish. Try it on pork roast hot from the oven. Or on boneless, stuffed and rolled, thinly sliced, cold roast of pork.

INGREDIENTS:	4	APPLES, CORED, PEELED AND SLICED
	2	CUPS FRESH CRANBERRIES
	1	CUP BROWN SUGAR
	$1\frac{1}{2}$	CUPS APPLE CIDER

METHOD: Place all the ingredients into a sauce pan and bring them to a boil. Reduce the heat and cook until the most of the berries have burst, about 10 minutes.

USE ON: Pork, grilled, broiled, fried or roasted.

YIELD: $3\frac{1}{2}$ cups.

NUTRITIONAL FACTS:

Serving Size: 1/3 cup	Total Fat: 0 g	Sodium: 0 mg	Sugar: 16 g
Calories Per Serving: 70	Sat Fat: 0 g	Total Carbs: 18 g	Protein: 0 g
Fat Calories: 0	Cholest: 0 mg	Fiber: 1 g	

CHERRY SAUCE

You can prepare this sauce from fresh tart cherries, but they will need to be pitted. So do that first.

INGREDIENTS:
1	16 OUNCE CAN PITTED TART CHERRIES, PUREED
$1/_2$	TEASPOON GROUND CINNAMON
$1/_2$	TEASPOON GROUND CLOVES
1	TEASPOON FRESHLY GRATED LEMON RIND
1	TABLESPOON HONEY
$1/_2$	CUP MADEIRA WINE

METHOD: Place the cherries, cinnamon, cloves, lemon rind and honey into a sauce pan and bring to a boil. Reduce the heat and cook for 5 minutes. Remove the sauce from the heat and stir in the Madeira wine.

USE ON: Pork chops, broiled, grilled or fried, pork steaks or shoulder chops.

YIELD: 1 $1/_4$ cups.

NUTRITIONAL FACTS:
Serving Size: 1/4 cup	Total Fat: 0 g	Sodium: 0 mg	Sugar: 2 g
Calories Per Serving: 0	Sat Fat: 0 g	Total Carbs: 6 g	Protein: 0 g
Fat Calories: 0	Cholest: 0 mg	Fiber: 0 g	

GRAPEFRUIT SAUCE

You either love grapefruit or you can leave it alone. For grapefruit lovers this sauce is a palate-pleasing surprise. If you are not excited by grapefruit, you owe it to yourself to give it a try.

INGREDIENTS:		
	$^1/_2$	CUP SUGAR
	2	TABLESPOONS CORN STARCH
	1	CUP WATER
	1	TEASPOON GRATED FRESH GRAPEFRUIT PEEL
	2	CUPS GRAPEFRUIT JUICE
	$^1/_4$	TEASPOON SALT

METHOD: Place all the ingredients into a sauce pan and thoroughly blend while bringing the mixture to a boil. Cook the sauce for 2 minutes or until it is thickened.

USE ON: Ham steaks, grilled or broiled.

YIELD: 3 cups.

NUTRITIONAL FACTS:

Serving Size: 3 T	Total Fat: 0 g	Sodium: 35 mg	Sugar: 6 g
Calories Per Serving: 30	Sat Fat: 0 g	Total Carbs: 7 g	Protein: 0 g
Fat Calories: 0	Cholest: 0 mg	Fiber: 0 g	

BRANDY SAUCE

INGREDIENTS:

1	TABLESPOON ROUX
	OR
1	TABLESPOON FLOUR
$^3/_4$	CUP WATER
2	TABLESPOONS BRANDY
2	TABLESPOONS ORANGE JUICE

OPTION: Replace the orange juice with triple sec.

METHOD:

1. If using a roux, place all the ingredients into a sauce pan and bring the sauce to a boil. Reduce the heat and cook until thickened.

2. If you saute your meat, whisk the flour into the pan juices and cook for 1 minute. Add the remaining ingredients and bring the sauce to a boil. Then reduce the heat and cook until thickened.

USE ON: Sauteed, broiled or grilled pork chops, pork steak or pork tenderloin medallions.

YIELD: 1 cup.

NUTRITIONAL FACTS:

Serving Size: 3 T	Total Fat: 0 g	Sodium: 0 mg	Sugar: 1 g
Calories Per Serving: 10	Sat Fat: 0 g	Total Carbs: 2 g	Protein: 0 g
Fat Calories: 0	Cholest: 0 mg	Fiber: 0 g	

PLUM SAUCE

For this sauce you can use canned plums, plumped pitted prunes or fresh Santa Rosa plums. When using fresh plums you'll need to add 1/2 cup water and possibly a little sugar while you cook them for 10 minutes over medium heat.

INGREDIENTS:	2	CUPS CANNED PLUMS
	$1\,^1/_2$	TABLESPOONS CORN STARCH
	$^1/_2$	TEASPOON GROUND ALLSPICE
	2	TABLESPOONS LEMON JUICE
	1	TABLESPOON BUTTER

METHOD:

1. Drain and reserve the plum juice/syrup.

2. Seed and quarter the plums, set aside.

3. Place the plum juice, corn starch, allspice and lemon juice into a sauce pan. Whisk to blend and dissolve the corn starch. Place the pan on the heat and bring the mixture to a boil. Reduce the heat to medium and whisking constantly, cook until the mixture thickens. Add the butter and plums to heat through, then remove the sauce from the heat.

USE ON: Pork, sauteed, broiled or roasted. Baked ham, grilled or broiled ham steaks.

YIELD: 2 cups.

NUTRITIONAL FACTS:

Serving Size: 1/4 cup	Total Fat: 1 g	Sodium: 15 mg	Sugar: 0 g
Calories Per Serving: 40	Sat Fat: 1 g	Total Carbs: 7 g	Protein: 0 g
Fat Calories: 10	Cholest: 5 mg	Fiber: 1 g	

CHAPTER 6

SAUCES AND GRAVIES MADE FOR VEAL

Veal is the meat of a calf and its qualifiers are, that it be 12 weeks old or younger and still nursing. Between 3 and 6 months, the meat begins to change color from pink to red. The taste also begins a slow change and at about six months both the color and taste is that of beef.

SOUR CREAM BASTING SAUCE

If you decide not to rub your veal with olive oil before roasting, this sauce makes an excellent basting medium and gives your roast an attractive finish.

INGREDIENTS:	1	CUP SOUR CREAM
	2	TABLESPOONS FLOUR
	1	TEASPOON MINCED FRESH THYME LEAVES, OR
	$1/4$	TEASPOON DRY THYME LEAVES, CRUMBLED
		PAPRIKA TO DUST AND GARNISH

METHOD:

1. Whisk the flour and thyme into the sour cream to make a paste.

2. Spread the paste over your veal, dust the past coating with paprika.

3. Preheat the oven using roasting chart guidelines for the type and size of your roast.

4. Put the roast in the oven.

5. Occasionally baste the roast with any remaining sauce and pan juices.

USE ON: Roast of veal leg and veal breast. Both may be stuffed.

YIELD: 1 cup.

NUTRITIONAL FACTS:

Serving Size: 3 T	Total Fat: 9 g	Sodium: 25 mg	Sugar: 2 g
Calories Per Serving: 100	Sat Fat: 6 g	Total Carbs: 4 g	Protein: 2 g
Fat Calories: 80	Cholest: 20 mg	Fiber: 0 g	

BEARNAISE SAUCE

INGREDIENTS:		
	1	CUP WHITE WINE
	3	EGG YOLKS
	2	TABLESPOONS WHITE WINE VINEGAR
	1	TABLESPOON CHOPPED PARSLEY
	1	TABLESPOON MINCED SHALLOTS
	1	TEASPOON TARRAGON
	1	TEASPOON CHERVIL
	$^1/_2$	TEASPOON SALT
		FRESHLY GROUND BLACK PEPPER TO TASTE
	$^1/_2$	CUP BUTTER

METHOD:

1. Beat the egg yolks into $^1/_4$ cup of the wine and set aside.

2. Place the remaining ingredients, except the butter, into a sauce pan and bring to a boil. Reduce the heat and simmer for 15 minutes.

3. Remove the pan from the heat and slowly whisk in the egg yolks. Now add the butter, 1 to 2 tablespoons at a time. When completed, strain the sauce.

USE ON: Calf liver, beef liver, pork liver...etc.

YIELD: 2 cups.

NUTRITIONAL FACTS:			
Serving Size: 3 T	Total Fat: 11 g	Sodium: 220 mg	Sugar: 0 g
Calories Per Serving: 120	Sat Fat: 6 g	Total Carbs: 1 g	Protein: 1 g
Fat Calories: 100	Cholest: 90 mg	Fiber: 0 g	

Brown Sauce

This sauce is so popular that it's name can be found in almost any restaurant. While the name is the same, the recipe varies greatly. You have probably realized by now that I have three sauces by this name in the book.

Chefs enjoy adding their own special touch to a sauce and that often leads to a different taste and a different recipe, without a different name. Cooks and chefs are drawn to a familiar name when the sauce has beef, beef broth or beef bouillon in it. After all how wrong can you be with "Brown Sauce". And therein lies the explanation as to why a sauce with a common name, tastes differently in various restaurants.

INGREDIENTS:

4	TABLESPOONS BUTTER
1	ONION, CHOPPED
$1/4$	CUP DICED CELERY
1	CARROT, CHOPPED
1	CLOVE GARLIC, CRUSHED
3	TABLESPOONS CORN STARCH
3	CUPS BEEF BOUILLON
2	TABLESPOONS MADEIRA WINE
$1/2$	TEASPOON GROUND THYME
8	BLACK PEPPERCORNS

Method: Saute the onion, celery, carrot and garlic in the butter for 5 minutes or until the onion begins to brown. Mix the corn starch with some of the bouillon, then add all the remaining ingredients to the pan and bring to a boil. Reduce the heat to simmer and cook for 20 minutes. Strain the sauce before serving.

Use On: Grilled or broiled veal cutlets, veal shoulder steaks or roasted veal breasts.

Yield: 3 cups.

NUTRITIONAL FACTS:			
Serving Size: 1/3 cup	Total Fat: 3.5 g	Sodium: 200 mg	Sugar: 1 g
Calories Per Serving: 60	Sat Fat: 2 g	Total Carbs: 6 g	Protein: 1 g
Fat Calories: 30	Cholest: 10 mg	Fiber: 0 g	

MADEIRA VEAL SAUCE

This sauce is best made in the pan in which you sauteed your veal. Since you probably have used an oil or butter to saute the veal, you can omit the 2 tablespoons of butter or oil in the sauce recipe.

INGREDIENTS:	2	TABLESPOONS BUTTER OR OLIVE OIL
	1	CUP SLICED MUSHROOMS
	1	SHALLOT, MINCED
	1	TEASPOON FLOUR
	$^1/_2$	CUP MADEIRA WINE
	1	CUP DEMI-GLAZE OR BEEF STOCK
	$^1/_2$	CUP WHIPPING CREAM
		FRESH CHOPPED PARSLEY TO GARNISH

METHOD: Saute the mushrooms and shallot in the butter or oil for 3 minutes. Blend in the flour and cook 1 minute. Add the wine and demi-glaze and bring the sauce to a boil. Reduce the heat and add the whipping cream. Cook for 2 additional minutes.

USE ON: Sauteed, broiled or grilled veal.

YIELD: 2 $^1/_2$ cups.

NUTRITIONAL FACTS:

Serving Size: 1/3 cup	Total Fat: 8 g	Sodium: 110 mg	Sugar: 1 g
Calories Per Serving: 100	Sat Fat: 3.5 g	Total Carbs: 3 g	Protein: 1 g
Fat Calories: 80	Cholest: 15 mg	Fiber: 0 g	

MARSALA VEAL SAUCE

This sauce works well for Veal Scaloppine, veal cutlets, or any other veal cut you prepare by sauteing. Just prepare the sauce in the same skillet so that when you deglaze the pan you're incorporating the meat juices into your sauce.

INGREDIENTS:	3	TABLESPOONS BUTTER
	1	CUP MUSHROOMS
	1	TEASPOON FLOUR
	$^1/_2$	CUP MARSALA WINE
	PINCH	SALT
		CHOPPED PARSLEY TO GARNISH

METHOD:

1. Saute the mushrooms in the butter for several minutes until the mushrooms release their liquid. Set aside.

2. Blend the flour and salt into the Marsala and set aside.

3. (Saute the veal, remove it from the pan and set aside.)

4. Pour the Marsala and the juice from the mushrooms into the pan. Deglaze the pan over high heat and add the mushrooms to heat through.

ALTERNATE: Replace the Marsala and the mushrooms with lemon juice and $^1/_4$ cup chopped parsley.

USE ON: Sauteed Veal Scaloppine or veal cutlets. On thicker cuts of veal such as veal shoulder chops that have been broiled or grilled.

This sauce can also be used on flattened chicken breasts and flattened medallions of pork tenderloin.

YIELD: 1 $^1/_4$ cups.

NUTRITIONAL FACTS:

Serving Size: 1/3 cup	Total Fat: 12 g	Sodium: 350 mg	Sugar: 0 g
Calories Per Serving: 140	Sat Fat: 7 g	Total Carbs: 1 g	Protein: 1 g
Fat Calories: 100	Cholest: 30 mg	Fiber: 0 g	

MARSALA VEAL SAUCE II

This sauce is a very flavorful demi-glaze. You need either a glaze (see Chapter 1) or a beef extract.

INGREDIENTS:

$1/4$	TEASPOON BEEF EXTRACT
	OR
1	TABLESPOON GLAZE
1	TABLESPOON BUTTER
$1/2$	CUP BEEF BROTH
$1/2$	CUP MARSALA

METHOD: Place all the ingredients into a sauce pan and bring to a boil. Remove the pan from the heat.

USE ON: Veal Scaloppine, veal cutlets and veal medallions. The cutlets and the medallions need to be pounded flat before sauteing.

YIELD: 1 cup.

NUTRITIONAL FACTS:

Serving Size: 3 T	Total Fat: 2 g	Sodium: 220 mg	Sugar: 0 g
Calories Per Serving: 45	Sat Fat: 1.5 g	Total Carbs: 1 g	Protein: 1 g
Fat Calories: 20	Cholest: 5 mg	Fiber: 0 g	

"This page is blank by Design"

CHAPTER 7

SAUCES AND GRAVIES MADE FOR LAMB OR MUTTON

WE TRIED THIS SAUCE ... AND

FRESH MINT SAUCE

Mint jelly and mint sauce are great "go togethers" with lamb. For this recipe buy fresh mint if you don't grow your own. Or if fresh mint is not available, buy mint jelly at the store.

INGREDIENTS:	3	TABLESPOONS MINCED FRESH MINT LEAVES
	2	TABLESPOONS POWDERED SUGAR
	6	TABLESPOONS DISTILLED VINEGAR
ALTERNATE:	6	TABLESPOONS WHITE WINE VINEGAR

METHOD: Blend all the ingredients in a small jar or bowl. Shake, it in the jar, or whisk it in the bowl. Let it rest for an hour at room temperature.

USE ON: Roast, sauteed or broiled lamb.

YIELD: 1 Cup.

NUTRITIONAL FACTS:

Serving Size: 3 T	Total Fat: 0 g	Sodium: 0 mg	Sugar: 6 g
Calories Per Serving: 30	Sat Fat: 0 g	Total Carbs: 9 g	Protein: 0 g
Fat Calories: 0	Cholest: 0 mg	Fiber: 0 g	

MINT SAUCE TOO!

What separates this sauce from the preceding one is that this version is cooked. The ingredient list is nearly identical, but now you have a syrup with mint leaves in it. It's not really a jelly, but it ain't far from it.

INGREDIENTS:	1	CUP CHOPPED FRESH MINT LEAVES (YOUR CHOICE OF VARIETY)
	$^1/_4$	CUP WATER
	3	TABLESPOONS SUGAR
	$^1/_3$	CUP VINEGAR

METHOD:

1. Chop the mint leaves and set aside.

2. Bring the water and sugar to a boil. Cook until the sugar is completely dissolved and the syrup is clear.

3. Remove the syrup from the heat and stir in the vinegar and the mint leaves. Let them steep for several hours, then strain before using.

USE ON: Lamb chops, roasted breast of lamb or roast leg of lamb, or use as a baste.

YIELD: 1 cup.

NUTRITIONAL FACTS:

Serving Size: 3 T	Total Fat: 0 g	Sodium: 0 mg	Sugar: 7 g
Calories Per Serving: 30	Sat Fat: 0 g	Total Carbs: 8 g	Protein: 0 g
Fat Calories: 0	Cholest: 0 mg	Fiber: 0 g	

CAPER SAUCE

INGREDIENTS: 2   CUPS WHITE SAUCE
                 $^1/_2$ CUP MINCED CAPERS

METHOD: Bring your white sauce to the boiling point. Lower the heat, add the capers to heat through and serve.

USE ON: Boiled mutton and lamb dishes.

YIELD: 2 $^1/_2$ cups.

NUTRITIONAL FACTS:

Serving Size: 1/4 cup	Total Fat: 7 g	Sodium: 75 mg	Sugar: 2 g
Calories Per Serving: 90	Sat Fat: 4 g	Total Carbs: 5 g	Protein: 2 g
Fat Calories: 60	Cholest: 20 mg	Fiber: 0 g	

SWEET ONION WHITE SAUCE

If sweet onions are not available you can still make this sauce by using leeks, or shallots. The taste won't be quite the same as onion, but it will be good.

INGREDIENTS:	2	CUPS WHITE SAUCE
	1	CUP CHOPPED ONION
	1	TABLESPOON WHITE WINE VINEGAR
	PINCH	FRESHLY GRATED NUTMEG

METHOD: Bring the white sauce to a scald and add the onion. Cook at a simmer for 6 to 8 minutes, then remove the sauce from the heat and stir in the nutmeg.

ALTERNATE: Saute the onion in a little extra light olive oil, or butter, for several minutes before adding it to a preheated white sauce.

USE ON: Grilled or broiled lamb cuts.

YIELD: 3 cups.

NUTRITIONAL FACTS:

Serving Size: 1/3 cup	Total Fat: 4 g	Sodium: 45 mg	Sugar: 4 g
Calories Per Serving: 70	Sat Fat: 2.5 g	Total Carbs: 7 g	Protein: 1 g
Fat Calories: 35	Cholest: 10 mg	Fiber: 1 g	

DILL SAUCE

You can choose to use the recipe as written, or replace the lamb broth with cream or milk.

INGREDIENTS:

1	CUP LAMB BROTH*
2	TABLESPOONS CIDER VINEGAR
2	TEASPOONS SUGAR
2	TABLESPOON FRESH DILL WEED (2 TEASPOONS DRIED) OR
$1/_2$	TEASPOON GROUND DILL SEED
1	EGG YOLK, SLIGHTLY BEATEN

* Drain the fat from the roasting pan. Add 1 cup water and deglaze the pan, then use as directed below.

METHOD:

1. To the hot broth, add the vinegar, sugar and dill and mix thoroughly.

2. Pour a little of the hot broth in the bowl containing your beaten egg and mix thoroughly.

3. Transfer the egg mixture back into the roasting pan with the broth. Whisk while cooking, until the sauce is thickened.

   Garnish with a sprig of fresh dill.

USE ON: Thinly sliced lamb.

YIELD: 1 $1/_2$ cups.

NUTRITIONAL FACTS:

Serving Size: 3 T	Total Fat: 1 g	Sodium: 120 mg	Sugar: 2 g
Calories Per Serving: 30	Sat Fat: 0 g	Total Carbs: 5 g	Protein: 1 g
Fat Calories: 10	Cholest: 30 mg	Fiber: 0 g	

CHAPTER 8

SAUCES FOR GAME AND GAME BIRDS

This chapter covers most of the available game such as deer, moose, boar, squirrel, rabbit and the game birds; pheasant, quail, squab, dove and partridge.

SWEET VENISON SAUCE

Admittedly, venison is generally not available unless you, or someone you know, is a hunter. Choose a sparkling wine for the dish, such as Asti Spumanti, or a Muscato or Port.

INGREDIENTS:

2 $\frac{1}{2}$	TABLESPOONS SWEET WINE
1	CUP RED CURRANT JELLY
1	SMALL CINNAMON STICK
1	WHOLE LEMON PEEL (PITH REMOVED)

METHOD: Place all the ingredients into a small pan and bring to a boil. Reduce the heat to simmer and cook 5 minutes. Strain and serve.

USE: On or under slices of venison.

YIELD: 1 cup

NUTRITIONAL FACTS:

Serving Size: 3 T	Total Fat: 0 g	Sodium: 30 mg	Sugar: 24 g
Calories Per Serving: 90	Sat Fat: 0 g	Total Carbs: 25 g	Protein: 0 g
Fat Calories: 0	Cholest: 0 mg	Fiber: 0 g	

BRANDY CREAM SAUCE

INGREDIENTS:

1	CUP CHICKEN BROTH
1	TABLESPOON CORN STARCH
$^1/_4$	CUP BUTTER
4	SHALLOTS, MINCED
1	CUP WHIPPING CREAM
1	TABLESPOON HORSERADISH
$^1/_2$	TEASPOON SALT
$^1/_4$	CUP BRANDY

METHOD:

1. Mix the chicken broth and corn starch and set aside.

2. Saute the shallots in butter for 5 minutes, add the whipping cream, horseradish, and salt and bring to a boil. Add the chicken broth and corn starch, reduce the heat and cook until thickened. Stir in the brandy.

USE ON: Pheasant or other game birds.

YIELD: $2\,^3/_4$ cups.

NUTRITIONAL FACTS:

Serving Size: 3 T	Total Fat: 8 g	Sodium: 160 mg	Sugar: 1 g
Calories Per Serving: 90	Sat Fat: 5 g	Total Carbs: 2 g	Protein: 1 g
Fat Calories: 70	Cholest: 25 mg	Fiber: 0 g	

GRAPE SAUCE

All nuts are not born equal some even have two names (hazelnuts are also known as filberts). But whatever they're called, you'll need some of them for the recipe. The Filbert is apparently named after Saint Philibert, a 5th century Frankish Abbot whose feast day is celebrated during the nutting season. I assume that refers to the harvest season, or that they're picked during an autumn full moon when nuts of all types are known to come out.

INGREDIENTS:	1	CUP WATER
	1	CUP SEEDLESS GRAPES (COLOR IS YOUR CHOICE)
	4	TABLESPOONS BUTTER
	$^1/_2$	CUP SWEET WINE (MUSCATO, PORT, DESSERT SHERRIES)
	PINCH	GROUND CLOVES
	$^1/_2$	CUP HAZELNUTS, FINELY CHOPPED

METHOD:

1. Place the water and grapes into a sauce pan and bring to a boil. Lower the heat and cook for 5 minutes, then drain and discard the water.

2. Add the butter, wine and cloves to the hot grapes and simmer for 5 minutes. Remove from the heat and add the chopped nuts.

USE ON: Quail.

YIELD: 2 cups.

NUTRITIONAL FACTS:			
Serving Size: 1/2 cup	Total Fat: 10 g	Sodium: 60 mg	Sugar: 0 g
Calories Per Serving: 120	Sat Fat: 4 g	Total Carbs: 4 g	Protein: 1 g
Fat Calories: 90	Cholest: 15 mg	Fiber: 1 g	

VENISON WHITE SAUCE

This is a flavored and slightly sweet white sauce made for venison.

INGREDIENTS:	2	CUPS WHITE SAUCE
	1	TABLESPOON SUGAR
	1	TABLESPOON VINEGAR
	$^1/_2$	TEASPOON CRUSHED ANISE SEED
	$^1/_4$	CUP DRY WHITE WINE

METHOD: Bring the white sauce to scald, add, and whisk in, all the ingredients. Cook for 2 minutes.

USE ON: Venison, moose and bison (buffalo).

YIELD: 2 $^1/_3$ cups.

NUTRITIONAL FACTS:

Serving Size: 3 T	Total Fat: 4 g	Sodium: 45 mg	Sugar: 2 g
Calories Per Serving: 60	Sat Fat: 2.5 g	Total Carbs: 4 g	Protein: 1 g
Fat Calories: 40	Cholest: 15 mg	Fiber: 0 g	

TUSCAN GAME SAUCE

This recipe calls for two cups of meat sauce. If you have some on hand, use it, but if not, buy one. However if you REALLY want to make one, and can't be talked out of it, then see Chapter 4 for the meat cooking sauce, or select a recipe from my best selling cookbook, "The Encyclopedia of Sauces For Your Pasta".

INGREDIENTS:		
	$1^1/_2$	CUPS WINE VINEGAR
	$1^1/_2$	CUPS DRY WHITE WINE
	$^1/_3$	CUP ONION, COARSELY CHOPPED
	1	BAY LEAF
	$^1/_2$	TEASPOON DRIED THYME
	2	TABLESPOONS CHOPPED PARSLEY
	2	TABLESPOONS BUTTER
	2	TABLESPOONS FLOUR
	2	CUPS TOMATO MEAT SAUCE
	2	TABLESPOONS PICKLE RELISH
	1	TABLESPOON CAPERS
	1	TABLESPOON CHOPPED PARSLEY
	1	TEASPOON DRIED MARJORAM
	$^1/_2$	TEASPOON SALT
	$^1/_4$	TEASPOON CRUSHED RED PEPPER

METHOD:

1. Place the first 6 ingredients into a sauce pan and bring the mixture to a boil. Cook uncovered until the liquid is reduced by 1/2. Discard the bay leaf. Strain the mixture or puree it in a blender. Return the mixture to your sauce pan and set it aside.

2. Make a roux of the flour and butter. Add the roux and all the remaining ingredients to the pureed mixture. Bring the sauce to a boil. Reduce the heat to simmer and cook for 10 minutes.

Use On: Rabbit, venison and boar.

Yield: 4 cups.

PEVERADA SAUCE

This game sauce is of northern Italian ancestry with a history that goes back to medieval times. It is a blend of flavors from stock, the liver of a game bird and dry Italian-style salami. The salami recommended is a Soppressa, particularly the Venetian Soppressa. But you can use whatever you can find.

INGREDIENTS:

3	TABLESPOONS OLIVE OIL
$^1/_2$	POUND OF ANY POULTRY LIVER, MINCED
6	OUNCES ITALIAN STYLE DRY SALAMI, MINCED
2	CUPS CHICKEN BOUILLON, BROTH OR STOCK
2	TABLESPOONS CHOPPED PARSLEY
	SALT AND FRESHLY GROUND BLACK PEPPER TO TASTE
1 $^1/_2$	TABLESPOONS LEMON JUICE

OPTIONS:

	ADD ONE OR ALL OF THE FOLLOWING:
$^1/_2$	CUP DRY BREAD CRUMBS, RAISINS, PINE NUTS.
$^1/_2$	TEASPOON CINNAMON.
	WINE AND MEAT JUICES FROM YOUR GAME.

METHOD: Saute the liver and salami in the oil for 3 minutes. Add all the ingredients, except lemon juice, and bring the mixture to a boil. Reduce the heat to low and cook uncovered for 30 minutes. Add the lemon juice.

For a smoother texture, puree the sauce in your blender before using.

USE ON: Game birds, venis on, boar and boiled beef.

YIELD: 3 $^1/_2$ cups.

NUTRITIONAL FACTS:

Serving Size: 1/3 cup	Total Fat: 9 g	Sodium: 440 mg	Sugar: 0 g
Calories Per Serving: 110	Sat Fat: 2.5 g	Total Carbs: 1 g	Protein: 7 g
Fat Calories: 80	Cholest: 90 mg	Fiber: 0 g	

WE TRIED THIS SAUCE ... AND

LOVED IT ( )
HATED IT ( )
MAYBE WE'LL TRY IT AGAIN ( )
WE'LL USE IT FOR UNWELCOME GUESTS ( )

GAME BIRD GREEN SAUCE

The green coloring in this sauce comes from the cucumber skin. You can also swap the small onion for an equal amount of green onion, (approximately 1/4 to 1/3 cup when chopped).

INGREDIENTS:

1	CUCUMBER, HALVED SEEDED AND CHUNKED
1	POTATO, BOILED OR MICROWAVED
1	SMALL ONION, CHOPPED
1	TABLESPOON ANCHOVY PASTE
1	CLOVE GARLIC
1	TEASPOON SALT
1	CUP OLIVE OIL
$1/4$	CUP VINEGAR

METHOD: Place all the ingredients into a blender and puree.

USE ON: Boiled, broiled, grilled or roasted pheasant, partridge (without the pear tree), quail, dove and squab.

YIELD: $3 \frac{1}{2}$ cups.

NUTRITIONAL FACTS:

Serving Size: 1/3 cup	Total Fat: 18 g	Sodium: 240 mg	Sugar: 1 g
Calories Per Serving: 180	Sat Fat: 2.5 g	Total Carbs: 5 g	Protein: 1 g
Fat Calories: 160	Cholest: 0 mg	Fiber: 1 g	

RABBIT WINE SAUCE

You can reverse the procedure of this recipe by sauteing the rabbit in the oil and garlic, then adding the remaining ingredients and cooking the rabbit in the sauce until tender. The wine however still needs to be reduced.

Rabbit and fresh rosemary are available year 'round in many super markets in America, but fennel is not. So when fennel is in season you can replace the rosemary with a sliced whole fennel bulb. You can also substitute the olives with fresh or frozen peas.

INGREDIENTS:		
	1	SPRIG FRESH ROSEMARY
	2	CUPS RED WINE
	2	TABLESPOONS OLIVE OIL
	3	CLOVES GARLIC, MINCED
	1	TABLESPOON TOMATO PASTE
		OR
	2	ITALIAN STYLE TOMATOES, PEELED, SEEDED AND CHOPPED
	$^1/_4$	CUP WATER
	$^1/_2$	TEASPOON SALT
	$^1/_2$	CUP CHOPPED\SLICED RIPE OLIVES

METHOD:

1. Place the rosemary and wine into a sauce pan. Bring to a boil to reduce by half, then remove from the heat and set aside.

2. Saute the garlic in the olive oil until lightly golden. Add tomato paste or tomatoes, water, salt and cook for 2 minutes. Add the wine and bring the sauce to a boil. Reduce the heat and cook for 5 minutes. Add the olives and cook 1 minute longer, then discard the rosemary.

USE ON: Sauteed, broiled or grilled rabbit.

YIELD: 2 $^1/_2$ cups.

NUTRITIONAL FACTS:			
Serving Size: 1/3 cup	Total Fat: 4.5 g	Sodium: 230 mg	Sugar: 0 g
Calories Per Serving: 80	Sat Fat: 0.5 g	Total Carbs: 3 g	Protein: 0 g
Fat Calories: 40	Cholest: 0 mg	Fiber: 0 g	

VENISON PEPPER SAUCE

Chop the ingredients into chunks for this sauce, because you will strain it prior to serving.

INGREDIENTS:		
	1	TABLESPOON BUTTER
	1	TABLESPOON FLOUR
	1	CUP BEEF BROTH OR CONSOMME
	1	ONION, CHOPPED
	1	CARROT RIB, CHOPPED
	1	CELERY, CHOPPED
	1	TEASPOON GRATED LEMON ZEST
	1	TEASPOON THYME
	2	SPRIGS PARSLEY
	$1/2$	CUP SHERRY
	$1/2$	TEASPOON SALT
	$1/2$	TEASPOON FRESHLY GROUND BLACK PEPPER
	PINCH	OF CAYENNE
	$1/2$	CUP CURRANT JELLY

METHOD:

1. Make a brown roux with the flour and butter.

2. Add the broth, onion, carrot, celery, lemon zest, thyme and parsley. Bring the mixture to a boil and reduce the heat. Cover the pan and simmer for 1 hour.

3. Add sherry, salt, pepper and currant jelly. Simmer 10 more minutes, then strain and serve.

USE ON: Venison. (When used on other game, omit the currant jelly.)

YIELD: 2 cups.

NUTRITIONAL FACTS:			
Serving Size: 1/3 cup	Total Fat: 1.5 g	Sodium: 210 mg	Sugar: 10 g
Calories Per Serving: 70	Sat Fat: 0.5 g	Total Carbs: 13 g	Protein: 1 g
Fat Calories: 10	Cholest: 5 mg	Fiber: 1 g	

"This page is blank by Design"

CHAPTER 9

SAUCES AND GRAVIES MADE FOR POULTRY

AND GAME BIRDS

The recipes in this chapter are usable with any fowl including game birds. For specific bird recipes see Chapters 10 through 13.

For new cooks: Giblets are the a collective name given to several parts of a bird, namely the heart, gizzard and liver. Generally you'll find them packed into the body cavity along with the neck.

POULTRY PAN GRAVY

This method for making gravy is identical to the pan gravy in chapter one. The difference is your choice of poultry and your liquid preference.

INGREDIENTS:	2	TABLESPOONS FAT FROM THE PAN DRIPPINGS
	2	TABLESPOONS FLOUR
	1	CUP OF ANY OF THE FOLLOWING:

PAN JUICES, MILK, HALF N' HALF, CREAM, WATER, WINE, STOCK, BROTH, OR POSSIBLY FRUIT JUICE.

SEASON TO TASTE; WITH 1, OR SEVERAL OF THE FOLLOWING:
SALT
PEPPER (BLACK, WHITE, CAYENNE OR PAPRIKA)
HERBS, MINCED IF FRESH, CRUMBLED IF DRY.
GRATED LEMON RIND, ORANGE RIND OR LIME RIND.

| OPTION: | 1 | CUP SLICED FRESH MUSHROOMS (YOU'LL NEED TO SIMMER THEM IN THE GRAVY FOR 5 TO 6 MINUTES). |
| | 1 | CUP OF COOKED AND CHOPPED GIBLETS. |

METHOD: Cook the fat and flour together for several minutes. Remove from the heat and slowly add your liquid while whisking. Return the pan to the heat and bring to a low boil. Season, add optional mushrooms and/or giblets and serve.

(To double the recipe, double the first three ingredients.)

USE ON: Poultry and/or mashed potatoes.

YIELD: 1 to 2 cups.

NUTRITIONAL FACTS:

Serving Size: 1/3 cup	Total Fat: 9 g	Sodium: 30 mg	Sugar: 3 g
Calories Per Serving: 120	Sat Fat: 3.5 g	Total Carbs: 6 g	Protein: 3 g
Fat Calories: 80	Cholest: 15 mg	Fiber: 0 g	

GAME BIRD WHITE SAUCE

INGREDIENTS:

2	CUPS MILK
1	WHOLE PEELED ONION
$1/_2$	CUP UNSEASONED BREAD CRUMBS
	SALT, PEPPER AND CAYENNE TO TASTE
PINCH	FRESHLY GRATED NUTMEG

METHOD:

1. Toast the bread crumbs in a dry skillet and set aside.

2. Place the milk and onion into a sauce pan, slowly bring it to a boil. Reduce the heat to simmer, cover and cook for 30 minutes. Remove and discard the onion, add the toasted bread crumbs and seasoning. Cook for 1 more minute and serve.

USE ON: Game birds or poultry.

YIELD: $2 \, 1/_4$ cups.

NUTRITIONAL FACTS:

Serving Size: 1/4 cup	Total Fat: 1 g	Sodium: 40 mg	Sugar: 2 g
Calories Per Serving: 35	Sat Fat: 0.5 g	Total Carbs: 5 g	Protein: 2 g
Fat Calories: 10	Cholest: 5 mg	Fiber: 0 g	

CELERY SAUCE

Celery and poultry are paired so wonderfully in this sauce that it can easily become a favorite. By the way, you're going to need 2 pans to make this one.

INGREDIENTS:	1	STALK CELERY HEART (NOT A RIB)
	3	CUPS CHICKEN OR TURKEY BROTH
	3	TABLESPOONS BUTTER
	3	TABLESPOONS FLOUR
	1	CUP MILK
	$^1/_4$	TEASPOON GROUND MACE
	$^1/_2$	CUP WHIPPING CREAM
		SEASON TO TASTE

METHOD:

1. Wash and trim the entire celery stalk and chop it into bite sized pieces. Place the celery and broth in a pan, cover and cook for about 30 minutes or until tender. Set aside.

2. Melt the butter in a sauce pan, whisk in the flour and cook for 3 minutes. Whisk in the milk and mace.

3. Strain the celery from its broth, set the celery aside. Add the broth to the milk and roux.

4. Bring the sauce to a boil, then reduce the heat and cook until the sauce thickens. Add the cooked celery and whipping cream. When the sauce returns to a boil remove it from the heat.

USE ON: Poached, broiled or roasted chicken or turkey. Hot chicken or turkey sandwiches.

YIELD: 4 cups.

NUTRITIONAL FACTS:

Serving Size: 1/2 cup	Total Fat: 6 g	Sodium: 220 mg	Sugar: 1 g
Calories Per Serving: 80	Sat Fat: 4 g	Total Carbs: 3 g	Protein: 2 g
Fat Calories: 60	Cholest: 20 mg	Fiber: 0 g	

ORANGE CRANBERRY SAUCE

INGREDIENTS:

2	TABLESPOONS BUTTER
1	MEDIUM ONION, CHOPPED
1	CELERY RIB, CHOPPED
8	OUNCE SLICED MUSHROOMS OR WHOLE SMALL BUTTON MUSHROOMS
1	TABLESPOON FLOUR
1 $^1/_2$	CUPS CHICKEN BROTH OR STOCK
$^3/_4$	CUP CRANBERRIES
1	TABLESPOON GRATED ORANGE ZEST
$^1/_2$	TEASPOON SALT
2	TABLESPOONS CANE SYRUP OR HONEY
$^1/_4$	CUP ORANGE JUICE
$^1/_2$	CUP STRAINED DRIPPINGS FROM THE COOKED POULTRY IF AVAILABLE

METHOD: Saute the onion, celery and mushrooms in the butter for 3 minutes then blend the flour into the broth. Add the broth and flour, cranberries, orange zest, salt, cane syrup and orange juice to the sauteed vegetables and bring the mixture to a boil. Cook for 15 minutes or until all the cranberries have burst.

If your sauce was prepared ahead of time and you want to add the strained juices from your roasted or broiled poultry you may need to add more flour. In that event add 1 tablespoon flour to 1 cup of the strained juices. Add that mixture to your sauce, bring the sauce to a boil and cook for 2 or 3 minutes. Remove from the heat and use. Or for a smooth sauce, strain or puree it before using.

USE ON: Roasted or broiled Cornish game hens, chicken or duck.

YIELD: 4 $^1/_2$ cups.

NUTRITIONAL FACTS:			
Serving Size: 1/2 cup	Total Fat: 2.5 g	Sodium: 130 mg	Sugar: 5 g
Calories Per Serving: 50	Sat Fat: 1.5 g	Total Carbs: 8 g	Protein: 1 g
Fat Calories: 20	Cholest: 5 mg	Fiber: 1 g	

SAUCE Á LA KING

This is the one! The sauce that lets you to use the left-overs of any roasted bird. It was very popular years ago (30's through the 50's) when chicken was expensive and a whole roast chicken was more than two people could eat. Back then they didn't come in parts. So you got the whole thing. All 3 to 6 pounds of it.

This is a basic white sauce with added vegetables for color. It makes a very attractive dish and can be served over toast, biscuits, noodles or rice.

The standard recipe for an "á la KING" calls for bell pepper, mushrooms and a little pimiento. The pimiento is there to add a dash of red. If you mix bell pepper colors you can omit the pimiento. Expand your thinking and add some sliced or diced carrot and fresh or frozen peas.

INGREDIENTS:

2	TABLESPOON BUTTER
$1/_3$	BELL PEPPER, CUT INTO STRIPS (USE SEVERAL COLORS)
4	OUNCES SLICED MUSHROOMS
2	TABLESPOONS FLOUR
3	CUPS LIQUID, YOUR CHOICE (YOU COULD USE $1/_2$ MILK AND $1/_2$ CHICKEN BROTH)
	SALT AND WHITE PEPPER TO TASTE

METHOD:

1. Saute the bell pepper and the mushrooms in the butter for about 5 minutes. Remove the vegetables from the pan and set aside.

2. Whisk the flour into the remaining butter and juices in the pan and cook for 2 minutes. Whisk in the milk or other liquids and cook until the sauce begins to thicken. Return the vegetables and the poultry to the sauce and heat through. Serve.

USE ON: About 2 cups of cooked and cubed chicken, turkey or Cornish hens.

YIELD: 3 $^3/_4$ cups.

NUTRITIONAL FACTS:

Serving Size: 1/2 cup	Total Fat: 3.5 g	Sodium: 160 mg	Sugar: 2 g
Calories Per Serving: 60	Sat Fat: 2 g	Total Carbs: 4 g	Protein: 2 g
Fat Calories: 35	Cholest: 10 mg	Fiber: 0 g	

GIBLET GRAVY

INGREDIENTS: 3   CUPS WATER (1 CUP CAN BE A WHITE WINE)
                 GIBLETS AND THE NECK
            $^1/_4$ CUP FAT FROM THE ROASTING PAN (SEPARATE FAT FROM THE
                 JUICES, RESERVE THE JUICES
            3   TABLESPOONS FLOUR
                 SALT AND PEPPER TO TASTE

OPTION: After you've removed the scum from the broth add several peppercorns, an onion studded with a couple cloves, 1 or 2 parsley sprigs and a carrot.

METHOD:

1. Rinse the giblets under running water and place them in a sauce pan with 3 cups of water. Bring the water to a boil then lower the heat to simmer. Partially cover and cook for 1 hour or until the gizzard is easily pierced with a fork.

2. Remove the pan from the heat. Remove the giblets, mince them and set aside. Strain the broth and set aside.

3. Make a light brown roux from the flour and fat.

4. Add the fat free juices from your roasting pan to the giblet broth, plus enough water to make 3 cups of broth.

5. Slowly whisk the 3 cups of broth into the roux and cook until slightly thickened. Add the minced giblets and season with salt and pepper. Cook for a few minutes to allow melding. Serve.

USE ON: All domestic fowl. Use the giblets from whatever bird you cook to make this gravy.

YIELD: 2 $^1/_2$ cups.

NUTRITIONAL FACTS:

Serving Size: 1/3 cup	Total Fat: 5 g	Sodium: 0 mg	Sugar: 0 g
Calories Per Serving: 70	Sat Fat: 1.5 g	Total Carbs: 2 g	Protein: 0 g
Fat Calories: 45	Cholest: 5 mg	Fiber: 0 g	

MUSTARD CREAM SAUCE

This is an uncooked sauce which is simply blended and served.

INGREDIENTS:	$^1/_2$	CUP DIJON MUSTARD
	1	CUP WHIPPING CREAM
	1	TEASPOON JUICE
		SALT AND PEPPER TO TASTE

METHOD: Whisk all the ingredients together.

USE ON: Cold chicken, cold turkey breast. Try warming the sauce to use on calamari steaks, ground beef/steak patties.

YIELD: $1 \, ^1/_2$ cups.

NUTRITIONAL FACTS:

Serving Size: 3 T	Total Fat: 9 g	Sodium: 370 mg	Sugar: 1 g
Calories Per Serving: 100	Sat Fat: 6 g	Total Carbs: 5 g	Protein: 1 g
Fat Calories: 80	Cholest: 35 mg	Fiber: 0 g	

MARENGO SAUCE

This sauce is usually poured over chicken and called "Chicken Marengo". It was created in 1800 by Napoleon's personal chef to commemorate his victory over the Austrians at Marengo in northwestern Italy.

I've put it in this chapter because the sauce is able to stand on it's own without the chicken. As such, it can be used on other poultry.

INGREDIENTS:		
	2	TABLESPOONS BUTTER
	$^1/_2$	CUP CHOPPED ONION
	4	OUNCES SLICED MUSHROOMS, OR 1 CUP BUTTON MUSHROOMS
	1	CLOVE GARLIC, MINCED OR BRUISED
	$^1/_2$	CUP WHOLE PITTED OLIVES (GREEN RIPE OLIVES IF YOU CAN FIND THEM)
	1	15 OUNCE CAN WHOLE TOMATOES, SQUISHED AND CHOPPED, OR DICED TOMATOES
	$1\,^1/_2$	CUPS CHICKEN STOCK
	$^1/_2$	CUP WHITE WINE

METHOD: Saute the onions, mushrooms and garlic in the butter for 5 minutes. If you used crushed garlic, discard it now. Add the olives, tomatoes and chicken stock and bring the sauce to a boil. Cook uncovered on medium heat for 20 minutes, then add the wine and cook 5 minutes longer. Serve.

OPTION: If you follow the original method, the chicken is browned in the butter and removed before starting the vegetable saute.

Then the chicken is returned to the pan with the tomatoes and the broth.

Use On: Sauteed, roasted or broiled chicken pieces. Split and broiled, or baked Cornish game hens. Sauteed boneless turkey thighs or slices of turkey breast.

Yield: 4 cups.

NUTRITIONAL FACTS:			
Serving Size: 1/3 cup	Total Fat: 2.5 g	Sodium: 380 mg	Sugar: 2 g
Calories Per Serving: 40	Sat Fat: 1 g	Total Carbs: 2 g	Protein: 1 g
Fat Calories: 20	Cholest: 5 mg	Fiber: 0 g	

"This page is blank by Design"

CHAPTER 10

SAUCES AND GRAVIES MADE FOR CHICKEN

In a number of sauces in this chapter, I suggest you use extra light olive oil because it gives you the health benefits, (i.e., no cholesterol, easily digested, monounsaturated) of olive oil without its characteristic taste.

TETRAZZINI SAUCE

For at least two hundred years restaurateurs often named or created dishes to honor their famous customers. This dish and its sauce is named after a Florentine coloratura soprano whose name was Lusia Tetrazzini. She was a diva during the late 1800's and early 20th Century who sang throughout America and spent several years with the Chicago Opera.

Chicken Tetrazzini is a boneless chicken and pasta dish, topped with a light covering of Parmesan cheese and bread crumbs (or possibly toasted almonds) and then finished, by browning, under a broiler. I think the sauce is marvelous and can stand on its own, so I offer it here, to be used in any creative way on poultry.

INGREDIENTS:

$1/4$	CUP BUTTER
$1/2$	POUND SLICED MUSHROOMS
$1/4$	CUP FLOUR
2	CUPS CHICKEN BROTH
$1/2$	CUP CREAM OR HALF-AND-HALF
$1/4$	CUP MARSALA OR SHERRY

METHOD:

1. Saute the mushrooms in the butter for 3 minutes, then remove the mushrooms and set aside.

2. Whisk the flour into the remaining butter and cook for 2 to 3 minutes. Add the remaining ingredients and bring the sauce to a boil. Reduce the heat and cook until thickened. Return the mushrooms to the sauce.

USE ON: Boneless pieces of chicken, or turkey, including chicken pieces used to flavor a broth. Also on Cornish Hens.

YIELD: $3 1/2$ cups.

NUTRITIONAL FACTS:

Serving Size: 1/3 cup	Total Fat: 7 g	Sodium: 160 mg	Sugar: 1 g
Calories Per Serving: 80	Sat Fat: 4 g	Total Carbs: 3 g	Protein: 2 g
Fat Calories: 60	Cholest: 20 mg	Fiber: 0 g	

RUM AND CHERRY SAUCE

Chicken like pork lends itself well to both sweet and non-sweet sauces. This is a slightly sweet one of unusual color and flavor.

INGREDIENTS:		
	2	CANS CHERRIES (TART ARE PREFERRED)
	$1/_4$	CUP BUTTER
	2	TABLESPOON FLOUR
	$1/_8$	TEASPOON ALLSPICE
	$1/_8$	TEASPOON CINNAMON
	$1/_8$	TEASPOON DRY MUSTARD
	1	TEASPOON SUGAR
	$1/_2$	TEASPOON SALT
	$1/_2$	CUP CRUSHED PINEAPPLE
	2	TABLESPOONS DARK RUM
	$1/_2$	CUP CHICKEN BROTH

METHOD:

1. Drain the cherries, save the juice and set both aside.

2. Make a roux of the butter and flour, add the cherry juice and all the remaining ingredients except the cherries. Bring the sauce to a boil and reduce the heat. Add the cherries and simmer for 5 minutes.

USE ON: Chicken: broiled, boiled, baked, sauted or roasted.

YIELD: 3 cups.

NUTRITIONAL FACTS:			
Serving Size: 1/3 cup	Total Fat: 3 g	Sodium: 130 mg	Sugar: 1 g
Calories Per Serving: 50	Sat Fat: 2 g	Total Carbs: 7 g	Protein: 1 g
Fat Calories: 25	Cholest: 10 mg	Fiber: 1 g	

CREAMED WHITE WINE SAUCE

INGREDIENTS:

1	TABLESPOON BUTTER OR EXTRA LIGHT OLIVE OIL
$^1/_2$	CUP WHITE WINE
$^1/_2$	POUND HALVED OR SMALL BUTTON MUSHROOMS
$^1/_2$	TEASPOON SALT
PINCH	WHITE PEPPER
1	CUP SOUR CREAM

METHOD:

Saute the mushrooms in the butter for 5 minutes. Add the white wine, salt and white pepper. Simmer for 2 additional minutes. Remove from the heat and stir in the sour cream.

If the sauce appears too thick, add a splash or two of wine.

USE ON:

Chicken halves or quarters sauteed, broiled or baked.

YIELD:

$2 ^1/_2$ cups.

NUTRITIONAL FACTS:

Serving Size: 1/3 cup	Total Fat: 8 g	Sodium: 180 mg	Sugar: 2 g
Calories Per Serving: 90	Sat Fat: 4.5 g	Total Carbs: 3 g	Protein: 2 g
Fat Calories: 70	Cholest: 15 mg	Fiber: 0 g	

CORN SAUCE

If you've ever wondered what you can do with the liquid from a can of corn (besides throw it out), here's a sauce you can use it in. Of course, I'm assuming you're going to use the corn as part of your meal.

INGREDIENTS:	$^3/_4$	CUP LIQUID FROM WHOLE KERNEL CANNED SWEET CORN
		OR
	$^3/_4$	CUP CREAM STYLE CORN PUREED IN YOUR BLENDER
	$^3/_4$	CUP WHIPPING CREAM
	1	TABLESPOON CORN STARCH
	PINCH	WHITE PEPPER OR
		FRESHLY GROUND BLACK PEPPER TO TASTE

METHOD: Dissolve the corn starch in the whipping cream. Place all the ingredients into a sauce pan and bring to a boil. Reduce the heat and cook until thickened.

USE ON: Chicken: boiled and skinned, or chicken custard.

YIELD: 1 $^1/_2$ cups.

NUTRITIONAL FACTS:

Serving Size: 1/3 cup	Total Fat: 11 g	Sodium: 130 mg	Sugar: 1 g
Calories Per Serving: 140	Sat Fat: 7 g	Total Carbs: 9 g	Protein: 2 g
Fat Calories: 100	Cholest: 40 mg	Fiber: 1 g	

IRISH MASKING SAUCE

"Masking" is a term for applying a thick sauce to cover a meat ... plain ol' chicken gravy won't do. The masking quality of this sauce is in it's thickness. It's like a pudding, and you spread it on as though you were frosting a cake.

This dish is traditionally served cold. In fact, if you want to do it the way the Irish would, you'll need two chickens. The first is boiled, boned, skinned and minced. The second chicken needs to be completely boned, except for the wing tips. Then stuff the body cavity and spaces where you have removed the bone, with minced chicken, ham and tongue (and if you have a truffle, throw that in too), tie up the legs and shape the stuffed bird to look like a chicken. Now wrap it all in cheese cloth and baste stitch the cheese cloth with a bright colored thread. Poach the bird for one hour in chicken broth along with a carrot and a sprig of parsley. Let the bird cool in the water. Remove the bright colored thread and the cheese cloth. Towel dry the bird, set it on a wire rack. Coat the bird with the Masking Sauce and allow it to set-up. Prepare a clear aspic. Garnish the bird with parsley and several rounds of a carrot that has been dipped into the clear aspic (allow the garnish to set-up). Now coat the whole bird again with the clear aspic. Chill the bird for twelve hours. To serve, slice the bird across the body. It will be beautiful! If what I've just described is more than you're willing to commit to, follow the recipe and use it on boneless chicken parts.

INGREDIENTS:	1	TEASPOON UNFLAVORED GELATIN
	$^1/_4$	CUP WHIPPING CREAM
	2	TABLESPOONS BUTTER
	2	TABLESPOONS FLOUR
	$^1/_2$	CUP CHICKEN BROTH
	$^1/_2$	CUP MILK
	PINCH	GROUND MACE

METHOD:

1. Thoroughly mix the cream and gelatin together and set aside.

2. Make a roux by melting the butter in a sauce pan, whisk in the flour and cook for 3 minutes. Add the chicken broth, milk and mace. Bring

10-6

the mixture to a boil. Reduce the heat and cook for about 5 minutes or until it thickens.

3.   Add the whipping cream and gelatin and continue cooking until the sauce begins to bubble again, then remove from heat.

USE ON: Cooked boneless chicken thighs, legs or breast.

YIELD: 1 $^1/_2$ cups.

NUTRITIONAL FACTS:			
Serving Size: 3 T	Total Fat: 6 g	Sodium: 90 mg	Sugar: 1 g
Calories Per Serving: 70	Sat Fat: 3.5 g	Total Carbs: 3 g	Protein: 2 g
Fat Calories: 50	Cholest: 20 mg	Fiber: 0 g	

WE TRIED THIS SAUCE ... AND

LOVED IT ( )
HATED IT ( )
MAYBE WE'LL TRY IT AGAIN ( )
WE'LL USE IT FOR UNWELCOME GUESTS ( )

MAPLE SAUCE

INGREDIENTS: $^1/_4$ CUP EXTRA LIGHT OLIVE OIL OR BUTTER
1   CLOVE GARLIC, MINCED
1   TEASPOON BALSAMIC VINEGAR
2   TABLESPOONS MAPLE SYRUP
$^1/_4$ TEASPOON EACH; SALT AND DRY MUSTARD

METHOD: Place all the ingredients into a sauce pan and cook for 3 minutes.

USE ON: Broiled chicken.

YIELD: $^1/_2$ cup.

NUTRITIONAL FACTS:

Serving Size: 3 T	Total Fat: 24 g	Sodium: 260 mg	Sugar: 11 g
Calories Per Serving: 250	Sat Fat: 3 g	Total Carbs: 12 g	Protein: 0 g
Fat Calories: 210	Cholest: 0 mg	Fiber: 0 g	

WE TRIED THIS SAUCE ... AND

LOVED IT ( )
HATED IT ( )
MAYBE WE'LL TRY IT AGAIN ( )
WE'LL USE IT FOR UNWELCOME GUESTS ( )

LEMON SAUCE

INGREDIENTS:
$^1/_4$	CUP EXTRA LIGHT OLIVE OIL
2	TABLESPOONS MINCED ONION
1	CLOVE GARLIC, BRUISED
$^1/_2$	CUP LEMON JUICE
$^1/_2$	TEASPOON THYME
$^1/_2$	TEASPOON SALT

METHOD: Saute the onion and garlic in the olive oil for 3 minutes. Stir in the lemon juice, thyme and salt. Remove from heat.

USE ON: Broiled or sauteed chicken breast, thighs, halves or quarters.

YIELD: $^3/_4$ cup.

NUTRITIONAL FACTS:
Serving Size: 3 T	Total Fat: 12 g	Sodium: 250 mg	Sugar: 1 g
Calories Per Serving: 110	Sat Fat: 1.5 g	Total Carbs: 3 g	Protein: 0 g
Fat Calories: 100	Cholest: 0 mg	Fiber: 0 g	

HUNTERS STYLE CHICKEN SAUCE

(POLLO ALLA CACCIATORA)

The most famous of all Italian-style sauces for chicken! In some areas of the country, and in many restaurants, it is better known by its mixed English\Italian name, Chicken Cacciatora. From recipe to recipe the name remains Chicken Cacciatora, but the ingredients will most assuredly vary.

INGREDIENTS:

2	TABLESPOON BUTTER
2	TABLESPOONS OLIVE OIL
$^1/_3$	CUP CHOPPED ONION
1	TABLESPOON FLOUR
$^1/_2$	POUND SLICED MUSHROOMS
$^1/_2$	CUP WHITE WINE
$^1/_2$	CUP CHICKEN BROTH
1	CUP CANNED AND SQUISHED WHOLE OR DICED TOMATOES
$^1/_3$	CUP CHOPPED PARSLEY

METHOD:

1. Saute the onion in the butter\oil until the onion wilts or the edges begin to brown. Sprinkle the flour over the onion and cook until the flour begins to color.

2. Add the mushrooms and cook for 2 minutes. Add the wine, broth and tomatoes and bring the sauce to a boil. Reduce the heat, and cook for 20 minutes. To serve, spoon the sauce over or under, your cooked chicken.

OPTION: If you sauted your chicken in a seasoned flour, use the wine to deglaze your pan. Then continue cooking the wine to reduce it by half. Set aside until tomato sauce is nearly cooked. Add your sauteed chicken and wine to the sauce during the last 10 minutes of cooking. Garnish with parsley and serve.

USE ON: Chicken, broiled, grilled, baked or sauteed.

YIELD: 3 cups.

"This page is blank by Design"

CHAPTER 11

SAUCES AND GRAVIES MADE FOR TURKEY

MARSALA PAN GRAVY

INGREDIENTS:

6	MUSHROOMS, SLICED
1/2	CUP MARSALA WINE
2	TABLESPOONS OF TURKEY STOCK
1	TEASPOON CORN STARCH
	SALT AND PEPPER TO TASTE

METHOD: Place the mushrooms and liquids into your saute pan. Poach the mushrooms for 2 to 3 minutes. Stir in the corn starch and cook the sauce 1 more minute. Season and use.

OPTION: To add an Italian touch, add some freshly grated Parmesan cheese over the turkey breasts, then broil until the cheese melts.

USE ON: Sauteed turkey breast slices.

YIELD: 1 cup.

NUTRITIONAL FACTS:

Serving Size: 1/3 cup	Total Fat: 0 g	Sodium: 240 mg	Sugar: 1 g
Calories Per Serving: 35	Sat Fat: 0 g	Total Carbs: 2 g	Protein: 1 g
Fat Calories: 0	Cholest: 0 mg	Fiber: 0 g	

BRANDIED TURKEY SAUCE

This is a method for dressing up a simple sauteed dish. It adds an interesting flavor and gives you the opportunity to show off your culinary skills by flaming your turkey breast slices. One-up-man-ship is good for the soul!

Dredge slices of turkey breasts through a seasoned flour, dip them in an egg wash and then press the slices on toasted bread crumbs to coat. Saute 'til golden.

INGREDIENTS: $\frac{1}{2}$ CUP BRANDY

METHOD:
1. Remove saute pan from the heat.

2. Deglaze your hot skillet with the brandy, then ignite the brandy in the pan and pour the sauce over the turkey slices.

USE ON: Slices of turkey breast. Pounded boneless thigh meat.

YIELD: $\frac{1}{2}$ cup.

NUTRITIONAL FACTS:			
Serving Size: 1 T	Total Fat: 0 g	Sodium: 0 mg	Sugar: 0 g
Calories Per Serving: 40	Sat Fat: 0 g	Total Carbs: 0 g	Protein: 0 g
Fat Calories: 0	Cholest: 0 mg	Fiber: 0 g	

CRANBERRY SAUCE

Cranberry sauce is America's favorite turkey accompaniment and it is available in your local grocery store in a dozen varieties (many of the varieties add citrus). Normally it is available in three forms;

1. A jellied sauce.

2. Chunky style.

3. Fresh whole berries.

This recipe uses the latter, because I recognize that sometimes you want to do it yourself.

INGREDIENTS:	2	CUPS SUGAR
	2	CUPS WATER
	1	POUND FRESH WHOLE CRANBERRIES

METHOD: Place the sugar and water into a sauce pan and cook over low heat until the sugar completely dissolves. Bring the syrup to a boil and cook for 5 additional minutes. Add the cranberries, return the syrup to a boil and cook for 5 additional minutes until the berry skins pop. Remove from the heat to cool before chilling.

USE ON: Roasted turkey, as a dressing on turkey sandwiches and as a sauce over barbecued turkey burgers.

YIELD: 4 cups.

NUTRITIONAL FACTS:

Serving Size: 1/3 cup	Total Fat: 0 g	Sodium: 5 mg	Sugar: 17 g
Calories Per Serving: 80	Sat Fat: 0 g	Total Carbs: 21 g	Protein: 0 g
Fat Calories: 0	Cholest: 0 mg	Fiber: 1 g	

BRANDY TURKEY SAUCE

INGREDIENTS:

1	CUP TURKEY BROTH
3	TABLESPOONS CHOPPED GREEN ONION
2	EGG YOLKS
1	CUP WHIPPING CREAM
$^1/_4$	CUP LIQUEUR (SUCH AS AN AMARETTO)
$^1/_4$	CUP BRANDY
1	TABLESPOON TARRAGON

METHOD:

1. Place the turkey broth and onion into a sauce pan. Bring the broth to a boil. Cook to reduce by half.

2. In a small mixing bowl, whisk the egg yolks and cream until well blended. While whisking, slowly add the hot broth to the egg and cream mixture.

3. Return the entire mixture to the sauce pan and cook over medium heat until the sauce thickens. Add the brandy, Amaretto and tarragon, then bring the sauce back to a boil and cook 1 additional minute.

USE ON: Turkey or chicken.

YIELD: 2 $^1/_2$ cups.

NUTRITIONAL FACTS:			
Serving Size: 3 T	Total Fat: 6 g	Sodium: 60 mg	Sugar: 1 g
Calories Per Serving: 80	Sat Fat: 3.5 g	Total Carbs: 3 g	Protein: 1 g
Fat Calories: 50	Cholest: 45 mg	Fiber: 0 g	

CRABAPPLE TURKEY SAUCE

INGREDIENTS:	1	CUP CRABAPPLE JELLY
	$^1/_4$	CUP LEMON JUICE
	$^1/_4$	CUP LIQUEUR (PREFERABLY AMARETTO)

METHOD: In a small sauce pan, melt the jelly. Stir in the lemon juice and liqueur. Cook 1 additional minute, stirring to blend well.

USE ON: Turkey, pork or ham.

YIELD: 1 $^1/_2$ cups.

NUTRITIONAL FACTS:

Serving Size: 1/4 cup	Total Fat: 0 g	Sodium: 30 mg	Sugar: 0 g
Calories Per Serving: 110	Sat Fat: 0 g	Total Carbs: 24 g	Protein: 0 g
Fat Calories: 0	Cholest: 0 mg	Fiber: 0 g	

PICCATA SAUCE

In Italian cookery this sauce is normally associated with veal, but it also goes well with turkey and chicken. Its' prerequisite (and its piquancy) is lemon. Anything else is an option of the cook, and that includes the use of capers to give added piquancy. Whatever your meat choice for this sauce, it is normally flattened by pounding, or by pressing it flat under a rolling pin. Then the meat is floured before sauteing. Deglaze the skillet with the broth and then add it where called for in the recipe.

INGREDIENTS:	$^1/_2$	CUP BUTTER
	8	OUNCES SLICED MUSHROOMS
	$1\,^1/_2$	TABLESPOONS FLOUR
	1	CUP BROTH (TURKEY OR CHICKEN) OR A WHITE WINE SUCH AS SAUVIGNON BLANC
	2	TABLESPOONS FRESHLY SQUEEZED LEMON JUICE
	6	PAPER THIN SLICES OF LEMON FOR GARNISH
	1	TABLESPOON CHOPPED PARSLEY TO GARNISH

METHOD:

1. Saute the mushrooms in the butter until the butter is absorbed and then released (about 3 minutes). Remove the mushrooms and set aside.

2. Whisk the flour into the butter and juices and cook for 2 minutes. Whisk in the broth. Bring the sauce to a boil and cook until it thickens. Return the mushrooms to the pan to heat through. Remove the pan from the heat and stir in the lemon juice.

USE ON: Sauteed turkey breast slices, broiled or sauteed boneless chicken pieces, or very thin veal scallops.

YIELD: $2\,^1/_2$ cups.

NUTRITIONAL FACTS:

Serving Size: 1/3 cup	Total Fat: 11 g	Sodium: 300 mg	Sugar: 1 g
Calories Per Serving: 120	Sat Fat: 7 g	Total Carbs: 3 g	Protein: 2 g
Fat Calories: 100	Cholest: 30 mg	Fiber: 0 g	

"This page is blank by Design"

CHAPTER 12

SAUCES AND GRAVIES MADE FOR DUCK

APRICOT SAUCE

Domestic duck, as well as goose, has a great deal of fat, and when cool, the fat congeals quickly into a very unappetizing collection of grease on your plate. But, when the fat is allowed to baste the bird in the oven, it creates a really crisp skin with a rich golden color. When the skin is eaten immediately, straight from oven, it is wonderful. Gravy made from duck or goose is not as flavorful as chicken or turkey gravy and therefore is bypassed for something more palatable, like this apricot sauce.

INGREDIENTS:	2 ¹/₂	CUPS APRICOTS (CANNED WORKS BETTER THAN FRESH)
	1	TEASPOON FRESH ORANGE RIND
	2	CUPS BLUSH, ROSE OR WHITE ZINFANDEL WINE
	6	TABLESPOONS BUTTER
		FRESHLY GROUND BLACK PEPPER TO TASTE

OPTION: DUCK LIVER(S) (SAUTE BEFORE ADDING TO SAUCE).

METHOD: Place all the ingredients into a blender and blend until smooth. Stirring constantly, cook over medium heat or on a diffuser until the sauce begins to boil. Lower the heat and cook until slightly thickened.

USE ON: Duck, roasted, broiled or braised.

YIELD: 3 ¹/₂ cups.

NUTRITIONAL FACTS:

Serving Size: 1/3 cup	Total Fat: 4.5 g	Sodium: 50 mg	Sugar: 0 g
Calories Per Serving: 70	Sat Fat: 3 g	Total Carbs: 3 g	Protein: 0 g
Fat Calories: 40	Cholest: 10 mg	Fiber: 1 g	

BLACK CHERRY SAUCE

If you can't find black cherries at the store, use any other canned cherries available. You can even use drained and rinsed maraschino cherries. But since maraschino cherries are bottled in pure sugar syrup, you don't want to add that to your sauce.

INGREDIENTS:	2	CANS BLACK CHERRIES
	$3/4$	CUP MARSALA OR CHERRY JUICE
	3	TABLESPOONS CORN STARCH
	4	TABLESPOONS BUTTER
	2	TABLESPOONS MINCED ONION
	$3/4$	MARSALA OR DRY SHERRY
	$1\,1/2$	CUPS CHICKEN BULLION
	1	BAY LEAF

METHOD:
1. Drain the cherries saving 3/4 cup of the juice. Mix the corn starch and cherry juice and set aside.

2. Saute the onion in the butter until it is transparent. Add the wine, bouillon and bay leaf and bring the mixture to a boil.

3. Discard the bay leaf and whisk the cherry juice into the pan, then cook until thickened. Add the cherries. Taste to adjust the seasoning and add salt and pepper if needed.

USE ON: Broiled or roasted duck quarters.

YIELD: 4 cups.

NUTRITIONAL FACTS:			
Serving Size: 1/3 cup	Total Fat: 2 g	Sodium: 120 mg	Sugar: 1 g
Calories Per Serving: 60	Sat Fat: 1.5 g	Total Carbs: 10 g	Protein: 1 g
Fat Calories: 20	Cholest: 5 mg	Fiber: 0 g	

BRANDIED ORANGE SAUCE

I'm giving you a chance to show off with this sauce, by flaming the brandy. It adds such a pretty touch to your entree and can even set the tone for a romantic evening.

INGREDIENTS:		
	$^1/_2$	CUP BRANDY
	1	ORANGE RIND, GRATED OR SHREDDED (ZEST ONLY)
	1	CLOVE GARLIC, MINCED
	2	TABLESPOONS BUTTER
	3	TABLESPOONS (POTATO) FLOUR OR CORN STARCH
	1	CUP DRY MARSALA WINE OR DRY SHERRY
	2	CUPS CHICKEN BROTH
	$^1/_2$	CUP JELLY (CRANBERRY, CURRANT OR LINGONBERRY)
	$^1/_2$	TEASPOON SALT

METHOD:

1. If you choose to flame the brandy, omit it from the sauce. If not, add the brandy along with the other liquids.

2. Saute the garlic and shredded orange peel in the butter for 2 to 3 minutes, then whisk in the flour and cook 2 additional minutes.

3. Blend in the wine, add all the remaining ingredients and bring the sauce to a boil. Reduce the heat to low and cook until thickened.

OPTION:

To flame the brandy, warm it first, then light it and pour it over the duck on your serving platter. When the flame has burned out, serve the duck with the sauce on the side.

If you don't have a large ladle to hold the flaming brandy, pour the warmed brandy over the hot duck and then light it.

USE ON: Roasted or broiled duck.

YIELD: 4 cups.

NUTRITIONAL FACTS:

Serving Size: 1/4 cup	Total Fat: 1.5 g	Sodium: 260 mg	Sugar: 6 g
Calories Per Serving: 70	Sat Fat: 1 g	Total Carbs: 7 g	Protein: 1 g
Fat Calories: 15	Cholest: 5 mg	Fiber: 0 g	

MUSHROOM PAPRIKA SAUCE

If you'd like an alternate to the sweet sauces usually served on duck, here's one I think you'll enjoy.

INGREDIENTS:	1	DUCK LIVER (IF PACKED IN THE DUCK)
	$1/4$	CUP FLOUR
	$1/2$	CUP WATER
	$1/2$	CUP BUTTER
	$1/2$	CUP MINCED ONION
	$1/2$	POUND SLICED MUSHROOMS
	$1/2$	CUP DRY SHERRY
	1	CUP TOMATO SAUCE
	1	TABLESPOON PAPRIKA
	$1/2$	TEASPOON SALT
		FRESHLY GROUND BLACK PEPPER TO TASTE

METHOD:

1. Saute the duck liver in the butter for 5 minutes. Remove it from the heat and let it cool, then mince the liver and set aside.

2. Mix the flour and water and set aside.

3. Saute the onion in the butter for 3 minutes. Add the mushrooms and saute an additional 3 minutes. Add all the remaining ingredients except the minced liver and bring the sauce to a boil. Reduce the heat to simmer and cook, stirring constantly, until thickened. Add the chopped liver and simmer for 5 more minutes.

USE ON: Roasted or broiled duck.

YIELD: 4 cups.

NUTRITIONAL FACTS:			
Serving Size: 1/4 cup	Total Fat: 6 g	Sodium: 220 mg	Sugar: 1 g
Calories Per Serving: 70	Sat Fat: 3.5 g	Total Carbs: 4 g	Protein: 1 g
Fat Calories: 50	Cholest: 30 mg	Fiber: 1 g	

PLUM SAUCE

If you have a hand-held wand-type blender, you can puree this sweet and sour sauce right in your pan when it's finished cooking.

INGREDIENTS:		
	2	POUNDS RIPE SANTA ROSA PLUMS, BLANCHED AND PEELED
	1	POUND APRICOTS
	1	CUP PINEAPPLE (FRESH OR CANNED)
	1	TEASPOON SHREDDED FRESH GINGER
	$^3/_4$	CUP DISTILLED WHITE VINEGAR
	$^3/_4$	CUP SUGAR

METHOD:

1. Place all the ingredients into a blender and whirl until smooth. If you prefer a chunkier sauce, stop anywhere along the way.

2. Transfer the mixture to a sauce pan and bring it to a boil. Reduce the heat to simmer and cook until the sauce thickens, approximately 2 hours. Taste to adjust the sweetness and cool before using.

USE ON: Duck roast, broiled or barbecued. It will also go nicely with chicken or pork.

YIELD: 5 cups.

NUTRITIONAL FACTS:			
Serving Size: 1/3 cup	Total Fat: 0 g	Sodium: 0 mg	Sugar: 9 g
Calories Per Serving: 50	Sat Fat: 0 g	Total Carbs: 13 g	Protein: 1 g
Fat Calories: 0	Cholest: 0 mg	Fiber: 1 g	

HONEY MINT SAUCE

INGREDIENTS:	1	CUP HONEY
	$1/4$	CUP WHITE WINE VINEGAR
	1	TEASPOON CORN STARCH
	1	TABLESPOON WATER
	3	TABLESPOONS LEMON JUICE
	1	OUNCE BOURBON WHISKEY
	$1/4$	CUP CHOPPED FRESH MINT LEAVES

METHOD:

1. Place the honey and the vinegar in a sauce pan and bring them to a boil. Reduce the heat to simmer and cook for 10 minutes.

2. Remove the honey mixture from the heat. Mix the corn starch, water and lemon juice and whisk into the honey. Return the sauce to the heat and bring it to a boil.

3. Remove the sauce from the heat, add the bourbon and mint leaves and blend thoroughly.

USE ON: Roast or broiled duck.

YIELD: $1\,3/4$ cups.

NUTRITIONAL FACTS:			
Serving Size: 3 T	Total Fat: 0 g	Sodium: 0 mg	Sugar: 26 g
Calories Per Serving: 100	Sat Fat: 0 g	Total Carbs: 26 g	Protein: 0 g
Fat Calories: 0	Cholest: 0 mg	Fiber: 0 g	

ORANGE SAUCE

When you order "Duck a' l'Orange" at your favorite restaurant, this is the sauce you'll get, or something close to it. It is quite simple, but it does require a brown stock. If you're not up to making brown stock, use a dehydrated beef bouillon or beef soup base. The pan juices require reduction and that takes a few minutes.

INGREDIENTS:		JUICES FROM THE ROASTED DUCK
	1	CUP WHITE WINE
	2	TABLESPOONS BUTTER
	2	TABLESPOONS FLOUR
	1	CUP BROWN STOCK
	$^1/_2$	CUP ORANGE JUICE
		ORANGE ZEST, GRATED OR JULIENNED

METHOD:

1. Grate the zest or peel the orange rind to julienne and set aside.

2. Strain the duck juices and remove the fat.

3. Place the wine and duck juices into a sauce pan and boil until reduced by half.

4. Make a roux by cooking the flour in the butter for 3 minutes.

5. To the roux add the reduced duck juices and wine, brown stock and orange juice and bring the sauce to a boil. Reduce the heat to a simmer and cook for 3 minutes or until slightly thickened, add the orange peel and serve.

USE ON: Roast duck.

YIELD: 2 cups.

NUTRITIONAL FACTS:			
Serving Size: 3 T	Total Fat: 2.5 g	Sodium: 30 mg	Sugar: 2 g
Calories Per Serving: 50	Sat Fat: 1.5 g	Total Carbs: 3 g	Protein: 0 g
Fat Calories: 25	Cholest: 5 mg	Fiber: 0 g	

"This page is blank by Design"

Chapter 13

Sauces And Gravies Made For Goose And Gander

(Geese if you're cooking more than one.)
(Gooses if you're trying to get the attention of the cook!)

There was a time when goose grease had practical, but limited use, as an ingredient in home remedies for hot rubs to cure something or other. Well here we're going to throw it out. It doesn't taste good, nor does it do a thing for you from a dietary or nutritional standpoint. Goose skin, like duck skin, is very, very fatty. If you roast a goose until it is quite golden in color, and the skin is very crisp, you might enjoy a few bites. If you let it cool and then bite into it, you find a rivulet of grease running down your throat. The moral of this story is; skin the sucker first!

MADEIRA SAUCE

INGREDIENTS:

1	TABLESPOON EXTRA LIGHT OLIVE OIL OR BUTTER
1	ONION, CHOPPED
3	CLOVES GARLIC
	GOOSE GIBLETS INCLUDING THE NECK
1	QUART CHICKEN STOCK OR BROTH
2	CELERY RIBS, CHUNKED
1	CARROT, PARED AND BROKEN
1	TABLESPOON TOMATO PASTE
12	SPRIGS PARSLEY
1	TEASPOON THYME
1	TEASPOON SAGE
6	WHOLE CLOVES
6	PEPPERCORNS
6	JUNIPER BERRIES (IF YOU HAVE THEM)
$^1/_2$	CUP MADEIRA
2	TABLESPOONS ROUX OR CORN STARCH

METHOD:

1. In a 6 to 8 cup sauce pan, saute the onion, garlic and giblets in the butter for 3 minutes. Then add all the remaining ingredients, except the Madeira and roux and bring the stock to a boil. Reduce the heat and simmer for 1 hour.

2. Thoroughly blend the Madeira and the roux together and set aside.

3. Remove the stock from the heat and strain. Slowly whisk the stock into the Madeira and roux mixture. Cook the sauce several minutes until it is slightly thickened. Serve.

OPTION:

If you are able to recover any juices (not fat) from the roasted goose, strain them and add to the sauce.

USE ON: Roasted goose (keep in mind that a sauce for a goose is a sauce for a gander).

YIELD: 3 cups.

CREAMY GARLIC SAUCE

Successful preparation of this recipe requires a double boiler. If you have one great, if not, slowly bring the milk to scald (just at the point of simmering) over direct heat, using a diffuser, before adding the other ingredients. With this sauce you can choose how you use the garlic. If you want it to remain in the sauce, use garlic paste, or mince it. If you don't want the garlic to remain in the sauce, use Step 3 below.

INGREDIENTS:

12	GARLIC CLOVES (BRUISED, MINCED OR AS A PASTE)
4	CUPS MILK
4	EGG YOLKS
1	TEASPOON SALT
PINCH	WHITE PEPPER

METHOD:

1. Whisk the egg yolks into 1 cup of milk and set aside.

2. Place the garlic cloves in 3 cups of milk and scald the milk.

3. If the garlic cloves are whole and bruised remove them and discard at this point.

4. Now slowly whisk the egg yolks into the hot milk. Add the salt and pepper and cook until the sauce thickens.

USE ON: Boiled or broiled goose.

YIELD: 4 $^1/_2$ cups.

NUTRITIONAL FACTS:

Serving Size: 3 T	Total Fat: 2 g	Sodium: 120 mg	Sugar: 2 g
Calories Per Serving: 35	Sat Fat: 1 g	Total Carbs: 2 g	Protein: 2 g
Fat Calories: 20	Cholest: 40 mg	Fiber: 0 g	

SOUR CREAM SAUCE

Goose is a very popular Christmas bird in eastern Europe and is usually prepared with lard. If it's a taste you like, feel free to use it.

INGREDIENTS:		
	3	TABLESPOONS EXTRA LIGHT OLIVE OIL
	2	ONIONS, SLICED
	1	CUP WATER, CHICKEN BROTH OR WHITE WINE
	1	LEMON, QUARTERED
	$^1/_2$	TEASPOON SALT
	10	PEPPERCORNS
	1	CUP SOUR CREAM

METHOD:

1. Saute the onions in the olive oil until the edges begin to brown, then add water, lemon, salt and pepper. Cover and simmer the mixture for $^1/_2$ hour.

2. Remove from the heat and strain. Discard the solids and save the liquid.

3. When the goose is done, separate the fat from the juices. Discard the fat and add the juices to the onion broth. Heat the liquids to boiling, then remove it from the heat. Stir in the sour cream and return the sauce to the stove to heat through. Serve.

USE ON: Roast goose, broiled disjointed pieces.

YIELD: 2 $^1/_2$ cups.

NUTRITIONAL FACTS:			
Serving Size: 3 T	Total Fat: 6 g	Sodium: 95 mg	Sugar: 2 g
Calories Per Serving: 70	Sat Fat: 2.5 g	Total Carbs: 3 g	Protein: 1 g
Fat Calories: 60	Cholest: 5 mg	Fiber: 0 g	

COUNTRY STYLE SAGE SAUCE

INGREDIENTS:	1	MEDIUM ONION, PRE-BOILED IN SALTED WATER, OR BROTH, AND COOLED
	2	TABLESPOONS BUTTER
	1	CUP BREAD CRUMBS
	1	TABLESPOON CHOPPED FRESH SAGE
	$^1/_2$	TEASPOON SALT

METHOD:

1. Mince the cooked onion and set aside.

2. In a sauce pan, melt the butter, then add the bread crumbs and cook until they begin to color. Add the onion, sage and salt and cook for 5 minutes.

OPTION: Add $^1/_4$ cup juices from your roast.

USE ON: Roast goose. This sauce can also be used on roast pork.

YIELD: 1 $^1/_2$ cups.

NUTRITIONAL FACTS:

Serving Size: 1/4 cup	Total Fat: 4.5 g	Sodium: 380 mg	Sugar: 2 g
Calories Per Serving: 110	Sat Fat: 2.5 g	Total Carbs: 15 g	Protein: 3 g
Fat Calories: 40	Cholest: 10 mg	Fiber: 2 g	

APPLE SAUCE

Apple sauce is readily available in grocery stores, but if you have a few extra apples, you might enjoy it freshly made.

INGREDIENTS:	2 OR 3	PEELED, CORED AND CHOPPED APPLES (CHOOSE YOUR FLAVOR, SWEET OR TART)
	$^1/_2$	CUP WATER
	$^1/_2$	TEASPOON LEMON JUICE
	1	TABLESPOON SUGAR
	$^1/_4$	TEASPOON GROUND CINNAMON

METHOD: Place the apples, water, lemon juice and sugar into a sauce pan and bring to a boil. Reduce the heat, cover and simmer until the apples are very soft. Remove from the heat and whisk in the cinnamon. Cool before serving or use warm.

USE ON: Roast goose, duck or with pork.

YIELD: 1 $^1/_2$ cups

NUTRITIONAL FACTS:			
Serving Size: 1/4 cup	Total Fat: 0 g	Sodium: 0 mg	Sugar: 7 g
Calories Per Serving: 30	Sat Fat: 0 g	Total Carbs: 8 g	Protein: 0 g
Fat Calories: 0	Cholest: 0 mg	Fiber: 1 g	

"This page is blank by Design"

CHAPTER 14

SAUCES MADE FOR SEAFOOD

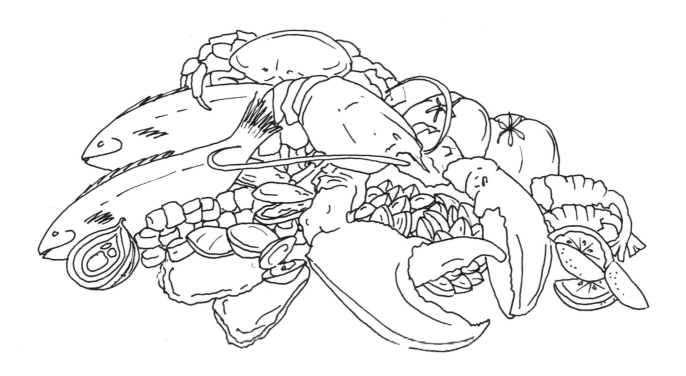

CIOPPINO SAUCE

Cioppino is a west coast stew of seafood in a tomato sauce. I believe it is actually an American version of a Ligurian fisherman's stew. I will also give you my unsolicited opinion, that Cioppino is good, very good in fact, and a marvelous way to serve a variety of seafood in a single dish. If this recipe sounds good to you, head for your seafood store and pick up a mixture of shrimp, crab, lobster, clams, mussels, scallops and a variety of cold-water fish fillets. Cut the fillets into bite size pieces, leave the clams and mussels intact and cut the crustaceans into chunks. All in all you'll need about 4 pounds of seafood. Now you're ready for the sauce.

INGREDIENTS:

$1/4$	CUP OLIVE OIL
4	CLOVES GARLIC, MINCED
1	LARGE ONION, CHOPPED
$1/4$	TEASPOON CRUSHED RED PEPPER
2	ANCHOVY FILLETS, MINCED
1	CUP FRESH CELERY LEAVES CHOPPED
1	TABLESPOON CHOPPED PARSLEY
2	CUPS LIQUID: WINE (BLUSH OR WHITE), OR A BROTH OF CHICKEN, VEGETABLE OR FISH (IF YOU USE THE FISH BROTH, OMIT THE ANCHOVY)
1	28 OUNCE CAN OF WHOLE TOMATOES, SQUISHED OR
2	POUNDS FRESH TOMATOES, PEELED, SEEDED AND CHOPPED
$1/2$	TEASPOON WHOLE LEAF OREGANO
1	TABLESPOON COARSELY CHOPPED FRESH BASIL LEAF LEMON WEDGES ON THE SIDE PARSLEY TO GARNISH

METHOD:

1. Saute the garlic, onion and crushed red pepper, until the garlic begins to turn golden and the onion begins to color. Add all the remaining ingredients and bring to a boil. Reduce the heat and cook for 15 minutes.

2. Add the seafood items as follows, at 1 minute intervals or each time the sauce returns to a boil:

Add the cold water fish first.

Next add the crab and lobster.

Third, add the shrimp, clams and mussels.

Fourth, add the scallops.

Bring the sauce to a low boil. When the clams and mussels open and the fish flakes, the Cioppino is done. Add the garnish and serve with lemon wedges on the side.

Use On: Serve this dish in large soup bowls along with a loaf of crusty Italian bread.

Or serve it in a bread bowl (do this at the table). Using small 6" round loaves of crusty Italian or French bread (either sweet or sourdough), slice off the top, scoop out the soft center and fill the bread bowl with the Cioppino.

Yield: 8 cups.

NUTRITIONAL FACTS:			
Serving Size: 3/4 cup	Total Fat: 6 g	Sodium: 240 mg	Sugar: 4 g
Calories Per Serving: 120	Sat Fat: 1 g	Total Carbs: 7 g	Protein: 2 g
Fat Calories: 50	Cholest: 0 mg	Fiber: 2 g	

CURRY SAUCE

INGREDIENTS:

2	TABLESPOONS BUTTER
1/2	CUP ONION, CHOPPED
1	CELERY RIB, CHOPPED
1	CLOVE GARLIC, THINLY SLICED
2	TABLESPOONS FLOUR
1	TABLESPOON CURRY POWDER
1	QUART CHICKEN STOCK
PINCH	THYME
1	RED, RIPE TOMATO, DICED
1	GREEN TOMATO, CHOPPED
1	TART APPLE, CORED AND CHOPPED
1/2	BANANA, CHOPPED

METHOD: Melt the butter in a sauce pan and saute the onion, celery and garlic until the onions edges begin to brown. Work the flour and curry powder into the sauce. When the mixture is fairly smooth, whisk in the chicken broth and bring to a boil. Cook until the sauce begins to thicken. Add the remaining ingredients and cook the sauce for 20 minutes. Strain and serve.

USE ON: Fish steaks, grilled, broiled or poached. Fish fillets, shrimp, scallops and steamed rice.

YIELD: 6 cups.

NUTRITIONAL FACTS:

Serving Size: 1/4 cup	Total Fat: 1 g	Sodium: 125 mg	Sugar: 2 g
Calories Per Serving: 25	Sat Fat: 0.5 g	Total Carbs: 3 g	Protein: 1 g
Fat Calories: 10	Cholest: 5 mg	Fiber: 0 g	

SEAFOOD CHAMPAGNE SAUCE

The champagne won't make this sauce taste any better than a white wine, but it sounds better.

INGREDIENTS:	1	CUP HALF AND HALF
	1 $^1/_2$	TABLESPOONS CORN STARCH
	$^1/_2$	TEASPOON LEMON JUICE
	$^1/_2$	CUP CHAMPAGNE
	1	TABLESPOON BUTTER
	2	TEASPOONS FRESHLY GRATED LEMON RIND

METHOD: Place the half-and-half, corn starch and lemon juice into a sauce pan over medium heat and while whisking constantly bring the mixture to a boil. Cook for 1 minute and add the champagne. When the sauce returns to a boil, remove it from the heat and whisk in the butter and lemon peel.

USE ON: Baked, sauteed or poached fish, sauteed or boiled shrimp, boiled lobster, imitation crab and lobster, seafood salad (use extra light olive oil instead of the butter), sauteed calamari steaks.

YIELD: 1 $^1/_2$ cups.

NUTRITIONAL FACTS:

Serving Size: 3 T	Total Fat: 4.5 g	Sodium: 25 mg	Sugar: 1 g
Calories Per Serving: 60	Sat Fat: 3 g	Total Carbs: 3 g	Protein: 1 g
Fat Calories: 40	Cholest: 15 mg	Fiber: 0 g	

CREOLE SEAFOOD SAUCE

Once upon a time in the 60's, I had a government job and one of the fellows I worked with was a Cajun named Joe. Joe and I enjoyed each others company and as a result we spoke on many subjects. Not only of cabbages and kings, but serious stuff like sports, tools and fishing. Frequently we'd also discuss food. I recall a comment Joe made one day about Louisiana cooking, when he quantified the whole of it by saying, "If it has the Louisiana Holy Trinity of onions, celery and green pepper in it, I'll eat it!" Well, that's what you get here, the Louisiana Holy Trinity and a few other items thrown in for good measure.

INGREDIENTS:	2	TABLESPOONS EXTRA LIGHT OLIVE OIL
	1	ONION, CHOPPED
	$^1/_2$	CUP CELERY, CHOPPED
	$^1/_2$	CUP BELL PEPPER, SEEDED AND CHOPPED
	2	CLOVES GARLIC, MINCED
	1	CUP FRESH TOMATOES, PEELED AND CHOPPED
	$^1/_4$	CUP TOMATO PASTE
	1	CUP WATER
	$^1/_2$	TEASPOON THYME, CRUMBLED
	$^1/_2$	TEASPOON SALT
	PINCH	CAYENNE PEPPER
	DASH	OF LOUISIANA STYLE HOT SAUCE

METHOD: In a skillet or sauce pan, saute the onion, celery, bell pepper and garlic in the olive oil until the vegetables are just soft. Add the remaining ingredients and bring the mixture to a boil. Reduce heat to simmer and cook for 20 minutes.

USE ON: Seafood, sauteed, broiled, baked or poached.

YIELD: 3 $^1/_2$ cups.

NUTRITIONAL FACTS:

Serving Size: 1/3 cup	Total Fat: 3 g	Sodium: 10 mg	Sugar: 2 g
Calories Per Serving: 45	Sat Fat: 0 g	Total Carbs: 5 g	Protein: 1 g
Fat Calories: 25	Cholest: 0 mg	Fiber: 1 g	

CHAPTER 15

SAUCES MADE FOR FISH

WE TRIED THIS SAUCE ... AND

LOVED IT ( )
HATED IT ( )
MAYBE WE'LL TRY IT AGAIN ( )
WE'LL USE IT FOR UNWELCOME GUESTS ( )

ANCHOVY SAUCE

A white sauce is the base for this recipe. What's more, as a bonus, it can also be used to brighten up limp vegetables.

INGREDIENTS: 1   CUP WHITE SAUCE
             3   FILLETS OF ANCHOVY (WASHED AND MASHED TO A PASTE)
                       OR
             1 $^1/_2$ TEASPOONS OF PREPARED ANCHOVY PASTE

METHOD: Blend the anchovy into the white sauce, heat and serve.

USE ON: Poached, steamed or broiled fish.

YIELD: 1 cup.

NUTRITIONAL FACTS:

Serving Size: 2 T	Total Fat: 3.5 g	Sodium: 90 mg	Sugar: 1 g
Calories Per Serving: 45	Sat Fat: 2 g	Total Carbs: 2 g	Protein: 1 g
Fat Calories: 30	Cholest: 10 mg	Fiber: 0 g	

ANCHOVY SAUCE II

Kissin' kin to the preceding sauce because of the anchovy, but the similarity stops there. This sauce is more of a Veloute with anchovy.

INGREDIENTS:		
	2	TABLESPOONS BUTTER
	1	ONION, CHOPPED
	1	TABLESPOON FLOUR
	1	CUP FUMET OR CHICKEN STOCK
	1	TUBE ANCHOVY PASTE (APPROXIMATELY 1.5 OUNCES)
	1	TABLESPOON LEMON JUICE
	1	EGG YOLK

METHOD:

1. Saute the onion in the butter until the onion is transparent. Stir in the flour and cook for 1 minute. Add the stock, lemon juice and anchovy and bring the sauce to a boil. Reduce the heat and cook for 5 minutes.

2. While the sauce is cooking, whip the egg yolk and set aside.

3. Remove the sauce from the heat. Mix a tablespoon or two of the hot sauce with the egg yolk. Now add that mixture slowly to the sauce, stirring constantly.

USE ON: Fish, broiled, poached or fried.

YIELD: $2 \frac{1}{4}$ cups.

NUTRITIONAL FACTS:			
Serving Size: 2 T	Total Fat: 2 g	Sodium: 140 mg	Sugar: 1 g
Calories Per Serving: 30	Sat Fat: 1 g	Total Carbs: 1 g	Protein: 1 g
Fat Calories: 20	Cholest: 20 mg	Fiber: 0 g	

SHRIMP SAUCE

(NANTUA SAUCE)

This sauce is not for shrimp, but rather a white sauce with a little shrimp added.

INGREDIENTS:	1	CUP WHITE SAUCE
	$^1/_2$	CUP WHIPPING CREAM
	1	TABLESPOON MASHED CANNED SHRIMP
	1	TABLESPOON BUTTER
	1	TABLESPOON WHOLE SHRIMP FOR GARNISH

METHOD: Bring the white sauce to a boil, add the remaining ingredients and stir. Remove from the heat and adjust the seasoning.

USE ON: Poached, steamed or baked fish.

YIELD: 1 $^1/_2$ cups.

NUTRITIONAL FACTS:

Serving Size: 3 T	Total Fat: 9 g	Sodium: 55 mg	Sugar: 2 g
Calories Per Serving: 100	Sat Fat: 6 g	Total Carbs: 3 g	Protein: 2 g
Fat Calories: 80	Cholest: 30 mg	Fiber: 0 g	

OYSTER SAUCE

No, this is not for oysters. Oysters are an ingredient added to the white sauce.

INGREDIENTS:	1	CUP WHITE SAUCE
	3	TABLESPOONS CHOPPED PARSLEY
	1	CUP MINCED OYSTERS AND THEIR LIQUOR

METHOD: Bring the white sauce to a boil. Add the parsley and oysters and remove from the heat. Adjust the seasoning and serve.

USE ON: Poached, steamed or baked fish.

YIELD: 2 cups.

NUTRITIONAL FACTS:

Serving Size: 1/3 cup	Total Fat: 5 g	Sodium: 90 mg	Sugar: 2 g
Calories Per Serving: 90	Sat Fat: 3 g	Total Carbs: 5 g	Protein: 5 g
Fat Calories: 45	Cholest: 35 mg	Fiber: 0 g	

FLORENTINE SAUCE

I read somewhere that Italian Florentines are puzzled as to why we label any sauce or dish made with spinach "Florentine". Spinach is not a major ingredient in the cuisine of Florence. But they may have been major contributors to the use of spinach in several dishes and sauces, including this one.

INGREDIENTS:	1	CUP WHITE SAUCE
	1	CUP FINELY CHOPPED FRESH SPINACH
	1	TABLESPOON CHOPPED PARSLEY
	PINCH	NUTMEG (FRESHLY GRATED IF POSSIBLE)

METHOD: Blend all the ingredients, heat through and serve.

USE ON: Fish (hot or cold).

YIELD: 1 $\frac{1}{2}$ cups.

NUTRITIONAL FACTS:			
Serving Size: 1/4 cup	Total Fat: 5 g	Sodium: 70 mg	Sugar: 2 g
Calories Per Serving: 70	Sat Fat: 3.5 g	Total Carbs: 4 g	Protein: 2 g
Fat Calories: 50	Cholest: 15 mg	Fiber: 0 g	

WHITE WINE SAUCE FOR FISH

You'll be using a white sauce as the base for this one.

INGREDIENTS:	$^1/_2$	CUP WHITE WINE
	1	BAY LEAF
	2	WHOLE CLOVES
	2	WHOLE BLACK PEPPERCORNS
	PINCH	GROUND GINGER
	1	TEASPOON CHOPPED ONION (ANY TYPE)
	1	CUP WHITE SAUCE

OPTION: Replace half the wine with fish stock.

METHOD: Place the first 6 ingredients into a sauce pan and bring them to a boil and reduce the volume by half. Strain, if desired and discard the bay leaf. Add the white sauce and bring it back to a boil. Remove the pan from the heat and serve.

USE ON: Fish, fried, poached, baked or steamed.

YIELD: 1 $^1/_2$ cups.

NUTRITIONAL FACTS:

Serving Size: 3 T	Total Fat: 3.5 g	Sodium: 35 mg	Sugar: 1 g
Calories Per Serving: 50	Sat Fat: 2 g	Total Carbs: 3 g	Protein: 1 g
Fat Calories: 30	Cholest: 10 mg	Fiber: 0 g	

AURORE SAUCE

The sauce is a Veloute with two additional flavors.

INGREDIENTS:	2	CUPS VELOUTE SAUCE
	2	TABLESPOONS TOMATO PUREE
	1	TABLESPOON BUTTER

METHOD: Blend the first 2 ingredients in a sauce pan and bring to the boiling point. Add the butter and swirl to melt, then serve.

USE ON: Fish, steamed, poached or baked. I especially recommended it for use on sole.

YIELD: 2 $\frac{1}{4}$ cups.

NUTRITIONAL FACTS:

Serving Size: 3 T	Total Fat: 2.5 g	Sodium: 140 mg	Sugar: 0 g
Calories Per Serving: 30	Sat Fat: 1.5 g	Total Carbs: 1 g	Protein: 1 g
Fat Calories: 25	Cholest: 5 mg	Fiber: 0 g	

DILL SAUCE

Among the wonderful smells in a kitchen, there are two scents that come from herbs that elevate my spirits and fairly lift me off the floor. The bouquet from fresh or dried dill weed is one and the other is fresh sweet basil. This sauce features one of my favorites.

INGREDIENTS:	2	TABLESPOONS BUTTER
	3	TABLESPOONS FLOUR
	1 1/2	CUPS MILK
	1/2	TEASPOON SALT
	1	TEASPOON DRIED DILL WEED
	DASH	WHITE OR BLACK PEPPER

METHOD:　Make a roux of the flour and butter. Add the milk while whisking and cook until the sauce thickens. Add the seasonings and cook 1 minute longer and serve.

USE ON:　Baked or poached fish .

YIELD:　1 3/4 cups.

NUTRITIONAL FACTS:			
Serving Size: 3 T	Total Fat: 4 g	Sodium: 170 mg	Sugar: 2 g
Calories Per Serving: 60	Sat Fat: 2.5 g	Total Carbs: 4 g	Protein: 2 g
Fat Calories: 35	Cholest: 10 mg	Fiber: 0 g	

DILL SAUCE II

No modified white sauce here, this is considerably richer. You can use this sauce in two ways. As a baste, before and during broiling/frying the fish, or by serving the sauce over or under the fish.

INGREDIENTS: $^1/_2$ CUP BUTTER
2   TABLESPOONS FRESH DILL WEED
1   TEASPOON DILL SEED
2   TABLESPOONS LEMON JUICE
1   TEASPOON PAPRIKA
SALT TO TASTE
FRESH CHOPPED PARSLEY TO GARNISH

METHOD: Melt the butter and when it begins to foam, add all the ingredients except the parsley. Remove the pan from the heat.

USE ON: Fish fillets or fish steaks.

YIELD: $^2/_3$ cup.

NUTRITIONAL FACTS:			
Serving Size: 2 T	Total Fat: 18 g	Sodium: 180mg	Sugar: 0 g
Calories Per Serving: 160	Sat Fat: 11 g	Total Carbs: 2 g	Protein: 1 g
Fat Calories: 160	Cholest: 45 mg	Fiber: 1g	

CHAMBORD SAUCE

There is also a liqueur called Chambord. It's a very good liqueur and it has nothing to do with this sauce. However, oysters do!

You have a choice of using fresh or bottled oysters. If you use bottled oysters, increase the liquid in the bottle with water or a white wine, 'til you have 2 cups.

INGREDIENTS:		
	12	OYSTERS, STEAMED AND MINCED
	2	CUPS LIQUOR FROM THE STEAMED OYSTERS
	1	TABLESPOON BUTTER
	1	ONION, MINCED
	3	TOMATOES, MINCED W/JUICES
	6	MUSHROOMS, SLICED
	2	TABLESPOONS PARSLEY, FINELY CHOPPED
	1	SPRIG FRESH THYME OR
	$^1/_2$	TEASPOON DRIED THYME, CRUMBLED
	1	BAY LEAF
	$^1/_8$	TEASPOON GROUND CLOVE
	$^1/_8$	TEASPOON GROUND ALLSPICE
		SALT AND PEPPER TO TASTE

METHOD:

1. Steam the oysters in the liquid until they open (about 10 minutes). Set aside and mince when cool.

2. Saute the onion in the butter until limp. Add the tomatoes, mushrooms, parsley, thyme, bay leaf, clove and allspice. Cook over medium heat for 10 minutes. Add the oyster liquid and the oysters and bring to a boil. Reduce the heat and cook for 20 minutes. Remove the bay leaf, season with salt and pepper and serve.

USE ON: Baked fish.

YIELD: 3 $^1/_2$ cups.

NUTRITIONAL FACTS:			
Serving Size: 1/3 cup	Total Fat: 1.5 g	Sodium: 190 mg	Sugar: 1 g
Calories Per Serving: 40	Sat Fat: 0 g	Total Carbs: 3 g	Protein: 4 g
Fat Calories: 10	Cholest: 15 mg	Fiber: 0 g	

PARSLEY BUTTER

INGREDIENTS:

1	POUND BUTTER AT ROOM TEMPERATURE
1	CUP PARSLEY, CHOPPED
$1/4$	CUP CHOPPED CHIVES
2	TEASPOONS LEMON JUICE
PINCH	GARLIC POWDER
	OR
$1/4$	TEASPOON GRANULATED GARLIC

METHOD: Cream all the ingredients together and use.

USE ON: Broiled or baked fish.

YIELD: 2 cups.

NUTRITIONAL FACTS:

Serving Size: 2 T	Total Fat: 21 g	Sodium: 210 mg	Sugar: 0 g
Calories Per Serving: 180	Sat Fat: 13 g	Total Carbs: 0 g	Protein: 0 g
Fat Calories: 190	Cholest: 55 mg	Fiber: 0 g	

PARSLEY BUTTER II

INGREDIENTS:

1	CUP BUTTER AT ROOM TEMPERATURE
2	TABLESPOONS CHOPPED PARSLEY
2	TABLESPOONS LEMON JUICE
$^1/_2$	TEASPOON FRESHLY GROUND BLACK PEPPER

METHOD: Cream the butter and add the remaining ingredients. Cream again and serve.

USE ON: Broiled or baked fish.

YIELD: 1 $^1/_4$ cups.

NUTRITIONAL FACTS:

Serving Size: 2 T	Total Fat: 21 g	Sodium: 210 mg	Sugar: 0 g
Calories Per Serving: 190	Sat Fat: 13 g	Total Carbs: 0 g	Protein: 0 g
Fat Calories: 190	Cholest: 55 mg	Fiber: 0 g	

BLACK FRUIT SAUCE

This sauce gets some of its color from pumpernickel bread. The raisins and prunes may be in your cupboard, the pumpernickel you might have to buy.

A historical note on pumpernickel. The name of this dark, nearly black bread is ascribed to Napoleon. On one occasion during the campaign toward Russia, his personal chef offered Napoleon some of the local black bread. Upon tasting the bread, Napoleon gave it back to his chef and said, "Ce pain est pour Nicole". Translation; this bread is for Nicole (his horse), hence pum-per-nickel. I swear I didn't make up this story, but someone may have. If it's true it's an interesting footnote. If not, it's still an interesting commentary on a man who has several famous dishes named for and about him, like Chicken Marengo.

INGREDIENTS:	$^1/_2$	POUND PITTED PRUNES
	$^1/_4$	CUP RAISINS AND WATER TO COVER
	1	CUP WATER OR BEER, OR WHITE WINE
	1	TABLESPOON FRESH LEMON ZEST
	2	TABLESPOONS SUGAR
	1	TABLESPOON BUTTER
	1	CUP CUBED PUMPERNICKEL BREAD
	$^1/_4$	TEASPOON GROUND GINGER
	2	TABLESPOONS SLICED ALMONDS

METHOD:

1. Place the prunes and raisins into a sauce pan and add enough water to cover. Bring it to a boil. Reduce the heat and cook for 10 minutes. Drain to reserve the liquid and transfer the prunes and raisins to a cutting board. When cool enough to handle, coarsely chop the prunes and raisins.

2. Return the reserved liquid to the sauce pan along with 1 cup of water, the lemon zest, sugar, butter, pumpernickel and ginger and bring to a boil. Reduce the heat and cook for 10 minutes. Blend the mixture in

the pan, using a hand held processor. Or transfer the ingredients into a blender, and process until smooth. Add the almonds before serving.

Use On: Fish, poached, baked or broiled.

Yield: 3 ¹/₂ cups.

NUTRITIONAL FACTS:			
Serving Size: 1/4 cup	Total Fat: 1.5 g	Sodium: 35 mg	Sugar: 7 g
Calories Per Serving: 80	Sat Fat: 0.5 g	Total Carbs: 16 g	Protein: 1 g
Fat Calories: 10	Cholest: 0 mg	Fiber: 2 g	

HORSERADISH SAUCE

This Russian style fish sauce is as easy as pie and it can be made in a blender.

INGREDIENTS:
2   APPLES, PEELED, CORED AND QUARTERED
2   TABLESPOONS SUGAR
$^1/_4$ CUP PREPARED HORSERADISH (MEASURE FIRST, THEN DRAIN OR SQUEEZE DRY)

METHOD: Place the apples, sugar and horseradish into your blender, then run it at puree speed for 2 minutes. Add a little white vinegar to thin, if needed.

USE ON: Halibut, cod, haddock or any other white-fleshed fish that has been broiled, steamed or poached .

YIELD: $1\,^3/_4$ cups.

NUTRITIONAL FACTS:

Serving Size: 2 T	Total Fat: 0 g	Sodium: 5 mg	Sugar: 4 g
Calories Per Serving: 20	Sat Fat: 0 g	Total Carbs: 5 g	Protein: 0 g
Fat Calories: 0	Cholest: 0 mg	Fiber: 0 g	

LOBSTER SAUCE

There are very few locations in this country where you can buy lobster at a price low enough that you'd be willing to use it to make this sauce. but you can use the "phoney phish" version of lobster, (made from an inexpensive white bodied fish). Besides, the taste is very acceptable.

INGREDIENTS:

$\frac{1}{2}$	POUND PHONEY PHISH LOBSTER MEAT
1	TABLESPOON BUTTER
$1\frac{1}{2}$	CUPS WHITE SAUCE
$\frac{1}{4}$	TEASPOON PAPRIKA

METHOD: Dice, mince or shred the lobster meat. Saute the meat in butter for 2 minutes. Add the white sauce and paprika, then bring the sauce to a boil. Remove from the heat and use.

USE ON: Fish loaves, salmon patties, baked or broiled haddock or halibut.

YIELD: 2 $\frac{1}{4}$ cups.

NUTRITIONAL FACTS:			
Serving Size: 1/4 cup	Total Fat: 5 g	Sodium: 60 mg	Sugar: 1 g
Calories Per Serving: 80	Sat Fat: 3 g	Total Carbs: 3 g	Protein: 5 g
Fat Calories: 50	Cholest: 20 mg	Fiber: 0 g	

EGG AND LEMON SAUCE

(AKA: AVGOLEMONO)

This creamy tart sauce is probably the most famous one given to America by its' Greek communities. It has very broad applications in Greek cookery where it is used in soups and stews, served over vegetables and used on many meat dishes (such as meatballs) and for our purposes here, fish. If you want to use the sauce for some of the above suggested dishes, be sure to use a chicken stock with chicken, beef stock with beef, et cetera. You get the idea.

INGREDIENTS:	3	EGGS
	1	TABLESPOON CORN STARCH
	3	TABLESPOONS LEMON JUICE (= TO 1 MEDIUM LEMON)
	$^1/_4$	TEASPOON WHITE PEPPER
	1	CUP HOT FISH STOCK

METHOD: Thoroughly beat the eggs until creamy. Continue beating while adding the lemon juice and corn starch. Slowly beat in the hot stock, add the white pepper and use.

OPTION: Omit the corn starch and white pepper. Separate the eggs, then beat the egg whites with a pinch of salt until they are stiff. Beat in the yolks one at a time. Next beat in the lemon juice, then slowly beat in the hot stock.

USE ON: Cold-water fish fillets.

YIELD: 2 cups.

NUTRITIONAL FACTS:

Serving Size: 3 T	Total Fat: 1.5 g	Sodium: 95 mg	Sugar: 0 g
Calories Per Serving: 30	Sat Fat: 0.5 g	Total Carbs: 1 g	Protein: 2 g
Fat Calories: 15	Cholest: 65 mg	Fiber: 0 g	

CURRY SAUCE

This is a great sauce for a salmon barbecue, or any other pink-bodied fish you have.

INGREDIENTS:

1	TEASPOON BUTTER
1	MEDIUM ONION, CHOPPED
1	GRANNY SMITH (OR OTHER PIE APPLE), CORED AND CHOPPED
1	CLOVE GARLIC
1	FRESH ITALIAN STYLE TOMATO CHOPPED
$^1/_2$	TEASPOON SALT
2	TEASPOONS CURRY POWDER
$^1/_2$	BANANA SLICED OR MASHED
4	CUPS FISH OR CHICKEN BROTH

METHOD:

1. Saute the onion, apple, garlic, tomato and salt in the butter for 10 minutes. Add the curry powder, banana and fish broth and bring this to a boil. Reduce the heat to medium and cook uncovered for 1 hour.

2. Puree the sauce in the pan, or press it through a colander. Check the viscosity and if necessary thicken the sauce over heat with a little corn starch dissolved in white wine.

USE ON: Barbecued pink-bodied fish.

YIELD: 5 cups.

NUTRITIONAL FACTS:

Serving Size: 1/4 cup	Total Fat: 0 g	Sodium: 150 mg	Sugar: 2 g
Calories Per Serving: 15	Sat Fat: 0 g	Total Carbs: 3 g	Protein: 1 g
Fat Calories: 0	Cholest: 0 mg	Fiber: 0 g	

WE TRIED THIS SAUCE ... AND

LOVED IT ( )
HATED IT ( )
MAYBE WE'LL TRY IT AGAIN ( )
WE'LL USE IT FOR UNWELCOME GUESTS ( )

GENOESE SAUCE

INGREDIENTS:		
	1	TABLESPOON FLOUR
	1	TABLESPOON BUTTER
	1	TABLESPOON EXTRA LIGHT OLIVE OIL OR BUTTER
	1	ONION, SLICED
	1	CARROT SHREDDED OR SLICED INTO ROUNDS
	$^1/_2$	CUP WINE (YOUR CHOICE WHITE OR RED)
	$^1/_2$	CUP FUMET OR WATER
	1	TABLESPOON CHOPPED PARSLEY

METHOD:

1. Make a roux or "beurre manie" using the first two ingredients and set aside.

2. Saute the onion and carrot in the extra light olive oil until the onions are wilted. Add the wine, fumet and parsley and cook the mixture uncovered over medium heat for about 10 minutes or until reduced $^1/_4$. Add the roux or beurre manie and cook the sauce several minutes more to thicken. Serve.

USE ON: Fish, baked, broiled or poached.

YIELD: 1 $^3/_4$ cups.

NUTRITIONAL FACTS:

Serving Size: 1/4 cup	Total Fat: 3 g	Sodium: 20 mg	Sugar: 2 g
Calories Per Serving: 50	Sat Fat: 1 g	Total Carbs: 4 g	Protein: 0 g
Fat Calories: 30	Cholest: 5 mg	Fiber: 1 g	

EGG SAUCE

INGREDIENTS: 2   EGG YOLKS
                1   TABLESPOON WATER
                2   TABLESPOONS MINCED OR GROUND ALMONDS
                1   CUP FUMET, OR THE BROTH FROM THE POACHED FISH

METHOD: Whisk the egg yolks and water until light in color. Whisk the fumet into the mixture and add the almonds. In a sauce pan, bring the sauce to a simmer and cook until it thickens. Serve.

OPTION: If you start with a hot broth from poached fish, reverse the mixing process. Slowly whisk the hot broth into the beaten egg yolks, add the almonds, return the sauce to the heat and cook until thickened. Serve.

USE ON: Fish, poached, boiled, sauteed, baked or broiled.

YIELD: 1 $\frac{1}{3}$ cups

NUTRITIONAL FACTS:

Serving Size: 3 T	Total Fat: 3 g	Sodium: 115 mg	Sugar: 0 g
Calories Per Serving: 40	Sat Fat: 0.5 g	Total Carbs: 1 g	Protein: 2 g
Fat Calories: 25	Cholest: 60 mg	Fiber: 0 g	

TARTAR SAUCE

Here are two Tartar sauces, the first tastes best and the simplified version is much quicker to make.

INGREDIENTS:	1	EGG YOLK
	$3/4$	TEASPOON DRY MUSTARD
	2	TABLESPOONS EXTRA LIGHT OLIVE OIL
	$1/2$	TEASPOON LEMON JUICE
	PINCH	CAYENNE
	2	TABLESPOONS MINCED CAPERS
	1	SMALL ONION, GRATED OR MINCED
	1	GERKIN, MINCED
	1	TEASPOON MINCED PARSLEY

METHOD:

1. Beat the egg yolk until light in color. Add the mustard and beat until well blended.

2. Drizzle the oil into the mixture while beating constantly. Continue beating while you slowly add the lemon juice and cayenne. You should now have a mayonnaise.

3. Add and whisk in the remaining ingredients.

OPTION: The easy version is to use $1/2$ cup prepared mayonnaise, add the grated onion and 2 tablespoons of pickle relish.

USE ON: Fish, breaded, sauteed broiled or poached,

YIELD: $2/3$ cup.

NUTRITIONAL FACTS:			
Serving Size: 3 T	Total Fat: 7 g	Sodium: 75 mg	Sugar: 2 g
Calories Per Serving: 70	Sat Fat: 1 g	Total Carbs: 4 g	Protein: 1 g
Fat Calories: 60	Cholest: 45 mg	Fiber: 1 g	

ALMOND BUTTER SAUCE

This recipe can be increased by any multiple you need.

INGREDIENTS:	$1/4$	POUND BUTTER
	2	TABLESPOONS SLICED ALMONDS
	1	TABLESPOON LEMON JUICE
	1	TABLESPOON CHOPPED PARSLEY FOR GARNISH

METHOD: Melt the butter, mix in the sliced almonds and lemon juice.

USE ON: Fish, poached, baked or sauteed.

YIELD: $2/3$ Cup.

NUTRITIONAL FACTS:

Serving Size: 3 T	Total Fat: 31 g	Sodium: 290 mg	Sugar: 0 g
Calories Per Serving: 280	Sat Fat: 18 g	Total Carbs: 2 g	Protein: 1 g
Fat Calories: 280	Cholest: 75 mg	Fiber: 1 g	

"This page is blank by Design"

CHAPTER 16

SAUCES MADE FOR CRUSTACEANS

I'm talking about shrimp and other wonderful things from the sea like shrimp lobster, crab, crayfish, (aka crawfish and crawdads), scampi and langostino.

SEAFOOD COCKTAIL SAUCE

This recipe requires a teaspoon of onion juice. You can buy it or make it. If you choose to make it, there are two ways to do it. The first is to grate a quarter onion into a small bowl, strain out the juice and throw away the pulp. The second way is a little easier on the eyes, but requires more clean-up. Place about 1/4 onion into a food processor and let'er rip. Strain the resulting mush.

INGREDIENTS:

1	CUP CATSUP
1	TABLESPOON LEMON JUICE
1	TABLESPOON PREPARED HORSERADISH
1	TABLESPOON SUGAR
1	TEASPOON ONION JUICE
$^1/_2$	TEASPOON SALT
	SEVERAL SHAKES OF A BOTTLED HOT SAUCE

METHOD: Blend all the ingredients and use.

USE ON: Shrimp and crab.

YIELD: 1 $^1/_4$ cups.

NUTRITIONAL FACTS:

Serving Size: 1/4 cup	Total Fat: 0 g	Sodium: 860 mg	Sugar: 7 g
Calories Per Serving: 60	Sat Fat: 0 g	Total Carbs: 16 g	Protein: 1 g
Fat Calories: 0	Cholest: 0 mg	Fiber: 1 g	

DRAWN BUTTER SAUCE

While this sauce may have other applications, here it is offered as a dipping sauce for broiled or boiled shrimp and lobster.

INGREDIENTS:	4	TABLESPOONS DRAWN BUTTER
	2	TABLESPOONS FLOUR
	$1/4$	TEASPOON FRESHLY GROUND BLACK PEPPER
	1	TEASPOON LEMON JUICE
	1	CUP HOT WATER

METHOD: Heat the butter in a small pan, then whisk in the flour, pepper and lemon juice until smooth. Add the water and bring to a boil. Reduce the heat and cook for 5 minutes while stirring constantly.

USE ON: Broiled or boiled shrimp and lobster.

YIELD: 1 $1/4$ **cups.**

NUTRITIONAL FACTS:

Serving Size: 1/4 cup	Total Fat: 36 g	Sodium: 360 mg	Sugar: 0 g
Calories Per Serving: 360	Sat Fat: 22 g	Total Carbs: 10 g	Protein: 2 g
Fat Calories: 320	Cholest: 95 mg	Fiber: 0 g	

LOUIS SAUCE

A sauce for Crab Louis, pronounced "lew-ee". I believe it was created on the west coast to accommodate a meal-sized salad made from dungeness crab and laid over a bed of iceberg lettuce, olives, tomato wedges and hardcooked eggs. It works on any fresh, frozen, canned or imitation crab meat. The sauce compliments the taste of the crab meat rather than overpowering it.

INGREDIENTS:	$^1/_2$	CUP MAYONNAISE
	$^1/_2$	CUP WHIPPING CREAM (WHIPPED IF YOU WISH)
		OR
	$^1/_2$	CUP SOUR CREAM
	2	TABLESPOONS CHILI SAUCE
	1	TABLESPOON LEMON JUICE
	2	TEASPOONS GRATED ONION
		SEVERAL DROPS TABASCO SAUCE
	1	TABLESPOON CHOPPED PARSLEY, EITHER IN THE SAUCE OR AS A GARNISH OR BOTH
OPTION:	1	TABLESPOON HORSERADISH

METHOD: Blend all the ingredients. Serve with lemon wedges on the side.

ALTERNATE: If you choose whipping cream and decide to whip it, fold it into the sauce last.

USE ON: Crab meat (or shrimp for a Shrimp Louis).

YIELD: 1 $^1/_4$ cups.

NUTRITIONAL FACTS:

Serving Size: 1/4 cup	Total Fat: 25 g	Sodium: 250 mg	Sugar: 1 g
Calories Per Serving: 240	Sat Fat: 6 g	Total Carbs: 3 g	Protein: 1 g
Fat Calories: 220	Cholest: 20 mg	Fiber: 0 g	

LOUIS SAUCE TOO!

This sauce is made without mayonnaise, but you still need to use an egg yolk.

INGREDIENTS:	1	EGG YOLK
	2	TEASPOONS DIJON MUSTARD
	DASH	WORCESTERSHIRE SAUCE
	2	TEASPOONS RED WINE VINEGAR
	$^1/_4$	TEASPOON SALT
	PINCH	FRESHLY GROUND BLACK PEPPER
	$^1/_2$	CUP OLIVE OIL
	1	TABLESPOON CHILI SAUCE
	2	WHOLE GREEN ONIONS OR SCALLIONS, FINELY CHOPPED
	6	OLIVES, PITTED AND CHOPPED (YOUR CHOICE FOR COLOR AND TYPE)
	1	HEAD ICEBERG LETTUCE

METHOD: In a mixing bowl, beat the yolk until light yellow. Add the mustard, worcestershire sauce, vinegar, salt and pepper and whisk until thoroughly blended. Slowly drizzle in the oil, beating the mixture until thickened. Then whisk in the chili sauce, onions and olives.

OPTION: Add the crab meat to the sauce, while still over the heat, to warm through.

USE ON: Pour the sauce over the meat from 1 dungeness crab (approximately 1 pound) that has been laid over a full, round, center cut of iceberg lettuce (about $^1/_2$ inch thick). If dungeness crab is not available where you live, use what is available, or use imitation crab. It's available everywhere and is quite good.

YIELD: 1 $^1/_4$ cups.

NUTRITIONAL FACTS:			
Serving Size: 1/4 cup	Total Fat: 14 g	Sodium: 85 mg	Sugar: 1 g
Calories Per Serving: 140	Sat Fat: 2 g	Total Carbs: 3 g	Protein: 1 g
Fat Calories: 130	Cholest: 25 mg	Fiber: 1 g	

ITALIAN DIPPING SAUCE

INGREDIENTS:

$1/2$	CUP OLIVE OIL
$1/2$	CUP RED WINE VINEGAR
2	TABLESPOONS CAPERS (DRAINED)
$1/4$	TEASPOON OREGANO
$1/2$	TEASPOON SALT
1	TABLESPOON WORCESTERSHIRE SAUCE OR AROMATIC BITTERS

METHOD: Place all the ingredients into a blender and pulse once or twice until the capers are minced.

USE ON: Lobster, shrimp, crab or assorted vegetables.

YIELD: 1 cup.

NUTRITIONAL FACTS:

Serving Size: 2 T	Total Fat: 13 g	Sodium: 0 mg	Sugar: 0 g
Calories Per Serving: 120	Sat Fat: 2 g	Total Carbs: 1 g	Protein: 0 g
Fat Calories: 120	Cholest: 0 mg	Fiber: 0 g	

BALSAMIC DIPPING SAUCE

Balsamic vinegar, Italy's aged sweet wine vinegar has become an American favorite in a very short period of time and has quickly spread throughout the menus of America. You can now find it served as an appetizer, in soups, salads, entree's and desserts. Here it plays a role as a dipping sauce for an informal meal.

INGREDIENTS:	$^1/_2$	CUP OLIVE OIL
	2	TABLESPOONS BALSAMIC VINEGAR
	2	TEASPOONS LEMON JUICE
	$^1/_2$	TEASPOON SALT
OPTIONS:		TRY THEM ALL, BUT ONLY ONE AT A TIME.
	$^1/_4$	TEASPOON DRIED OREGANO, CRUMBLED
	1	TEASPOON FRESH, CHOPPED BASIL
	1	TABLESPOON CAPERS, MINCED
	$^1/_2$	TEASPOON CRUSHED RED PEPPER
	PINCH	OF FRESHLY GROUND BLACK PEPPER

METHOD: Place all the ingredients into a cruet or closeable jar, seal and shake thoroughly until emulsified.

USE ON: Shrimp, lobster, seafood salad, vegetables.

YIELD: $^2/_3$ cup.

NUTRITIONAL FACTS:			
Serving Size: 1 T	Total Fat: 0.5 g	Sodium: 10 mg	Sugar: 0 g
Calories Per Serving: 5	Sat Fat: 0 g	Total Carbs: 0 g	Protein: 0 g
Fat Calories: 5	Cholest: 0 mg	Fiber: 0 g	

NEWBURG SAUCE

This sauce is very creamy, rich and non-slenderizing. The name "Newburg", when associated with food, normally refers to lobster, but it needn't be. It is also usable with other seafood.

Whatever your choice of seafood for this sauce, it needs to be precooked and possibly diced. In this case, you can add the diced seafood to the sauce to warm through, before serving over toast. One exception is using this as a dipping sauce for broiled lobster or shrimp.

INGREDIENTS:	$^1/_4$	CUP BUTTER
	1	TABLESPOON FLOUR
	1	CUP WHIPPING CREAM OR HALF-AND-HALF
	2	EGG YOLKS, BEATEN
	2	TABLESPOONS SHERRY
	1	TEASPOON LEMON JUICE
	$^1/_4$	TEASPOON SALT
	PINCH	PAPRIKA

METHOD:

1. In a sauce pan, cook the butter and flour for 2 minutes to make a thin roux.

2. Whisk in the whipping cream and bring to a scald. Use a small amount of the hot cream to mix into the egg yolks, then add the yolks to the mixture in the sauce pan. Cook until the sauce thickens, then stir in the sherry, lemon juice, salt and paprika. Remove the sauce from the heat.

USE ON: Two cups of diced boiled, poached or broiled lobster meat. Firm-bodied cold-water white fish, shrimp or scallops.

YIELD: $1\,^2/_3$ cups.

NUTRITIONAL FACTS:

Serving Size: 1/3 cup	Total Fat: 28 g	Sodium: 250 mg	Sugar: 2 g
Calories Per Serving: 270	Sat Fat: 17 g	Total Carbs: 3 g	Protein: 3 g
Fat Calories: 250	Cholest: 175 mg	Fiber: 0 g	

NO FAT NEWBURG SAUCE

(AUTHORS HEALTHIER AND SLENDERIZING VERSION)

This is my outstanding version of a "Newburg Sauce". It is a variation on the "Low Fat Butter and Cream Sauce" that can be found in my best selling book, "The Encyclopedia of Sauces for Your Pasta".

INGREDIENTS:	8	OUNCES OF "NO FAT CREAM CHEESE"
	2	CUPS LOW FAT OR SKIM MILK
	2	TABLESPOONS (1/2 OUNCE) OF A BUTTER SUBSTITUTE (BUTTER BUDS/MOLLY MCBUTTER)
	$^1/_2$	CUP EGG BEATERS
	$^1/_4$	TEASPOON SALT
	PINCH	PAPRIKA
	2	TABLESPOONS SHERRY
	1	TEASPOON CORN STARCH

METHOD: Place all the ingredients, except the sherry, into a processor or blender and puree until smooth. Transfer the mixture into a sauce pan and bring to a scald. Cook until the sauce thickens. If the sauce is too thin, mix corn starch with an equal amount of water and whisk into the sauce. Remove from the heat and stir in the sherry.

OPTION: Add cooked and diced seafood to the sauce, to heat through. Serve on toast or in shallow soup bowls.

USE ON: Two cups of diced seafood. Lobster, shrimp, cold water white fish, scallops, imitation lobster, imitation crab. Or on a grouping of several seafood items.

YIELD: 3 $^1/_2$ cups.

NUTRITIONAL FACTS:			
Serving Size: 1/3 cup	Total Fat: 0 g	Sodium: 320 mg	Sugar: 3 g
Calories Per Serving: 45	Sat Fat: 0 g	Total Carbs: 5 g	Protein: 5 g
Fat Calories: 0	Cholest: 5 mg	Fiber: 0 g	

THERMIDOR SAUCE

Lobster Thermidor is generally served only in expensive restaurants. The reason? It's labor intensive and that makes it costly. Today with imitation lobster available, you can have it at home served on toast, or wide egg noodles and forego serving it in the empty lobster shell.

This sauce is not as intimidating as the ingredients list appears.

INGREDIENTS:		
	$1/4$	CUP BUTTER
	1	CUP THINLY SLICED MUSHROOMS
	$1/2$	TEASPOON SALT
	PINCH	FRESHLY GROUND BLACK PEPPER
	1	SLICE SOFT WHITE BREAD DICED, CRUST DISCARDED
	1	TEASPOON AROMATIC BITTERS
	PINCH	CAYENNE PEPPER
	1	TABLESPOON CHOPPED PARSLEY
	$1/4$	CUP BRANDY
	$1/2$	CUP SHERRY
	2	CUPS WHIPPING CREAM
	4	EGG YOLKS
	$1/2$	CUP FRESHLY GRATED PARMESAN CHEESE
		PAPRIKA

METHOD:

1. Saute the mushrooms in the butter for 3 minutes and set aside.

2. Place the second set of ingredients into a blender and puree until fairly smooth. Transfer the mixture from the blender to the sauce pan with the mushrooms. Bring the sauce to a simmer and cook until it thickens. Add the seafood, to heat through and remove from heat. Place the mixture into an oven-proof serving dish and sprinkle it with

Parmesan cheese. Place the dish under a broiler until the cheese turns golden. Remove from the broiler and garnish with paprika. Serve.

USE ON: Chunked imitation or real lobster. Ditto for crab, shrimp, cold water white fish.

YIELD: 3 ³/₄ cups.

NUTRITIONAL FACTS:

Serving Size: 1/3 cup	Total Fat: 20 g	Sodium: 240 mg	Sugar: 2 g
Calories Per Serving: 220	Sat Fat: 12 g	Total Carbs: 2 g	Protein: 4 g
Fat Calories: 180	Cholest: 135 mg	Fiber: 0 g	

"This page is blank by Design"

CHAPTER 17

SAUCES MADE FOR INVERTEBRATES

(IF YOU LIKE SPINELESS THINGS, YOU'LL LOVE THIS CHAPTER.)

CALAMARI SAUCE

You can use this sauce in two ways. The first is to poach whole baby calamari in the sauce. Or serve it over or under sauteed calamari steaks.

INGREDIENTS:		
	$^1/_2$	CUP OLIVE OIL
	1	MEDIUM ONION, CHOPPED
	2	CLOVE GARLIC, CRUSHED
	1	TABLESPOON ANCHOVY PASTE
	$^1/_2$	CUP WHITE WINE
	$^1/_2$	CUP DICED TOMATOES
	1	TEASPOON TOMATO PASTE

METHOD: Saute the onion and garlic in the olive oil for 2 to 3 minutes. Add the remaining ingredients and bring the sauce to a boil. Reduce the heat to low and cook for 10 minutes.

(If you poach your calamari in the sauce, add them to the pan along with the remaining ingredients.)

USE ON: Sauteed or grilled calamari steaks, boiled baby squid, or poached as suggested above.

YIELD: 2 $^1/_3$ cups.

NUTRITIONAL FACTS:

Serving Size: 1/4 cup	Total Fat: 13 g	Sodium: 105 mg	Sugar: 2 g
Calories Per Serving: 130	Sat Fat: 1.5 g	Total Carbs: 3 g	Protein: 1 g
Fat Calories: 110	Cholest: 0 mg	Fiber: 0 g	

Octopus Lemon Sauce

This is not a cooked and prepared sauce, but a mix and serve. To vary the taste of the sauce, vary the type of acid you use. Try different herb flavored vinegars or a Balsamic vinegar.

INGREDIENTS:	$^1/_2$	CUP OLIVE OIL
	$^1/_4$	CUP LEMON JUICE
	1	TEASPOON FRESHLY GROUND BLACK PEPPER

METHOD: Mix and use.

USE ON: Boiled baby octopus.

YIELD: $^3/_4$ cup.

NUTRITIONAL FACTS:

Serving Size: 2 T	Total Fat: 19 g	Sodium: 0 mg	Sugar: 0 g
Calories Per Serving: 170	Sat Fat: 2.5 g	Total Carbs: 1 g	Protein: 0 g
Fat Calories: 170	Cholest: 0 mg	Fiber: 0 g	

CALAMARI DIJON SAUCE

INGREDIENTS:		
	1	TEASPOON DIJON MUSTARD
	3	TABLESPOON WINE VINEGAR
	1	TEASPOON CORN STARCH
	$^1/_2$	CUP OLIVE OIL
	$^1/_2$	TEASPOON SALT
	PINCH	WHITE PEPPER
	$1^1/_2$	TABLESPOONS CHOPPED PARSLEY

Method:

1. Place dijon mustard, wine vinegar and corn starch into a small sauce pan. Cook it briefly until the mixture begins to thicken.

2. Remove the pan from the heat and thoroughly blend in the remaining ingredients.

USE ON: Sauteed calamari steaks.

YIELD: $^3/_4$ cup.

NUTRITIONAL FACTS:

Serving Size: 2 T	Total Fat: 20 g	Sodium: 240 mg	Sugar: 0 g
Calories Per Serving: 180	Sat Fat: 2.5 g	Total Carbs: 1 g	Protein: 0 g
Fat Calories: 180	Cholest: 0 mg	Fiber: 0 g	

ITALIAN STYLE CALAMARI SAUCE

INGREDIENTS:

2	TABLESPOONS OLIVE OIL
1	ONION, CHOPPED
2	CLOVES GARLIC, CRUSHED
1	TABLESPOON ANCHOVY PASTE
$1/2$	CUP WHITE WINE
1	TOMATO, PEELED AND CHOPPED
1	TEASPOON TOMATO PASTE

METHOD: Saute the onion and garlic in olive oil until the edges begin to brown. Add the remaining ingredients and bring the sauce to a simmer. Cook for 10 minutes and taste to adjust the seasoning. Serve as is, or strain and serve.

USE ON: Poached or sauteed squid rings or octopus (in wine or a mixture of wine and water for about 10 minutes or until tender. Don't over cook).

YIELD: $1 1/2$ cups.

NUTRITIONAL FACTS:

Serving Size: 3 T	Total Fat: 3 g	Sodium: 35 mg	Sugar: 1 g
Calories Per Serving: 45	Sat Fat: 0 g	Total Carbs: 3 g	Protein: 1 g
Fat Calories: 25	Cholest: 0 mg	Fiber: 0 g	

CALAMARI POACHING SAUCE

INGREDIENTS:

$^1/_4$	CUP OLIVE OIL
2	TABLESPOONS TOMATO PASTE
$^1/_2$	CUP WHITE WINE
$^1/_2$	CUP WATER
2	TABLESPOONS CHOPPED PARSLEY

METHOD: Mix all the ingredients in a blender until smooth.

USE ON: Whole calamari (squid) rounds cut from the tentacles, calamari steaks or octopus.

For stove top use: Using a skillet, put a single layer of raw calamari or octopus in the pan. Pour the sauce over the seafood and bring it to a boil. Reduce the heat to simmer, cover and cook for approximately 30 minutes. For calamari steaks, cook for 20 minutes.

To bake: In an ovenproof baking dish, put the raw calamari or octopus in the dish and cover with the sauce. Bake at 325 F., for 1 hour, then test for tenderness. Bake longer if necessary.

YIELD: 1 $^1/_3$ cups.

NUTRITIONAL FACTS:

Serving Size: 3 T	Total Fat: 7 g	Sodium: 0 mg	Sugar: 0 g
Calories Per Serving: 80	Sat Fat: 1 g	Total Carbs: 1 g	Protein: 0 g
Fat Calories: 70	Cholest: 0 mg	Fiber: 0 g	

CHAPTER 18

SAUCES FOR VARIETY MEATS

Variety meat is the American term for "innards" or "organ meats". Whichever word you use it means the same thing and refers to the sweetbreads, kidneys, liver, tongue, tripe and heart. So if you eat any of the organ meats named, this is your chapter. For an absolutely outstanding tripe and sauce recipe, see my best selling book, The Encyclopedia of Sauces for Your Pasta, for the "Roman Style Tripe Sauce".

There are other sauces, interspersed throughout the book, that you might enjoy using on sweetbreads and organ meats. Beginning with Chapter 1, refer to the Glaze recipe and read the "Use" comments on how to turn a glaze into a demi-glaze. In Chapter 3 there is the Brown Butter Sauce, Black Butter Sauce and Ravigote Sauce. Try the Horseradish Sauce in Chapter 4 or the

Raisin Sauce for tongue in Chapter 7.

SWEETBREADS

When your taste buds desire sweetbreads, you can choose from lamb, beef or calf. Calf sweetbreads are the odds on favorite for tenderness and sweetness. Dip the sweetbreads into an egg wash and then into bread crumbs and then skewer them on a spit separated by mushrooms, bell pepers, onions and possibly a little bacon. Baste with butter while broiling and serve with the Manor House Sauce.

There are many ways to serve sweetbreads when not using a sauce. Such as braising, broiling or breading and frying them.

Sweetbreads may require some cleaning before using. Ask your butcher if they have been par-boiled and cleaned. If the answer is no, parboil them for 15 minutes in water to which 1 tablespoon vinegar and 1 teaspoon salt has been added for each quart of water. Cool, then remove and discard the connecting tissue. Flatten the sweetbreads by using a plate with a weight on it before refrigerating.

BRAINS

When brains are part of your menu, you can choose calf, beef, lamb or pork. Calf brains have the most delicate flavor. All brains require precooking, so cover them with cold water to which you've added 2 tablespoons vinegar, 1 teaspoon salt, several pepercorns, 1/2 an onion, 1 carrot and a little thyme. Bring them to a simmer and cook for at least 30 minutes. Allow the broth and brains to cool, then refrigerate together until needed.

Additional sauces, for use on sauteed or broiled brains, are found in Chapter Two. Specifically, BROWN BUTTER SAUCE (SAUCE AUX BEURRE NOISETTE) AND BLACK BUTTER SAUCE (BEURRE NOIR).

Precooked brains can be diced or minced and then scrambled with eggs. Season the eggs with a dash of hot sauce or ketchup, a dash of worcestershire and a little salt. Serve on toast. They can also be breaded and fried until goldenbrown.

LIVER

Beef and calf liver need no pre-preparation. Straight from the package is fine. But if you choose lamb or pork you'll need to drop them into boiling water for 1 minute, then drain and use.

A suitable sauce for whole roasted calf liver is the BEARNAISE SAUCE in Chapter Three.

TONGUE

Tongue should be parboiled for about 10 minutes. This allows you to skin the tongue for further cooking. There are a variety of ways to prepare tongue, like braising, roasting, spit barbecuing or boiling.

To braise, saute some onion in butter, then add the tongue along with parsley, thyme, several cloves and several cups of white wine or beef broth. Keep a low level of liquid in the covered pan until the tongue is cooked, about $1^1/_2$ to 2 hours. Serve it with the PIQUANT SAUCE in Chapter Four.

MANOR HOUSE SAUCE

In France, this would be called a "Chateau Sauce", I like that better. A Chateau is a large country house, sometimes with turrets and things and it looks like a small castle.

INGREDIENTS:		
	$1/4$	CUP CHOPPED MUSHROOMS
	$1/4$	CUP WHITE WINE
	$3/4$	CUP BUTTER (MELT 1/2 CUP AND SET ASIDE)
	3	TABLESPOONS ONION
	3	TABLESPOONS CHOPED SHALLOTS
	$1/4$	CUP FLOUR
	3	CUPS BEEF BOUILLON
	$1/2$	CUP TOMATO PASTE
OPTION:	2	TABLESPOONS BEEF TEA (AKA MEAT EXTRACT).

METHOD:

1. Poach the mushrooms in the wine for about 5 minutes and set aside.

2. Saute the onion and shallots in $1/4$ cup butter until golden. Add the flour and cook until brown. Then add the bouillon, tomato paste and beef tea and cook until the sauce thickens. Add the mushrooms, wine and remaining $1/2$ cup melted butter.

3. At this point thoroughly blend, or puree the sauce until smooth.

USE ON: Breaded and broiled or sauteed sweetbreads.

YIELD: 5 cups.

NUTRITIONAL FACTS:			
Serving Size: 1/4 cup	Total Fat: 7 g	Sodium: 200 mg	Sugar: 0 g
Calories Per Serving: 90	Sat Fat: 4.5 g	Total Carbs: 5 g	Protein: 1 g
Fat Calories: 70	Cholest: 20 mg	Fiber: 0 g	

SHERRY CREAM SAUCE

INGREDIENTS:

4	TABLESPOONS BUTTER
8	OUNCES SLICED MUSHROOMS
$^1/_2$	CUP DRY SHERRY
1	CUP WHIPING CREAM
$^1/_2$	TEASPOON SALT
	FRESHLY GROUND BLACK PEPPER TO TASTE

METHOD: Saute the mushrooms in the butter until the butter is absorbed and released. Add the sherry and whiping cream and simmer the ingredients for 5 minutes. Serve.

USE ON: Sauteed or baked sweetbreads. If desired the sweetbreads can be placed on toast before saucing.

YIELD: 2 $^1/_2$ cups.

NUTRITIONAL FACTS:

Serving Size: 1/4 cup	Total Fat: 11 g	Sodium: 160 mg	Sugar: 1 g
Calories Per Serving: 120	Sat Fat: 7 g	Total Carbs: 2 g	Protein: 1 g
Fat Calories: 100	Cholest: 35 mg	Fiber: 0 g	

CAPERED EGG SAUCE

This sauce will serve three pairs of precooked and cubed brains.

INGREDIENTS:	$^1/_4$	CUP BUTTER
	$^1/_4$	CUP MINCED OR GRATED ONION
	2	TABLESPOONS FLOUR
	2	CUPS BEEF BOUILLON
	2	EGG YOLKS, BEATEN
	1	TOMATO, PEELED, SEEDED AND CHOPED
	1	TABLESPOON CHOPED ITALIAN, ANAHEIM CHILI OR BELL PEPPER
	2	TABLESPOONS CAPERS
	1	TABLESPOON LEMON JUICE
	1	TEASPOON SALT

METHOD:

1.   Briefly saute the onions in the butter, whisk in the flour and cook for 1 or 2 minutes. Add the bouillon and cook until slightly thickened.

2.   Blend a little of the hot bouillon into the beaten egg yolks. Then slowly add the egg mixture into the bouillon and simmer the mixture for 2 or 3 minutes. Add the brains and remaining ingredients. Simmer the sauce for 15 minutes and serve.

USE ON: To find sauces for sauteed or broiled brains see my comments at the beginning of this chapter.

YIELD: 3 $^1/_2$ cups.

NUTRITIONAL FACTS:

Serving Size: 1/4 cup	Total Fat: 4 g	Sodium: 310 mg	Sugar: 1 g
Calories Per Serving: 60	Sat Fat: 2.5 g	Total Carbs: 4 g	Protein: 1 g
Fat Calories: 40	Cholest: 40 mg	Fiber: 0 g	

BRAINS Á LA KING

For this preparation you'll need about one pound of precooked and cubed brains. For an added touch, serve over your favorite toasted bread.

INGREDIENTS:	2	TABLESPOONS EXTRA LIGHT OLIVE OIL OR BUTTER
	2	BELL PEPPERS, CHOPPED (COLOR IS YOUR CHOICE)
	1	TABLESPOON GRATED ONION
	$^1/_2$	CUP FINELY CHOPED CELERY
	2	TABLESPOONS CHOPED PIMENTO OR RED BELL PEPPER
	$^1/_2$	TEASPOON SALT
	PINCH	FRESHLY GROUND BLACK PEPPER
	2	TABLESPOONS EXTRA LIGHT OLIVE OIL OR BUTTER
	2	TABLESPOONS FLOUR
	2	CUPS MILK

OPTION: You can exchange a Veloute Sauce for the White Sauce normally used in this recipe.

METHOD:

1. Saute the bell pepper, onion and celery in the olive oil for 3 minutes. Add the pimento, salt and pepper and cook 1 additional minute. Set aside.

2. Make a light roux of the butter and flour, then slowly add the milk while whisking to blend. When the sauce is thoroughly blended and smooth, add the sauteed vegetables and precooked and cubed brains.

   Heat through and serve over toast.

YIELD: $2^1/_2$ cups.

NUTRITIONAL FACTS:			
Serving Size: 1/2 cup	Total Fat: 10 g	Sodium: 210 mg	Sugar: 4 g
Calories Per Serving: 130	Sat Fat: 2.5 g	Total Carbs: 8 g	Protein: 3 g
Fat Calories: 90	Cholest: 10 mg	Fiber: 1 g	

SAUCE Á LA POULETTE

This is a very old sweetbread sauce recipe. The word a'la Poulette refers to the fact that there are eggs in the sauce.

INGREDIENTS:	1	TABLESPOON BUTTER
	1	TABLESPOON FLOUR
	1	CUP WATER OR CONSOMME
	1/2	CUP ONION JUICE (GRATE THE ONION, STRAIN TO EXTRACT THE JUICE, DISCARD THE PULP)
	3	TABLESPOONS LEMON JUICE
		SALT AND FRESHLY GROUND PEPPER TO TASTE
	2	EGG YOLKS, BEATEN
	1	TABLESPOON CHOPPED PARSLEY

METHOD:

1. Make a light roux of the butter and flour. Add the water, onion juice and lemon juice and bring the mixture to a boil. Cover and allow to simmer for 20 minutes.

2. Add the salt and pepper, stir a small amount of the hot mixture into the beaten egg yolks and mix well.

3. Add the yolks into the sauce while whisking, then add the parsley and serve at once.

USE ON: Sweetbreads.

YIELD: 2 cups.

NUTRITIONAL FACTS:

Serving Size: 1/4 cup	Total Fat: 4 g	Sodium: 240 mg	Sugar: 1 g
Calories Per Serving: 60	Sat Fat: 2 g	Total Carbs: 2 g	Protein: 3 g
Fat Calories: 35	Cholest: 80 mg	Fiber: 0 g	

WINE SAUCE FOR BAKED LIVER

If you're the type who loves liver briefly fried and pink on the inside, this recipe may not be for you. On the other hand, for those times when you don't want to fry the liver, it gives you a nice taste change.

INGREDIENTS:	2	ONIONS, SLICED TOP TO BOTTOM
	$^1/_2$	CUP BUTTER
	$^1/_2$	CUP RED WINE
	$^1/_4$	CUP CHOPED PARSLEY
	1	TEASPOON THYME
		SALT AND FRESHLY GROUND BLACK PEPPER TO TASTE
	$^1/_2$	CUP FLOUR

METHOD:

1. Briefly saute the onions in the butter until wilted. Add the wine, parsley, thyme, salt and pepper. Cover and simmer until the onions are thoroughly cooked, about 15 to 20 minutes.

2. Place the sauce in a coverable baking dish/pan. Dredge about 6 liver slices in the flour. Lay the floured liver on the onions. Bake for $^1/_2$ hour in a moderate oven. Remove the cover and bake 10 minutes longer. Serve.

USE ON: If you've come this far you'll know.

YIELD: 2 $^3/_4$ cups.

NUTRITIONAL FACTS:			
Serving Size: 1/3 cup	Total Fat: 14 g	Sodium: 140 mg	Sugar: 3 g
Calories Per Serving: 150	Sat Fat: 8 g	Total Carbs: 5 g	Protein: 1 g
Fat Calories: 120	Cholest: 35 mg	Fiber: 1 g	

RAISIN SAUCE

INGREDIENTS:

$^1/_2$	CUP WHITE WINE
2	TABLESPOONS CORN STARCH
2	CUPS VEGETABLE STOCK
	OR
2	CUPS STOCK MADE THE LAMBS TONGUE
$^1/_2$	CUP RAISINS
$^1/_2$	TEASPOON SALT

METHOD:

1. Blend the white wine and the corn starch and set aside.

2. Place the stock, raisins and salt into a sauce pan and bring to a boil. Reduce the heat and cook for 5 minutes or until the raisins are plump.

3. Stir in the corn starch and wine mixture and cook until thickened.

USE ON: Lamb tongues.

YIELD: 3 cups.

NUTRITIONAL FACTS:

Serving Size: 1/4 cup	Total Fat: 0 g	Sodium: 240 mg	Sugar: 4 g
Calories Per Serving: 45	Sat Fat: 0 g	Total Carbs: 9 g	Protein: 1 g
Fat Calories: 0	Cholest: 0 mg	Fiber: 0 g	

RAISIN SAUCE TOO!

This raisin sauce differs substantially from the preceding raisin sauce. For starters, it's sweet.

INGREDIENTS:		
	1	TABLESPOON CORN STARCH
	1$^1/_2$	CUPS WATER, OR BROTH FROM BOILED TONGUE OR HAM
	$^1/_4$	TEASPOON GROUND CLOVES
	$^3/_4$	CUP BROWN SUGAR, FIRMLY PACKED
	$^3/_4$	CUP RAISINS
	1	TABLESPOON BUTTER
	1	TABLESPOON LEMON JUICE

METHOD:
In a sauce pan, blend a little broth and the corn starch. Add the remaining broth, ground cloves and brown sugar. Bring the sauce to a boil. Reduce the heat to simmer and cook for 3 minutes or until the sauce thickens. Remove the sauce from the heat and stir in the butter and lemon juice. Serve.

USE ON:
Tongue or ham.

YIELD:
2 $^3/_4$ cups.

NUTRITIONAL FACTS:

Serving Size: 1/4 cup	Total Fat: 1 g	Sodium: 15 mg	Sugar: 1.7 g
Calories Per Serving: 90	Sat Fat: 0.5 g	Total Carbs: 20 g	Protein: 0 g
Fat Calories: 10	Cholest: 5 mg	Fiber: 0 g	

"This page is blank by Design"

Chapter 19

Barbecue Sauces

(aka: BBQ)

Barbecuing goes way beyond cooking over hot coals or an open flame, I firmly believes it rekindles and satisfies some primitive instinct in men. I love it! And if you love it too, this chapter's for you!

The barbecue is such a unique and fun method of cooking meats, as are the many vegetables that can be cooked along with the meat. Corn-on-the-cob (with or without the husk) eggplant slices, tomatoes, zucchini, carrots, peppers and potatoes to name my favorites. Be creative.

There are sauces that are endowed by their creators as a "basting" sauce.

Others are designated "barbecue" sauces. Marinades are also a contender in this type of cookery. The differences are important and you should be familiar with them.

Marinade: A sauce in which you marinate (soak) the meat for several minutes to several days prior to cooking. These are generally acidic mixtures. The more acid a marinade contains, the faster the flavors and tenderizers penetrate into the meat.

Basting sauce: A sauce you brush on your meat during the last 30 minutes of cooking. These are a mixed bag. Some are sweet and some are not. They can also be used to flavor smoking meats.

Barbecue sauce: A sauce you put on your meat after cooking, normally at the time of serving. These come in all flavors and temperaments.

Men truly come into their own with the barbecue, indoors or outdoors. It really is an enjoyable style of cookery. It has an element of showmanship! And if you make a good sauce, it gives you a sense of mastery and can earn you a round of applause from appreciative diners. Barbecue and basting sauces are limited only by your imagination. There may be thousands of them, but I'm going to hold it down to fifty recipes. I've tried to avoid overloading your sensory organs while providing you with as wide of choice of barbecue sauces as possible and I hope I've succeeded. So, if you don't find a sauce that captures your imagination and whets your appetite from this selection, buy one!

As a point of interest, I want to bring your attention to something I'm sure you know, even if you're not sure why; that the word "Ketchup" is spelled variously as "Catsup" and "Catch-Up". You may not know that it comes from the the Chinese language (taken from the Malay language). What's more, you may not care. Catsup and Catch-Up are considered variants of Ketchup. While I generally use a brand called Catsup, to standardize things I will use the word Ketchup.

You use what you like. Ketchup in barbecue sauces is a frequently used ingredient, so I think the explanation is worth while.

Beginner Cooks Alert!

A basting sauce containing any type of sugar should be applied only during the last 30 minutes of cooking. (Experienced cooks know that sugar will burn - and with it, your barbecue!)

Medical point of interest:

I have read in several publications that Worcestershire Sauce interferes with high blood pressure medication and may bring on sustained hypertension. If you are taking this medicine, you may wish to confirm this information with your doctor. If you do not use high blood pressure medication, feel free to add Worcestershire Sauce to any of the following recipes.

BASIC BARBECUE SAUCE

INGREDIENTS:

$1/2$	CUP TOMATO KETCHUP
$1/4$	CUP WATER
2	TABLESPOONS BROWN SUGAR
2	TABLESPOONS VINEGAR
1	TEASPOON PAPRIKA
$1/2$	TEASPOON SALT
$1/2$	TEASPOON CELERY SEED
$1/4$	TEASPOON HOT PEPPER SAUCE

METHOD: Blend all the ingredients in a small sauce pan and bring the mixture to a boil. Reduce the heat to simmer and cook for 10 minutes and serve.

USE ON: Chicken or ribs.

YIELD: 1 cup.

NUTRITIONAL FACTS:

Serving Size: 2 T	Total Fat: 0 g	Sodium: 330 mg	Sugar: 4 g
Calories Per Serving: 25	Sat Fat: 0 g	Total Carbs: 7 g	Protein: 0 g
Fat Calories: 0	Cholest: 0 mg	Fiber: 0 g	

LOUISIANA BAYOU SAUCE

INGREDIENTS:	3	TABLESPOONS VEGETABLE OIL
	1	CUP CHOPPED ONION
	1	CUP CANNED TOMATO SAUCE
	$1/4$	CUP WATER
	$1/2$	CUP MOLASSES
	$1/4$	CUP LEMON JUICE
	2	TABLESPOONS PREPARED MUSTARD
	2	TEASPOONS SALT
	$1/2$	TEASPOON FRESHLY GROUND BLACK PEPPER

METHOD: Saute the onion for 5 minutes then add the remaining ingredients and bring the sauce to a boil. Reduce the heat and simmer for 15 minutes.

USE ON: Pork spareribs, or loin back ribs.

YIELD: 3 cups.

NUTRITIONAL FACTS:

Serving Size: 2 T	Total Fat: 1.5 g	Sodium: 260 mg	Sugar: 4 g
Calories Per Serving: 35	Sat Fat: 0 g	Total Carbs: 6 g	Protein: 0 g
Fat Calories: 15	Cholest: 0 mg	Fiber: 0 g	

HOT MOLASSES SAUCE

INGREDIENTS:

$\frac{1}{2}$	CUP LIGHT MOLASSES
$\frac{1}{2}$	CUP PREPARED MUSTARD
$\frac{1}{2}$	CUP LEMON JUICE
$\frac{1}{4}$	CUP KETCHUP
2	TEASPOONS BOTTLED HOT SAUCE
1	TEASPOON GARLIC SALT

METHOD: Blend all the ingredients together and heat the sauce to boiling. Remove from the heat.

ALTERNATES:

1. Equal amounts of honey and water for the molasses.

2. Vinegar for the lemon juice.

3. Chili sauce or steak sauce for the ketchup.

USE ON: Pork spareribs or back ribs.

YIELD: $1\,\frac{3}{4}$ cups.

NUTRITIONAL FACTS:

Serving Size: 2 T	Total Fat: 0 g	Sodium: 220 mg	Sugar: 7 g
Calories Per Serving: 40	Sat Fat: 0 g	Total Carbs: 9 g	Protein: 0 g
Fat Calories: 0	Cholest: 0 mg	Fiber: 0 g	

LOUISIANA DIPPING SAUCE

Langostino is Spanish for crayfish. It comes from the French word for Spiny Lobster "Langouste". It got its name because of its similarity to the European Spiny Lobster and is found in Central and South American waters. The suffix "ino" means small or little, i.e., crayfish).

INGREDIENTS:

$1/_2$ CUP BUTTER

2   TABLESPOONS LIME JUICE

SEVERAL DROPS BOTTLED HOT SAUCE

METHOD: Melt the butter and add the remaining ingredients. Use some of the sauce to baste your crustaceans while barbecuing. Use the remainder as a dipping sauce.

ALTERNATE: Exchange lemon juice for the lime juice.

USE ON: Shrimp, crayfish and langostino.

YIELD: $2/_3$ cup.

NUTRITIONAL FACTS:			
Serving Size: 1 T	Total Fat: 10 g	Sodium: 100mg	Sugar: 0 g
Calories Per Serving: 90	Sat Fat: 6 g	Total Carbs: 5 g	Protein: 0 g
Fat Calories: 90	Cholest: 25 mg	Fiber: 0 g	

SOUTHERN BELLE BARBECUE SAUCE

When you make this recipe and you want it to be very smooth, puree the sauce before or after cooking.

INGREDIENTS:	1	12 OUNCE JAR PRESERVES (APRICOT OR PEACH)
	3	TABLESPOONS WINE VINEGAR
	2	TABLESPOONS BOTTLED STEAK SAUCE

METHOD: Place all the ingredients into a sauce pan and bring to a boil. Remove the pan from the heat and serve.

ALTERNATE: Exchange steak sauce for an equal amount of honey.

USE ON: Pork roasts, pork chops, spareribs and pork loin, ham steaks chicken and fish.

YIELD: 1 $^3/_4$ cups.

NUTRITIONAL FACTS:

Serving Size: 2 T	Total Fat: 0 g	Sodium: 45 mg	Sugar: 0 g
Calories Per Serving: 50	Sat Fat: 0 g	Total Carbs: 13 g	Protein: 0 g
Fat Calories: 0	Cholest: 0 mg	Fiber: 0 g	

MOLASSES BARBECUE SAUCE

INGREDIENTS:	1	CUP LIGHT OR DARK MOLASSES
	$1/2$	CUP PREPARED MUSTARD
	1	CUP CIDER VINEGAR
	1	TEASPOON SALT

METHOD: Combine all the ingredients and blend well.

USE ON: Chicken or beef.

YIELD: $2 1/2$ cups.

NUTRITIONAL FACTS:

Serving Size: 2 T	Total Fat: 0 g	Sodium: 85 mg	Sugar: 4 g
Calories Per Serving: 20	Sat Fat: 0 g	Total Carbs: 5 g	Protein: 0 g
Fat Calories: 0	Cholest: 0 mg	Fiber: 0 g	

SWEET AND SOUR BARBECUE SAUCE

INGREDIENTS:

4	CUPS BOTTLED CHILI SAUCE
1	CUP VINEGAR
$^1/_2$	CUP SOY SAUCE
1 $^1/_2$	CUPS WATER
2	TABLESPOONS PREPARED MUSTARD
1	TEASPOON SALT
2	TEASPOONS HORSERADISH
1	CUP BROWN SUGAR
2	CUPS CHOPPED ONION

METHOD: Place all the ingredients into a sauce pan and bring to a boil. Reduce the heat and simmer for 15 minutes.

USE ON: Pork back ribs, beef ribs and spit roasted cuts of beef.

YIELD: 8 to 9 cups.

NUTRITIONAL FACTS:

Serving Size: 2 T	Total Fat: 0 g	Sodium: 150 mg	Sugar: 2 g
Calories Per Serving: 25	Sat Fat: 0 g	Total Carbs: 6 g	Protein: 0 g
Fat Calories: 0	Cholest: 0 mg	Fiber: 0 g	

TEXAS HORSERADISH SAUCE

INGREDIENTS:

$^1/_2$	CUP CHILI SAUCE
3	TABLESPOONS LEMON JUICE
$^1/_2$	CUP WATER
2	TABLESPOONS SUGAR
$^1/_2$	TEASPOON GARLIC SALT
$^1/_2$	TEASPOON BOTTLED HOT SAUCE
1	TABLESPOON HORSERADISH

METHOD: Place all the ingredients, except the horseradish, into a sauce pan and bring to a boil. Reduce the heat and simmer for 15 minutes. Remove the pan from the heat and add the horseradish.

USE ON: Burgers, steak and shrimp.

YIELD: 1 $^1/_3$ cups.

ORANGE BARBECUE SAUCE

INGREDIENTS:	2	TEASPOONS FRESHLY GRATED ORANGE PEEL
	$1/_2$	CUP ORANGE JUICE
	$1/_3$	CUP LEMON JUICE
	$1/_3$	CUP KETCHUP
	$1/_4$	CUP BROWN SUGAR
	1	TABLESPOON FINELY CHOPPED ONION
	1	TABLESPOON SOY SAUCE
	PINCH	SALT

METHOD: Place all the ingredients into a sauce pan and bring them to a boil. Then remove the pan from the heat.

USE ON: Pork spareribs.

YIELD: 1 $3/_4$ cups.

NUTRITIONAL FACTS:

Serving Size: 2 T	Total Fat: 0 g	Sodium: 160 mg	Sugar: 5 g
Calories Per Serving: 25	Sat Fat: 0 g	Total Carbs: 7 g	Protein: 0 g
Fat Calories: 0	Cholest: 0 mg	Fiber: 0 g	

ORANGE BASTING SAUCE

INGREDIENTS:

$^1/_2$	CUP GRATED ORANGE RIND
1	CUP WATER
1	CUP SORGHUM SYRUP (OR SIMPLE SUGAR SYRUP)
$^1/_2$	CUP FINELY CHOPPED ONION
1	TEASPOON SALT
1	TEASPOON FRESH GRATED GINGER
4	ORANGES, JUICED
$^1/_3$	CUP SOY SAUCE

METHOD: Place the first 6 ingredients into a sauce pan and bring them to a boil. Reduce the heat to low and cook for 20 minutes. Remove the pan from the heat, add the orange juice and the soy sauce.

USE ON: Ham steaks, pork, pork spareribs and chicken.

YIELD: 5 cups.

NUTRITIONAL FACTS:

Serving Size: 2 T	Total Fat: 0 g	Sodium: 180 mg	Sugar: 5 g
Calories Per Serving: 30	Sat Fat: 0 g	Total Carbs: 8 g	Protein: 0 g
Fat Calories: 0	Cholest: 0 mg	Fiber: 0 g	

ORANGE-MUSTARD BASTING SAUCE

INGREDIENTS:

1	SMALL CAN (6 OUNCES) FROZEN ORANGE JUICE
$1^1/_4$	CUPS WATER
1	CUP PACKED LIGHT BROWN SUGAR
$^1/_4$	CUP CIDER VINEGAR
2	TABLESPOONS PREPARED MUSTARD

METHOD: Place all the ingredients into a sauce pan and bring them to a boil. Reduce the heat and simmer for 20 minutes.

USE ON: Ham steaks, pork spareribs.

YIELD: 3 cups.

NUTRITIONAL FACTS:

Serving Size: 2 T	Total Fat: 0 g	Sodium: 15 mg	Sugar: 8 g
Calories Per Serving: 35	Sat Fat: 0 g	Total Carbs: 9 g	Protein: 0 g
Fat Calories: 0	Cholest: 0 mg	Fiber: 0 g	

LEMON BASTING SAUCE

INGREDIENTS:
$^1/_2$	CUP VEGETABLE OIL
$^3/_4$	CUP FRESH LEMON JUICE
$^1/_4$	CUP WATER
1	TABLESPOONS SALT
2	TABLESPOONS SUGAR
$1^1/_2$	TEASPOONS BOTTLED HOT SAUCE

METHOD: Place all the ingredients into a sauce pan and bring them to a boil. Remove from heat.

USE ON: Chicken and fish.

YIELD: $1\,^2/_3$ cups.

NUTRITIONAL FACTS:

Serving Size: 1 T	Total Fat: 4 g	Sodium: 270 mg	Sugar: 1 g
Calories Per Serving: 40	Sat Fat: 1 g	Total Carbs: 1 g	Protein: 0 g
Fat Calories: 35	Cholest: 0 mg	Fiber: 0 g	

HONEY-ROSEMARY BASTING SAUCE

INGREDIENTS:	$3/4$	CUP FINELY CHOPPED ONION
	1	CLOVE GARLIC, MINCED
	$1/4$	CUP VEGETABLE OIL
	$1\,1/2$	CUPS FRUIT JUICE (YOUR CHOICE, BUT PEAR IS RECOMMENDED)
	$1/2$	WHITE WINE VINEGAR
	$1/4$	CUP HONEY
	1	TEASPOON DRY MUSTARD
	1	TEASPOON SALT
	$1/4$	TEASPOON CRUMBLED ROSEMARY
	$1/4$	TEASPOON WHITE PEPPER

METHOD: Saute the onion and garlic in the oil for about 3 minutes. Add the remaining ingredients and bring to a boil. Reduce the heat and simmer for 5 minutes. Let the sauce cool before using.

USE ON: Chicken.

YIELD: 3 cups.

NUTRITIONAL FACTS:

Serving Size: 2 T	Total Fat: 2.5 g	Sodium: 105 mg	Sugar: 5 g
Calories Per Serving: 45	Sat Fat: 0 g	Total Carbs: 6 g	Protein: 0 g
Fat Calories: 20	Cholest: 0 mg	Fiber: 0 g	

TOMATO BARBECUE SAUCE

Make this sauce about 24 hours before you need it. Early preparation will help the uncooked ingredients meld.

INGREDIENTS:		
	1	CUP CANNED TOMATO SAUCE
	$1/_4$	CUP WHITE VINEGAR
	1	ONION FINELY CHOPPED
	2	CLOVES GARLIC, CRUSHED
	1	TABLESPOON SALT
	1	TABLESPOON SUGAR
	$1/_2$	TEASPOON FRESHLY GROUND BLACK PEPPER
	$1/_4$	TEASPOON CAYENNE PEPPER
	1	TABLESPOON DRY MUSTARD
	1	TEASPOON BOTTLED HOT SAUCE
	1	TEASPOON SORGHUM SYRUP

METHOD: Blend all The ingredients.

USE ON: Beef and lamb.

YIELD: 2 $1/_3$ cups.

NUTRITIONAL FACTS:			
Serving Size: 2 T	Total Fat: 0 g	Sodium: 510 mg	Sugar: 2 g
Calories Per Serving: 15	Sat Fat: 0 g	Total Carbs: 3 g	Protein: 0 g
Fat Calories: 0	Cholest: 0 mg	Fiber: 0 g	

HAM BASTE SAUCES, ONE, TWO AND THREE

Two of these bastes require no preparation other than blending two ingredients. So I'll group these three together and number them 1 through 3.

INGREDIENTS: #1   1   CUP ORANGE JUICE AND 1/2 CUP SHERRY OR SYRUP OF GRENADINE

                   #2   1   BOTTLE OF COLA, FLAVORED ONES TOO!

                   #3   1   CUP PINEAPPLE JUICE W/BROWN SUGAR TO TASTE

METHOD: Blend, if more than 1 ingredient, and it's ready to use.

USE ON: Ham, ham steaks, ham loaf, smoked pork chops.

YIELD: #1 - 1 $^1/_2$ cups.
                   #2 - 1 $^1/_2$ cups.
                   #3 - 1 $^1/_4$ cups.

NUTRITIONAL FACTS:			
Serving Size: 1 T	Total Fat: 0 g	Sodium: 0 mg	Sugar: 1 g
Calories Per Serving: 10	Sat Fat: 0 g	Total Carbs: 1 g	Protein: 0 g
Fat Calories: 0	Cholest: 0 mg	Fiber: 0 g	

LIGHT MOLASSES SAUCE

INGREDIENTS:

$^1/_2$	CUP LIGHT MOLASSES (CANE IS PREFERRED)
$^1/_2$	CUP WINE OR CIDER VINEGAR
$^1/_2$	CUP PREPARED MUSTARD
2	TABLESPOONS BOTTLED HOT SAUCE

METHOD: Blend all the ingredients and then use.

USE ON: Chicken.

YIELD: $1\,^2/_3$ cups.

NUTRITIONAL FACTS:

Serving Size: 2 T	Total Fat: 0 g	Sodium: 110 mg	Sugar: 7 g
Calories Per Serving: 40	Sat Fat: 0 g	Total Carbs: 9 g	Protein: 0 g
Fat Calories: 0	Cholest: 0 mg	Fiber: 0 g	

HOLIDAY BARBECUE SAUCE

INGREDIENTS:

$1/_2$	CUP BUTTER
$1/_2$	CUP LIGHT BROWN SUGAR
2	CUPS KETCHUP
$1/_4$	CUP CHILI SAUCE
$1/_4$	CUP LEMON JUICE
1	CUP CORN OIL
2	CLOVES GARLIC, CRUSHED
$1/_4$	TEASPOON CAYENNE PEPPER
1	TEASPOON DRY MUSTARD

METHOD: Place all the ingredients into a sauce pan and bring to a boil. Reduce the heat to simmer and cook for 15 minutes.

USE ON: Chicken, beef, lamb or veal.

ADDITIONAL USES: As a marinade, or as a basting sauce while cooking or smoking meats.

YIELD: 4 $1/_4$ cups.

NUTRITIONAL FACTS:

Serving Size: 2 T	Total Fat: 9 g	Sodium: 220 mg	Sugar: 4 g
Calories Per Serving: 110	Sat Fat: 3 g	Total Carbs: 7 g	Protein: 0 g
Fat Calories: 80	Cholest: 5mg	Fiber: 0 g	

KANSAS CITY BARBECUE SAUCE

INGREDIENTS:

3	CUPS KETCHUP
2	TABLESPOONS PREPARED HORSERADISH
2	TABLESPOONS HOT MUSTARD
2	TEASPOONS LEMON JUICE
$^1/_2$	TEASPOON CELERY SEED
PINCH	ONION POWDER
PINCH	CAYENNE PEPPER
PINCH	SALT
2-3	DROPS LIQUID SMOKE
	OIL FROM 1 CLOVE PRESSED GARLIC

METHOD: Place all the ingredients into a sauce pan and bring to a boil. Remove from the heat.

USE ON: Pork spareribs

YIELD: 3 $^1/_4$ cups.

NUTRITIONAL FACTS:

Serving Size: 2 T	Total Fat: 0 g	Sodium: 320 mg	Sugar: 3 g
Calories Per Serving: 30	Sat Fat: 0 g	Total Carbs: 8 g	Protein: 1 g
Fat Calories: 0	Cholest: 0 mg	Fiber: 0 g	

TEXAS STYLE BARBECUE RIBS

Here's one sauce that does it all. It's used as a marinade, a basting sauce or a barbecue sauce.

INGREDIENTS:	2	CUPS COFFEE
	1	CUP KETCHUP
	$1/_2$	CUP CIDER VINEGAR
	$1/_2$	CUP BROWN SUGAR
	1	TEASPOON CAYENNE PEPPER
	$1/_2$	TEASPOON GROUND CUMIN
	$1/_2$	TEASPOON DRIED OREGANO (CRUMBLED)
	2	TABLESPOONS LEMON JUICE
	2	TEASPOONS SALT
	2	MEDIUM ONIONS, CHOPPED
	6	CLOVES GARLIC, CRUSHED

METHOD: Place all the ingredients into a sauce pan and bring them to a boil. Reduce the heat, cover and simmer for 20 minutes. Remove and discard the garlic.

USE ON: Beef ribs.

YIELD: 5 cups.

NUTRITIONAL FACTS:

Serving Size: 2 T	Total Fat: 0 g	Sodium: 390 mg	Sugar: 3 g
Calories Per Serving: 15	Sat Fat: 0 g	Total Carbs: 4 g	Protein: 0 g
Fat Calories: 0	Cholest: 0 mg	Fiber: 0 g	

KENTUCKY BOURBON BASTING SAUCE

If your taste buds preferred a sour mash, you could call this a Tennessee Mash basting sauce. If it makes you happy, do it!

INGREDIENTS:	1	CUP KETCHUP
	$^1/_3$	CUP BOURBON
	$^1/_4$	CUP CIDER VINEGAR
	$^1/_4$	CUP MOLASSES
	2	CLOVES GARLIC, CRUSHED
	1	TABLESPOON LEMON JUICE
	1	TABLESPOON SOY SAUCE
	$^1/_2$	TEASPOON DRY MUSTARD
	$^1/_4$	TEASPOON FRESHLY GROUND BLACK PEPPER

METHOD: Blend all the ingredients and use.

USE ON: Beef and pork.

YIELD: 2 cups.

NUTRITIONAL FACTS:

Serving Size: 2 T	Total Fat: 0 g	Sodium: 190 mg	Sugar: 4 g
Calories Per Serving: 45	Sat Fat: 0 g	Total Carbs: 7 g	Protein: 0 g
Fat Calories: 0	Cholest: 0 mg	Fiber: 0 g	

HONEY MUSTARD BASTE

INGREDIENTS: $^3/_4$ CUP MUSTARD (YOUR CHOICE, BUT DIJON IS RECOMMENDED)
$^3/_4$ CUP HONEY
$^1/_2$ CUP ORANGE JUICE
2 TABLESPOONS VEGETABLE OIL

METHOD: Blend all the ingredients and use for basting.

USE ON: Ribs, pork or beef.

YIELD: 2 cups.

NUTRITIONAL FACTS:

Serving Size: 2 T	Total Fat: 1.5 g	Sodium: 220 mg	Sugar: 11 g
Calories Per Serving: 60	Sat Fat: 0 g	Total Carbs: 14 g	Protein: 0 g
Fat Calories: 15	Cholest: 0 mg	Fiber: 0 g	

CHINESE STYLE PORK BASTE

INGREDIENTS:		
	$^1/_2$	CUP HONEY
	1	CUP SOY SAUCE
	1	CUP KETCHUP
	4	CLOVES GARLIC, MINCED
	1	TABLESPOON FRESH GRATED GINGER
	$^1/_2$	TEASPOON CRUSHED RED PEPPER
		SESAME SEEDS TO GARNISH

METHOD: Blend all the ingredients. Use for basting.

USE ON: Spareribs and other cuts of pork.

YIELD: 2 $^1/_2$ cups.

NUTRITIONAL FACTS:

Serving Size: 2 T	Total Fat: 0 g	Sodium: 810 mg	Sugar: 7 g
Calories Per Serving: 40	Sat Fat: 0 g	Total Carbs: 10 g	Protein: 1 g
Fat Calories: 0	Cholest: 0 mg	Fiber: 0 g	

PLUM OR PRUNE BASTING SAUCE

INGREDIENTS:

3	TABLESPOONS SOY SAUCE
1	CUP RED WINE
$1/4$	CUP RED WINE VINEGAR
$1/4$	CUP VEGETABLE OIL
$1/2$	CUP PLUM JAM
	OR
$1/2$	CUP PRUNE BUTTER (LEKVAR)
2	CLOVES GARLIC, PRESSED OR MINCED
1	ONION, FINELY CHOPPED
PINCH	DRIED THYME LEAF, CRUMBLED

METHOD: Place all the ingredients into a sauce pan and bring to a boil. Remove the from the heat.

USE ON: Spareribs.

YIELD: 4 cups.

NUTRITIONAL FACTS:

Serving Size: 2 T	Total Fat: 2.5 g	Sodium: 130 mg	Sugar: 4 g
Calories Per Serving: 50	Sat Fat: 0 g	Total Carbs: 6 g	Protein: 0 g
Fat Calories: 20	Cholest: 0 mg	Fiber: 0 g	

KENTUCKY STYLE BARBECUE SAUCE

INGREDIENTS:

1 ³/₄	CUPS WATER
1	CUP KETCHUP
1 ¹/₂	TEASPOONS CAYENNE PEPPER
1	TEASPOON PAPRIKA
1	TEASPOON DRY MUSTARD
1	TEASPOON GARLIC SALT
¹/₂	TEASPOON ONION POWDER
¹/₂	TEASPOON FRESHLY GROUND BLACK PEPPER

METHOD: Place all the ingredients into a sauce pan and bring to a boil. Reduce the heat to simmer and cook 20 minutes.

USE ON: Chicken and spareribs.

YIELD: 3 cups.

NUTRITIONAL FACTS:

Serving Size: 2 T	Total Fat: 0 g	Sodium: 130 mg	Sugar: 1 g
Calories Per Serving: 10	Sat Fat: 0 g	Total Carbs: 3 g	Protein: 0 g
Fat Calories: 0	Cholest: 0 mg	Fiber: 0 g	

PAPRIKA BARBECUE SAUCE

INGREDIENTS:		
	1	CUP KETCHUP
	$^1/_2$	CUP CIDER VINEGAR
		JUICE FROM 2 LEMONS
	$^1/_2$	CUP BUTTER
	$^1/_4$	CUP PAPRIKA
	$^1/_4$	CUP DARK BROWN SUGAR
	1	TABLESPOON FRESHLY GROUND BLACK PEPPER
	1	TABLESPOON PREPARED HORSERADISH
	2	TEASPOONS DRY MUSTARD
	1	CLOVE GARLIC, MINCED
		SEVERAL SHAKES BOTTLED HOT SAUCE

METHOD: Place all the ingredients into a sauce pan and bring to a boil. Reduce the heat and cook 10 minutes.

USE ON: Beef, spareribs and chicken.

YIELD: 3 cups.

NUTRITIONAL FACTS:

Serving Size: 2 T	Total Fat: 4 g	Sodium: 170 mg	Sugar: 3 g
Calories Per Serving: 60	Sat Fat: 2.5 g	Total Carbs: 6 g	Protein: 0 g
Fat Calories: 40	Cholest: 10 mg	Fiber: 0 g	

WE TRIED THIS SAUCE ... AND

ORIGINAL BARBECUE SAUCE

INGREDIENTS:		
	1	ONION, CHOPPED
	2	CLOVES GARLIC, MINCED
	2	TABLESPOONS BUTTER
	1	26 OUNCE CAN TOMATOES
	$1/2$	CUP CHOPPED CELERY W/LEAVES
	$1/3$	CUP VINEGAR
	$1/2$	BELL PEPPER, CHOPPED
	1	BAY LEAF
	3	TABLESPOONS MOLASSES
	$1\,1/2$	TEASPOONS SALT
	2	TEASPOONS DRY MUSTARD
	2	TEASPOONS BOTTLED HOT SAUCE
	$1/2$	TEASPOON GROUND CLOVES
	$1/2$	TEASPOON GROUND ALLSPICE
	$1/4$	LEMON WEDGE

METHOD: Saute the onion and the garlic in butter until the onion begins to turn color. Add the remaining ingredients and bring to a boil. Reduce the heat and simmer 30 minutes. Strain the sauce.

USE ON: Chicken.

YIELD: 5 cups.

NUTRITIONAL FACTS:

Serving Size: 2 T	Total Fat: 0.5 g	Sodium: 140 mg	Sugar: 2 g
Calories Per Serving: 15	Sat Fat: 0 g	Total Carbs: 3 g	Protein: 0 g
Fat Calories: 5	Cholest: 0 mg	Fiber: 0 g	

HAWAIIAN STYLE BASTING SAUCE

Hawaiian style means it has pineapple juice in it. But you knew that!

INGREDIENTS:		
	$3/4$	CUP PINEAPPLE JUICE
	$1/2$	CUP VEGETABLE OIL
	$1/3$	CUP SOY SAUCE
	$1/4$	CUP LEMON JUICE
	$1/4$	CUP MOLASSES
	1	TEASPOON GROUND GINGER

METHOD:　　　Blend all the ingredients.

USE ON:　　　Chicken, lamb and pork.

YIELD:　　　2 cups.

NUTRITIONAL FACTS:

Serving Size: 2 T	Total Fat: 6 g	Sodium: 310 mg	Sugar: 4 g
Calories Per Serving: 80	Sat Fat: 1 g	Total Carbs: 5 g	Protein: 0 g
Fat Calories: 60	Cholest: 0 mg	Fiber: 0 g	

TEXAS BBQ BASTING SAUCE

INGREDIENTS:

1	POUND MELTED BUTTER
2	TABLESPOONS DRY MUSTARD
$^1/_2$	CUP WINE VINEGAR (GARLIC FLAVORED IF YOU HAVE IT)
3	TABLESPOONS LEMON JUICE
2	TEASPOONS BOTTLED HOT SAUCE
$^1/_2$	TEASPOON CAYENNE PEPPER

METHOD: Blend all the ingredients.

USE ON: Chicken, beef and pork.

YIELD: 2 $^3/_4$ cups.

NUTRITIONAL FACTS:

Serving Size: 2 T	Total Fat: 17 g	Sodium: 200 mg	Sugar: 0 g
Calories Per Serving: 160	Sat Fat: 3 g	Total Carbs: 1 g	Protein: 0 g
Fat Calories: 150	Cholest: 0 mg	Fiber: 0 g	

SWEET AND SOUR BASTING SAUCE

INGREDIENTS: 1 $^1/_2$ CUPS ORANGE MARMALADE
1 $^1/_2$ CUPS CHILI SAUCE
$^1/_4$ CUP CIDER VINEGAR
1 $^1/_2$ TEASPOONS CELERY SEED

METHOD: Blend all the ingredients.

USE ON: Chicken, lamb and spareribs.

YIELD: 3 $^1/_4$ cups.

NUTRITIONAL FACTS:

Serving Size: 2 T	Total Fat: 0 g	Sodium: 180 mg	Sugar: 0 g
Calories Per Serving: 50	Sat Fat: 0 g	Total Carbs: 13 g	Protein: 0 g
Fat Calories: 0	Cholest: 0 mg	Fiber: 0 g	

TENNESSEE BASTING SAUCE

INGREDIENTS:

3	CUPS CIDER VINEGAR
$1/2$	CUP SOY SAUCE
$1/2$	CUP WINE (ANY COLOR)
$1/4$	CUP DRY MUSTARD
$1/4$	CUP KETCHUP
$1/4$	CUP MARGARINE
1	ONION, QUARTERED
1	LEMON, QUARTERED
16	WHOLE CLOVES
10	BAY LEAVES
5	CLOVES GARLIC
1	TABLESPOON SALT
1	TEASPOON WHOLE DRIED OREGANO LEAF
1	TEASPOON WHOLE DRIED ROSEMARY
$1/2$	TEASPOON BLACK PEPPER
$1/4$	TEASPOON CAYENNE PEPPER
$1/4$	TEASPOON BOTTLED HOT SAUCE

METHOD: Place all the ingredients into a sauce pan and bring to a boil. Reduce the heat to simmer and cook for 15 minutes. Strain the sauce and discard the solid ingredients.

USE ON: Fresh ham or fresh picnic ham, boneless shoulder roast, boneless pork butt or pork spareribs.

YIELD: 5 cups.

NUTRITIONAL FACTS:

Serving Size: 2 T	Total Fat: 1 g	Sodium: 370 mg	Sugar: 0 g
Calories Per Serving: 20	Sat Fat: 0 g	Total Carbs: 2 g	Protein: 0 g
Fat Calories: 10	Cholest: 0 mg	Fiber: 0 g	

HORSERADISH BARBECUE SAUCE

INGREDIENTS:

1	ONION, FINELY CHOPPED
1	CUP WATER
1	CUP KETCHUP
$^1/_2$	CUP CIDER VINEGAR
1	TABLESPOON CHOPPED PARSLEY
1	TABLESPOON BROWN SUGAR
1	TABLESPOON PREPARED HORSERADISH
1	TABLESPOON MUSTARD
1	TEASPOON BLACK PEPPER

METHOD: Place all the ingredients into a sauce pan and bring to a boil. Reduce the heat and simmer for 10 minutes.

USE ON: Beef and pork.

YIELD: 3 $^1/_2$ cups.

NUTRITIONAL FACTS:

Serving Size: 2 T	Total Fat: 0 g	Sodium: 115 mg	Sugar: 2 g
Calories Per Serving: 15	Sat Fat: 0 g	Total Carbs: 4 g	Protein: 0 g
Fat Calories: 0	Cholest: 0 mg	Fiber: 0 g	

BEER BASTING SAUCE

There are those who add beer to almost anything. If that's you, this is your recipe.

INGREDIENTS:

1 ¹/₂	CUPS CHILI SAUCE
1	CUP BEER
2	TABLESPOONS GRATED ONION
2	TABLESPOONS CIDER VINEGAR
2	TEASPOONS WHITE SUGAR
2	TEASPOONS CHILI POWDER

METHOD: Place all the ingredients into a sauce pan and bring to a boil. Let it boil for 1 minute. Remove from the heat.

USE ON: Beef, chicken, spareribs.

YIELD: 3 cups.

NUTRITIONAL FACTS:

Serving Size: 2 T	Total Fat: 0 g	Sodium: 230 mg	Sugar: 0 g
Calories Per Serving: 25	Sat Fat: 0 g	Total Carbs: 5 g	Protein: 0 g
Fat Calories: 0	Cholest: 0 mg	Fiber: 0 g	

CREOLE BARBECUE SAUCE

There is a substantial difference between Creole and Cajun cooking. Many Americans confuse the terms because they have never experienced the difference between the two kinds of cookery. There are times the differences can be confusing. Creole food is a blend of French, Spanish and some Indian cooking, taught to Blacks and then re-interpreted by them. The result is a very satisfying combination of flavors with visual and gustatory appeal. On the other hand Cajun food (Acadian) is French Celtic* cooking adapted to a whole range of game, seafood and crops found in Louisiana.

* Most of the Acadians from Nova Scotia and New Brunswick who found their way to the bayous of Louisiana were originally from Brittany. That region of France was historically peopled by the Celtics.

INGREDIENTS:	2	CUPS WATER
	2	CUPS VINEGAR
	$1/2$	CUP MARGARINE
	$1/4$	CUP SUGAR
	$1/4$	CUP KETCHUP
	2	SHAKES BOTTLED HOT SAUCE
	1	LARGE ONION, CHOPPED
	6	RIBS CELERY, CHOPPED
	1	LEMON, THINLY SLICED
	1	BAY LEAF
	1	TABLESPOON SALT
	2	TABLESPOONS CAYENNE PEPPER
	2	TABLESPOONS CELERY SEED
	$1/4$	TEASPOON GRANULATED GARLIC
	1	TEASPOON DRY MUSTARD
	1	TEASPOON BLACK PEPPER

METHOD: Place all the ingredients into a sauce pan and bring to a boil. Reduce the heat and simmer for 30 minutes. Strain the sauce.

USE ON: Chicken, beef and pork.

YIELD: 8 cups.

NUTRITIONAL FACTS:

Serving Size: 2 T	Total Fat: 2 g	Sodium: 160 mg	Sugar: 1 g
Calories Per Serving: 25	Sat Fat: 0 g	Total Carbs: 2 g	Protein: 0 g
Fat Calories: 15	Cholest: 0 mg	Fiber: 0 g	

MUSTARD BARBECUE AND BASTING SAUCE

INGREDIENTS:

2	CUPS PREPARED MUSTARD
1	CUP MAYONNAISE
$1/_2$	CUP WATER
$1/_3$	CUP KETCHUP
$1/_4$	CUP MARGARINE
2	TABLESPOONS SUGAR
1	TEASPOON SALT
$1/_4$	TEASPOON BLACK PEPPER
$1/_4$	TEASPOON LIQUID SMOKE

METHOD: Place all the ingredients into a sauce pan and bring to a boil. Reduce the heat to simmer and cook for 10 minutes.

USE ON: Chicken, pork, beef, lamb and ribs.

YIELD: 4 $1/_4$ cups.

NUTRITIONAL FACTS:

Serving Size: 2 T	Total Fat: 7 g	Sodium: 340 mg	Sugar: 1 g
Calories Per Serving: 80	Sat Fat: 1 g	Total Carbs: 2 g	Protein: 1 g
Fat Calories: 70	Cholest: 5 mg	Fiber: 0 g	

WE TRIED THIS SAUCE ... AND

LOVED IT ( )
HATED IT ( )
MAYBE WE'LL TRY IT AGAIN ( )
WE'LL USE IT FOR UNWELCOME GUESTS ( )

MUSTARD BASTING SAUCE

INGREDIENTS: 1   POUND MARGARINE (2 CUPS)
              1   CUP WHITE VINEGAR
              $^1/_3$ CUP PREPARED MUSTARD
              $^1/_4$ CUP SOY SAUCE

METHOD: Melt the margarine and add the remaining ingredients.

USE ON: Chicken.

YIELD: 3 $^1/_2$ cups.

NUTRITIONAL FACTS:

Serving Size: 2 T	Total Fat: 13 g	Sodium: 330 mg	Sugar: 0 g
Calories Per Serving: 120	Sat Fat: 2.5 g	Total Carbs: 1 g	Protein: 0 g
Fat Calories: 120	Cholest: 0 mg	Fiber: 0 g	

WINE BARBECUE SAUCE

INGREDIENTS:		
	1	CUP WHITE WINE
	1	CUP CANNED TOMATOES OR TOMATO SAUCE
	1 1/2	CUPS BEEF BOUILLON
	1	TABLESPOON LEMON JUICE
	1/4	CUP WORCESTERSHIRE SAUCE
	1/2	TEASPOON TABASCO SAUCE
	1/2	CUP OLIVE OIL
	1	TABLESPOON SUGAR
	1	BAY LEAF
	1	TEASPOON SALT
	1/2	TEASPOON FRESHLY GROUND BLACK PEPPER
	1	TEASPOON SPANISH SEASONING OR CHILI POWDER
	2	CLOVES GARLIC, MINCED
	1/2	ONION, CHOPPED
	1/2	CUP CHOPPED CELERY
	1	CUP OKRA
	1/2	TEASPOON OREGANO LEAF
	1/2	TEASPOON DRIED BASIL

METHOD: Combine all the ingredients in a sauce pan and bring to a boil. Reduce the heat to simmer and cook for 45 minutes.

At this point you can either:

1.   Strain the sauce and discard the solids and use as is.

Or

2.   Remove and discard the bay leaf. Blenderize the sauce until it's fairly smooth.

USE ON: Chicken, ham, hot dogs, grilled pork steaks, lamb shoulder chops.

YIELD: 8 cups.

NUTRITIONAL FACTS:			
Serving Size: 2 T	Total Fat: 2.5 g	Sodium: 150 mg	Sugar: 1 g
Calories Per Serving: 30	Sat Fat: 0 g	Total Carbs: 1 g	Protein: 0 g
Fat Calories: 25	Cholest: 0 mg	Fiber: 0 g	

PONG BASTING SAUCE

In the late 50's, my first sales job in the food industry was selling Stokley-Van Camp products. At that time Stokley had a group of mixed juices, featuring pineapple paired with a citrus. Specifically pineapple/grapefruit, pineapple/orange and pineapple/lime. Stokley abbreviated the blended juices respectively to the cutesy names of Ping, Pong and Pili.

This is a round-about way of explaining the name of this basting sauce.

INGREDIENTS:

1	CUP PINEAPPLE JUICE
1	CUP ORANGE JUICE
$^1/_2$	CUP KETCHUP
2	TEASPOONS PREPARED MUSTARD
$^1/_4$	CUP HONEY
1	TABLESPOON BUTTER
2	TEASPOON SALT

METHOD: Place all the ingredients into a sauce pan and bring the sauce to a boil. Reduce the heat to simmer and cook for 30 minutes or until the sauce is slightly thickened.

USE ON: Chicken or pork.

YIELD: 3 cups.

NUTRITIONAL FACTS:

Serving Size: 2 T	Total Fat: 0.5 g	Sodium: 260 mg	Sugar: 6 g
Calories Per Serving: 30	Sat Fat: 0 g	Total Carbs: 7 g	Protein: 0 g
Fat Calories: 0	Cholest: 0 mg	Fiber: 0 g	

"This page is blank by Design"

CHAPTER 20

SAUCES MADE FOR EGG DISHES

Have you ever considered how wonderful eggs really are? They are one of the few foods that can be eaten for breakfast, lunch, snacks, dinner, dessert and beverages. Wow! They are virtually indispensable to baking and they act as a binder for many foods as well as an outstanding thickening agent. Well right here in Chapter 19, you'll find recipes that will allow you to add a variety of flavors to your eggs.

Also scan Chapter 2 for additional sauces to be used on egg dishes.

HOLLANDAISE SAUCE

Hollandaise is probably the worlds most famous sauce for eggs. It is the stuff Eggs Benedict are covered with. It used to be an elegant dish served in many of America's fine restaurants, particularly during brunch. If you've never eaten Eggs Benedict, it is a slice of boiled ham or Canadian bacon, sauted in butter and laid on one half of an English muffin. Then a poached egg is placed on the ham and the whole thing is covered with Hollandaise sauce. It is always served in pairs, garnished with a sprinkle of chopped parsley or paprika pepper or both. Now you can buy it in sandwich form without the Hollandaise where it is known far and wide as an "Egg McMuffin". Gottcha!

It is really important that a double boiler be used in the preparation of this sauce. It can also be done very carefully over direct heat if you use a diffuser to keep your cooking pan above the heat (especially needed if you have an electric stove). Recognize that you are adding egg yolks to melted butter to make the sauce and if your pan gets too warm, the eggs will cook..., and the sauce is ruined. Then you'll have to throw it out and start over.

INGREDIENTS:	1	CUP BUTTER
	3	EGG YOLKS, LIGHTLY BEATEN
	$^1/_4$	CUP LEMON JUICE
	$^1/_2$	TEASPOON SALT
	SMALL	PINCH OF CAYENNE PEPPER

METHOD: Melt the butter in a double boiler, keeping the upper unit from touching the hot water. Whisk in the egg yolks, lemon juice, salt and cayenne pepper. Continue whisking the mixture until it begins to thicken. Remove from the heat and use at once. This sauce will not keep.

USE ON: Eggs Benedict, poached eggs on toast, or steamed asparagus.

YIELD: 1 $^1/_2$ cups (multiply this recipe as many times as needed).

NUTRITIONAL FACTS:

Serving Size: 3 T	Total Fat: 26 g	Sodium: 410 mg	Sugar: 0 g
Calories Per Serving: 240	Sat Fat: 16 g	Total Carbs: 1 g	Protein: 1 g
Fat Calories: 240	Cholest: 150 mg	Fiber: 0 g	

HOLLANDAISE SAUCE II

In this version you can substantially vary the taste by swapping the cream with either sweet cream or sour cream. If you want to ease up on the cholesterol content, swap the cream for yogurt or a synthetic sour cream.

Again it is probably best to use a double boiler to make the sauce. But that is not an absolute. You can get by if you use a heat diffuser between your pan and the heat.

INGREDIENTS:		
	$^1/_4$	CUP BUTTER
	$^1/_4$	CUP CREAM
	2	EGG YOLKS, BEATEN
	1	TABLESPOON LEMON JUICE
		SALT TO TASTE
	PINCH	CAYENNE PEPPER

METHOD: Melt the butter, then add the cream and beaten egg yolks while whisking. Add the remaining ingredients and continue whisking until the sauce thickens. Remove from the heat and whisk for a moment longer.

USE ON: Poached egg dishes, asparagus and other green vegetables.

YIELD: $^3/_4$ cup.

NUTRITIONAL FACTS:

Serving Size: 3 T	Total Fat: 20 g	Sodium: 135 mg	Sugar: 1 g
Calories Per Serving: 190	Sat Fat: 12 g	Total Carbs: 1 g	Protein: 2 g
Fat Calories: 180	Cholest: 170 mg	Fiber: 0 g	

MOCK HOLLANDAISE SAUCE

This sauce is the same as the preceding, with one exception. You'll exchange the cream for flour and milk. It is a few calories less than regular hollandaise. but not much. Or you could look at it as though it were a white sauce with egg yolks. It won't change the calorie count, but it may change your opinion about it. It also has a small cooking plus — you can use direct heat.

INGREDIENTS:

$1/4$	CUP BUTTER
3	TABLESPOONS FLOUR
$1/2$	TEASPOON SALT
1	CUP MILK
1	TABLESPOON LEMON JUICE
PINCH	CAYENNE PEPPER
2	EGG YOLKS, BEATEN

METHOD:

1. Melt the butter in a sauce pan and whisk in the flour and salt, then add the milk while whisking constantly until the sauce has thickened.

2. Remove the sauce from the heat and whisk in the lemon juice and cayenne. Pour the mixture into the beaten egg yolks, whisking constantly until smooth.

USE ON: Poached egg dishes and green vegetables.

YIELD: 1 $1/2$ cups.

NUTRITIONAL FACTS:

Serving Size: 3 T	Total Fat: 8 g	Sodium: 210 mg	Sugar: 2 g
Calories Per Serving: 90	Sat Fat: 4.5 g	Total Carbs: 4 g	Protein: 2 g
Fat Calories: 70	Cholest: 70 mg	Fiber: 0 g	

MADEIRA SAUCE

If you were around in the fifties, you may remember a novelty song that had a short but popular run, with lyrics sung by an aging lothario encouraging a sweet young thing to "have some Madeira m'dear...,". I don't remember if she ever did drink the Madeira, but there was a lot of giggling and chortling going on between the inducements and it was a cute song. Which by the way, has absolutely nothing to do with this sauce.

INGREDIENTS:	2	TABLESPOONS BUTTER
	2	TABLESPOONS FLOUR
	2	CUPS BOUILLON
		SALT TO TASTE (YOU MAY WISH TO PASS ON THE SALT IF YOUR BOUILLON IS SALTY)
		FRESHLY GROUND BLACK PEPPER TO TASTE
	$^1/_2$	CUP MADEIRA WINE

OPTION: For a thicker sauce omit 1 cup of the bouillon.

METHOD: 1.   Make a roux using the butter and flour.

2. Add the bouillon, salt and pepper. Cook while whisking constantly until the sauce has thickened.

3. Whisk in the Madeira and remove the sauce from the heat.

USE ON: Shirred or poached eggs.

YIELD: 2 $^1/_2$ cups.

NUTRITIONAL FACTS:

Serving Size: 3 T	Total Fat: 7 g	Sodium: 1020 mg	Sugar: 1 g
Calories Per Serving: 100	Sat Fat: 4 g	Total Carbs: 4 g	Protein: 1 g
Fat Calories: 60	Cholest: 15 mg	Fiber: 0 g	

CREAM SAUCE

This is an extra rich white sauce using cream instead of milk. It also comes with several optional flavor enhancers. Each one gives your sauce a different taste.

INGREDIENTS:	1	TABLESPOON BUTTER
	1	TABLESPOON FLOUR
	1	CUP WHIPPING CREAM
	$1/_2$	TEASPOON SALT
		FRESHLY GROUND BLACK PEPPER TO TASTE
OPTIONS:		ADD 1, SEVERAL OR ALL;
	PINCH	GROUND CLOVES
	PINCH	CAYENNE PEPPER
	$1/_2$	TEASPOON DRY MUSTARD
	1	BAY LEAF
	1	CUP MUSHROOMS, CANNED OR PRECOOKED

METHOD:

1. Make a roux by cooking the flour in the butter for several minutes over low heat.

2. Whisk in the whipping cream and cook while whisking until thickened.

3. Add your choice(s) of the option(s) and cook for several additional minutes.

4. Remove and discard the bay leaf if used, serve.

USE ON: Poached eggs or omelets.

YIELD: 1 cup.

NUTRITIONAL FACTS:			
Serving Size: 2 T	Total Fat: 10 g	Sodium: 160 mg	Sugar: 1 g
Calories Per Serving: 90	Sat Fat: 6 g	Total Carbs: 1 g	Protein: 1 g
Fat Calories: 90	Cholest: 35 mg	Fiber: 0 g	

RUM SAUCE

When you get tired of maple syrup or powdered sugar on your french toast, try this sauce.

INGREDIENTS:	$^1/_4$	CUP DARK RUM
	$^1/_2$	CUP WATER
	2	TABLESPOONS BUTTER
	1	CUP SUGAR

METHOD: Combine all the ingredients into a sauce pan and bring the sauce to a boil. Reduce the heat to simmer and cook until the sugar is completely dissolved. Use it warm or at room temperature.

USE ON: French toast, any filled sandwich dipped into eggs and grilled.

YIELD: 1 $^1/_4$ cups.

NUTRITIONAL FACTS:

Serving Size: 2 T	Total Fat: 2 g	Sodium: 25 mg	Sugar: 11 g
Calories Per Serving: 80	Sat Fat: 1 g	Total Carbs: 12 g	Protein: 0 g
Fat Calories: 20	Cholest: 5 mg	Fiber: 0 g	

CHEESE SAUCE

This sauce is not far removed from a non-alcoholic fondue, and it makes a nice taste change for your egg dishes. The cheese choice is yours to make. For an Italian touch, use Parmesan, Asiago, Gorgonzola or Romano. For a Greek taste try Feta or Mizithra. Go Scandinavian with a goat cheese, Swiss with Swiss cheese or even Gruyere, go English with Cheddar, go..., well, you get the idea.

INGREDIENTS:	2	TABLESPOONS BUTTER
	2	TABLESPOONS FLOUR
	1	CUP MILK
	$^1/_2$	CUP FRESHLY GRATED OR SHREDDED SHARP CHEESE
	PINCH	NUTMEG OR MACE

METHOD: If you have some roux, put 2 tablespoons into a sauce pan.

Or, melt the butter, whisk in the flour and cook for about 3 minutes. Add the milk, bring it to scalding and whisk in the cheese. Cook until the sauce is smooth. Add nutmeg and taste for salt.

USE ON: Poached eggs, plain omelets.

YIELD: $1\,^2/_3$ cups.

NUTRITIONAL FACTS:

Serving Size: 3 T	Total Fat: 7 g	Sodium: 90 mg	Sugar: 2 g
Calories Per Serving: 80	Sat Fat: 4 g	Total Carbs: 3 g	Protein: 3 g
Fat Calories: 60	Cholest: 20 mg	Fiber: 0 g	

CHAPTER 21

SAUCES FOR SANDWICH FILLINGS

SAUCE FOR SLOPPY JOES

My mother often made sloppy joes during the 40's whenever ground beef was available (meat was rationed back then). She made it for two reasons, first because it is good, and second because my sister and I loved the slightly sweet, sloppy sandwiches they made. If it's new to you, try it, you' may love it too.

Try this sauce with cooked and crumbled ground chicken, turkey, veal, pork or for that matter, lamb.

INGREDIENTS:	2	TABLESPOONS BUTTER
	$1/_2$	CUP MINCED ONION
	$1/_2$	CUP CHOPPED CELERY
	$1/_2$	CUP CHOPPED BELL PEPPER
	$1/_2$	CUP CHOPPED MUSHROOMS
	$1/_4$	CUP CHILI SAUCE
	$1/_2$	CUP WATER
		SEASON TO TASTE

METHOD: Saute the onion, celery, bell pepper and mushrooms until limp. Add the remaining ingredients and cook covered for about 10 minutes.

USE ON: 1 pound cooked, crumbled and drained ground beef.

When you add the ground beef, bring the sauce to a boil. Reduce the heat and simmer for 5 minutes. Serve on big barbecue or hamburger buns.

YIELD: 2 $1/_4$ cups.

NUTRITIONAL FACTS:

Serving Size: 2 T	Total Fat: 1.5 g	Sodium: 75 mg	Sugar: 1 g
Calories Per Serving: 20	Sat Fat: 1 g	Total Carbs: 2 g	Protein: 0 g
Fat Calories: 15	Cholest: 5 mg	Fiber: 0 g	

SLOPPY JOES SAUCE TOO!

This sauce is somewhat sweeter than the preceding one and uses a fair amount of cheese.

INGREDIENTS:

2	TABLESPOONS EXTRA LIGHT OLIVE OIL
$1/_2$	CUP CHOPPED ONION
$3/_4$	CUP CHILI SAUCE
$1/_2$	CUP WATER
1	TABLESPOON VINEGAR
PINCH	CRUSHED RED PEPPER
1	TEASPOON DRY MUSTARD
$1\,1/_2$	CUPS SHREDDED CHEESE YOUR CHOICE; CHEDDAR, COLBY, JACK, JARLSBERG

METHOD: Saute the onion in the oil until the edges begin to brown. Add the chili sauce, water, vinegar, crushed red pepper and mustard. Blend well and continue cooking for about 5 minutes. Stir in the cheese. When the cheese is melted, mix it in with your cooked meat.

USE ON: Cooked, crumbled ground meat such as beef, pork, chicken or turkey.

YIELD: 2 $1/_2$ cups.

NUTRITIONAL FACTS:

Serving Size: 2 T	Total Fat: 4 g	Sodium: 190 mg	Sugar: 0 g
Calories Per Serving: 60	Sat Fat: 2 g	Total Carbs: 3 g	Protein: 2 g
Fat Calories: 35	Cholest: 10 mg	Fiber: 0 g	

CHEESE SAUCE

If you have a double broiler, use it for this sauce. If not, use a diffuser to raise your pan off the direct heat.

INGREDIENTS:	$^1/_2$	POUND CHEDDAR CHEESE OR ANY OTHER CHEESE
	1	CUP MILK OR BEER
	1	TEASPOON DRY MUSTARD
	$^1/_5$	TEASPOON DRY BASIL LEAF

METHOD: Place all the ingredients into a sauce pan and cook until the cheese is melted and the sauce is smooth.

USE ON: Grilled or broiled hamburgers, or mixed with cooked and crumbled hamburger.

YIELD: 3 cups.

NUTRITIONAL FACTS:			
Serving Size: 2 T	Total Fat: 5 g	Sodium: 90 mg	Sugar: 0 g
Calories Per Serving: 70	Sat Fat: 3 g	Total Carbs: 1 g	Protein: 4 g
Fat Calories: 45	Cholest: 15 mg	Fiber: 0 g	

WE TRIED THIS SAUCE ... AND

LOVED IT (   )
HATED IT (   )
MAYBE WE'LL TRY IT AGAIN (   )
WE'LL USE IT FOR UNWELCOME GUESTS (   )

SAUCE FOR ITALIAN STYLE SLOPPY JOES

I love Italian sausage and I eat them for breakfast, lunch or dinner, whether fried, roasted, broiled, grilled or barbecued. A special favorite of mine is when they're slowly simmered in tomatoes. In this recipe they are used to make the filling for sloppy joes.

INGREDIENTS:

1	POUND COOKED AND CRUMBLED ITALIAN SAUSAGE (YOU CAN USE THE OIL FROM THE COOKED SAUSAGE TO SAUTE THE VEGETABLES. IF YOU DO, THEN OMIT THE OLIVE OIL.)
2	TABLESPOONS OLIVE OIL
1	BELL PEPPER, CHOPPED
1	ONION, CHOPPED
1	CLOVE GARLIC
1	CUP SLICED MUSHROOMS
$^1/_4$	TEASPOON WHOLE LEAF OREGANO
1	8 OUNCE CAN TOMATO SAUCE
	OR
4	CHOPPED ITALIAN STYLE TOMATOES (CANNED OR FRESH)

METHOD:

1. Cook and crumble the sausage as suggested above.

2. Saute the bell pepper, onion and garlic in the oil. When the onion wilts or begins to color add the mushrooms and cook for 3 minutes. Then add the tomatoes, oregano and the sausage. Simmer for 10 minutes more.

USE ON: As a sandwich filling on large barbecue buns, sweet Italian or French sandwich rolls.

Or open faced as a mini pizza on English muffins. Add a little shredded mozzarella and broil until the cheese melts.

YIELD: 2 $^3/_4$ cups.

NUTRITIONAL FACTS:

Serving Size: 2 T	Total Fat: 4.5 g	Sodium: 170 mg	Sugar: 1 g
Calories Per Serving: 60	Sat Fat: 1.5 g	Total Carbs: 1 g	Protein: 3 g
Fat Calories: 40	Cholest: 10 mg	Fiber: 0 g	

CREAMY CHEESE SANDWICH FILLING

With this sandwich filling you can choose from three soft and creamy cheeses.

INGREDIENTS:	8	OUNCES RICOTTA, COTTAGE OR CREAM CHEESE
	$1/_3$	CUP SHREDDED SWISS, JACK OR PROVOLONE
	2	TEASPOONS HORSERADISH
		OR
	$1/_4$	TEASPOON OF A LOUISIANA HOT SAUCE
	3	TABLESPOONS MILK
	1	TEASPOON CHOPPED PARSLEY OR GREEN ONION

METHOD: Cream the cottage cheese, if used. Let the cheeses warm to room temperature and thoroughly blend all the ingredients. Use at room temperature.

USE ON: Toast (as a sandwich), toast points (as a canape), crackers, or use as a great filling for celery ribs.

YIELD: 1 $1/_2$ cups.

NUTRITIONAL FACTS:

Serving Size: 2 Tsp	Total Fat: 1.5 g	Sodium: 10 mg	Sugar: 0 g
Calories Per Serving: 20	Sat Fat: 1 g	Total Carbs: 0 g	Protein: 1 g
Fat Calories: 10	Cholest: 5 mg	Fiber: 0 g	

CHAPTER 22

MARINADES

A Marinade is a sauce in which you pickle (marinate) meat from several minutes to several days prior to cooking. The more acid a marinade contains, the faster the flavor and tenderizers penetrate into the meat.

The best marinating containers are glass, crockery, stainless steel or high quality plastic.

MARINADE FOR BEEF

(AKA: SAUERBRATEN)

You may know this marinade and sauce by it's German name, Sauerbraten. If you do it's not because there is a German restaurant on every corner, but because Americans of German heritage make up the largest single ethnic group in the United States (those of British heritage are actually a larger number, but that includes four groups, English, Scot, Welsh and Irish). Germans love sour foods and that is an extensive list spanning the entire spectrum of German cookery and includes all manner of pickled vegetables.

Historical note: There is a story that during the revolutionary war the Continental Congress came within a single vote of replacing English with German as our national language. This situation came about because the revolutionaries were angry with King George III over his excessive taxation without representation. Since 97% of the colonists at that time were British the notion of these English speaking people summarily rejecting their native language for German was highly unlikely.

INGREDIENTS:	2	CUPS CIDER VINEGAR
	2	CUPS WATER
	1	ONION, SLICED
	$^1/_4$	CUP SUGAR
	2	TEASPOONS SALT
	12	WHOLE PEPPERCORNS OR 1/2 TEASPOON CRACKED PEPPER
	3	WHOLE CLOVES
	2	BAY LEAVES
	1	LEMON, QUARTERED

METHOD:
1. Place all the ingredients into a stainless steel sauce pan and bring to scalding (don't boil). Remove from the heat.

2. Place your uncooked meat into a coverable non-aluminum container

and pour the hot marinade over it, then let it cool before refrigerating.

3.   Marinate for 4 days before you cook the meat.

USE ON: Any cut of beef or venison suitable for pot roast.

YIELD: 5 cups.

NUTRITIONAL FACTS:			
Serving Size: 2 Tsp	Total Fat: 0 g	Sodium: 40 mg	Sugar: 0 g
Calories Per Serving: 0	Sat Fat: 0 g	Total Carbs: 1 g	Protein: 0 g
Fat Calories: 0	Cholest: 0 mg	Fiber: 0 g	

Marinade For Lamb

INGREDIENTS:		
	1	CUP LEMON JUICE
	$^1/_2$	CUP OLIVE OIL
	1 $^1/_2$	TABLESPOONS SALT
	1	TABLESPOON CRACKED BLACK PEPPER
	1	CLOVE GARLIC
	6	GREEN ONIONS
	2	TEASPOONS WHOLE CORIANDER SEED
	PINCH	CAYENNE

METHOD: Blend all the ingredients.

USE ON: Leg of lamb or other large lamb pieces. Marinate for a minimum of 4 hours and up to 24 hours before cooking.

Cooking can be done on a spit, oven roasted or barbecued.

YIELD: 2 cups.

NUTRITIONAL FACTS:

Serving Size: 2 Tsp	Total Fat: 2.5 g	Sodium: 230 mg	Sugar: 0 g
Calories Per Serving: 25	Sat Fat: 0 g	Total Carbs: 1 g	Protein: 0 g
Fat Calories: 20	Cholest: 0 mg	Fiber: 0 g	

HERBED LEMON MARINADE

INGREDIENTS:

$1/3$	CUP VEGETABLE OIL
$1/3$	CUP LEMON JUICE
1	TEASPOON FRESHLY GRATED LEMON RIND
1	CLOVE GARLIC, MINCED
1	TEASPOON SALT
1	TEASPOON DRIED ROSEMARY, CRUMBLED
$1/4$	TEASPOON FRESHLY GROUND BLACK PEPPER

METHOD: Blend all the ingredients and pour the marinade over your meat. Marinate 4 to 24 hours in the refrigerator, turning pieces occasionally.

ALTERNATE: Substitute the lemon juice with cider vinegar and/or the garlic with 1/2 teaspoon dried basil leaf.

USE ON: Chicken, beef or lamb.

YIELD: $3/4$ cup.

NUTRITIONAL FACTS:

Serving Size: 2 Tsp	Total Fat: 4.5 g	Sodium: 150 mg	Sugar: 0 g
Calories Per Serving: 40	Sat Fat: 1 g	Total Carbs: 0 g	Protein: 0 g
Fat Calories: 40	Cholest: 0 mg	Fiber: 0 g	

BEER AND HONEY MARINADE

INGREDIENTS:	2	12 OUNCE CANS BEER
	1	CUP HONEY
	2	TEASPOONS DRY MUSTARD
	1	TEASPOON CHILI POWDER
	2	TABLESPOONS LEMON JUICE
	1	TEASPOON SALT
	2	TEASPOONS FRESHLY GROUND BLACK PEPPER
	1	TEASPOON RUBBED SAGE
	1	TEASPOON SUGAR

METHOD: Blend all the ingredients and pour the marinade over your meat. Marinate 1 to 24 hours in the refrigerator, turning pieces occasionally.

USE ON: Spareribs.

YIELD: $2\,^2/_3$ cups.

NUTRITIONAL FACTS:

Serving Size: 2 Tsp	Total Fat: 0 g	Sodium: 20 mg	Sugar: 3 g
Calories Per Serving: 10	Sat Fat: 0 g	Total Carbs: 3 g	Protein: 0 g
Fat Calories: 0	Cholest: 0 mg	Fiber: 0 g	

POLYNESIAN MARINADE

INGREDIENTS:

$1/4$	CUP HONEY
$1/4$	CUP ORANGE JUICE
2	TABLESPOONS LEMON JUICE
$1/4$	CUP SOY SAUCE
6	KUMQUATS, MINCED
2	TABLESPOON FRESH GRATED ORANGE PEEL
$1/2$	TEASPOON GINGER
$1/4$	TEASPOON BLACK PEPPER

METHOD: Blend all the ingredients and pour the marinade over your meat. Marinate 4 to 24 hours in the refrigerator, turning pieces occasionally.

USE ON: Chicken.

YIELD: $1\,1/4$ cups.

NUTRITIONAL FACTS:

Serving Size: 2 Tsp	Total Fat: 0 g	Sodium: 110 mg	Sugar: 2 g
Calories Per Serving: 10	Sat Fat: 0 g	Total Carbs: 3 g	Protein: 0 g
Fat Calories: 0	Cholest: 0 mg	Fiber: 0 g	

SHERRY MARINADE

INGREDIENTS:

$^1/_2$	CUP SHERRY
$^1/_3$	CUP HONEY
3	TABLESPOONS LEMON JUICE
1 $^1/_2$	TEASPOONS CINNAMON

METHOD: Blend all the ingredients and pour the marinade over your meat. Marinate 4 to 24 hours in the refrigerator, turning pieces occasionally.

USE ON: Chicken, pork loin and spareribs.

YIELD: $^3/_4$ cup.

NUTRITIONAL FACTS:

Serving Size: 2 Tsp	Total Fat: 0 g	Sodium: 0 mg	Sugar: 3 g
Calories Per Serving: 15	Sat Fat: 0 g	Total Carbs: 3 g	Protein: 0 g
Fat Calories: 0	Cholest: 0 mg	Fiber: 0 g	

RABBIT MARINADE

This is a good marinade for rabbit which is dipped in batter and then deep fried, or rolled in seasoned flour and sauteed.

INGREDIENTS:	$^1/_2$	CUP OIL
	3	TABLESPOONS LEMON JUICE
	2	TABLESPOONS CHOPPED ONION
	$1\,^1/_2$	TABLESPOONS SALT
	$^1/_2$	TEASPOON CRACKED BLACK PEPPER

METHOD: Blend all the ingredients and pour the marinade over your rabbit. Marinate for 2 hours, turning occasionally.

USE ON: Disjointed rabbit.

YIELD: $^3/_4$ cup.

NUTRITIONAL FACTS:

Serving Size: 2 Tsp	Total Fat: 5 g	Sodium: 500 mg	Sugar: 0 g
Calories Per Serving: 45	Sat Fat: 1 g	Total Carbs: 0 g	Protein: 0 g
Fat Calories: 45	Cholest: 0 mg	Fiber: 0 g	

GILLY, GILLY, HASENPFEFFER MARINADE

My name for this recipe reminds me of a song by the name of "Gilly, Gilly, Hasenpfeffer — something — Bogen By The Sea". It was popular about the same time people were singing other songs with nonsense lyrics like "Hut Sut Ralt Sittin On A Rilla Ra And A Sue It, Sue It, Sue It." Or the ever popular "Flat Foot Floogie With A Floy Floy". You may be one of the few readers of this recipe who remembers the real titles to those songs. Well, that's why I write things down.

Hasenpfeffer is the German word for a pickled rabbit dish, sauteed and served up in sour cream. My recipe is from the Pennsylvania Dutch so there may be some differences from a continental German recipe.

INGREDIENTS:
2	CUPS CIDER VINEGAR
2	CUPS WATER
1	LARGE ONION SLICED
$^1/_2$	TEASPOON SALT
$^1/_2$	TEASPOON CRACKED BLACK PEPPER
3	WHOLE CLOVES
1	BAY LEAF

METHOD: Blend all the ingredients in a glass bowl, crock pot or plastic marinating container. Place the rabbit quarters or halves into the marinade. Refrigerate for 48 hours, turning occasionally.

Brown the rabbit by sauteing. After browning, use some of the marinade to baste it during cooking. When the rabbit is fully cooked remove it from the pan and blend 1 cup of sour cream into the pan juices. Serve.

USE ON: Hasen (rabbit).

YIELD: 5 cups.

NUTRITIONAL FACTS:
Serving Size: 2 Tsp	Total Fat: 0 g	Sodium: 10 mg	Sugar: 0 g
Calories Per Serving: 0	Sat Fat: 0 g	Total Carbs: 0 g	Protein: 0 g
Fat Calories: 0	Cholest: 0 mg	Fiber: 0 g	

Chapter 23

Cheese Sauces And Cheese Dips

DIPPING CHEESE SAUCE

This sauce is somewhat different than fondue. Historically fondue originated in Switzerland (The Swiss were reluctant to throw usable, albeit-stale, food away). So they used aged and substantially dried cheese scraps melted in wine to create a dip to soften stale bread so that it could be eaten. Then sometime during the sixties America discovered fondue and it became popular as a party food. This recipe is more than a simple fondue, here the cheese is melted in whipping cream and bouillon which sets it apart from fondue.

INGREDIENTS:		
	$^1/_4$	CUP BUTTER
	2	TABLESPOONS GRATED ONION
	6	TABLESPOONS FLOUR
	2	TEASPOONS CHICKEN SOUP BASE OR 2 CUBES CHICKEN SOUP BASE
	2	CUPS WHIPPING CREAM
	$^1/_2$	POUND SHREDDED CHEESE: CHOOSE FROM SWISS, BRICK, MUENSTER, GOUDA, HARVARTI JARLSBERG OR SIMILAR CHEESES. MIX OR MATCH IF YOU WISH.
	$^1/_4$	POUND GRATED PARMESAN CHEESE

METHOD:

1. Saute the onions in the butter until soft and whisk in the flour. Cook for 2 minutes. Remove from the heat and set aside.

2. In a separate pan, scald the cream, add the chicken base and whisk until dissolved.

3. Return the onion roux to the heat. Add the cream mix, then return the mixture to a boil. Reduce the heat, add the cheeses and stir until the cheese is melted and the sauce is smooth.

USE ON:

Rolled slices of boiled ham, cocktail franks, apple wedges, pear wedges or cubes of somewhat stale, but crusty breads and as a dip for shrimp.

Add some cayenne or diced jalapeno and pour over corn chips to use as a nacho sauce. Or use it as a dip.

Yield: 2¹/₂ cups.

NUTRITIONAL FACTS:

Serving Size: 1/2 cup	Total Fat: 37 g	Sodium: 810 mg	Sugar: 3 g
Calories Per Serving: 420	Sat Fat: 23 g	Total Carbs: 8 g	Protein: 15 g
Fat Calories: 330	Cholest: 120 mg	Fiber: 0 g	

WELSH RAREBIT

If you have a double boiler, it's a good idea to use it. If you don't, use a diffuser to keep the pan off the direct heat and stir constantly until it's done.

INGREDIENTS:	1	CUP BEER
	2	TABLESPOONS BUTTER
	$^1/_2$	TEASPOON DRY MUSTARD
	PINCH	CAYENNE PEPPER
	1	POUND CHEDDAR CHEESE, SHREDDED

METHOD: Place all the ingredients, except the cheese, into a sauce pan. Bring them to a boil and slowly whisk in the cheese. Cook until the cheese is completely melted.

USE ON: Usually poured over toast for a light lunch or supper. Try it on English muffins, split and toasted bagles, buttermilk biscuits, or crackers.

YIELD: 3 cups.

NUTRITIONAL FACTS:

Serving Size: 1/2 cup	Total Fat: 29 g	Sodium: 510 mg	Sugar: 1 g
Calories Per Serving: 350	Sat Fat: 18 g	Total Carbs: 2 g	Protein: 19 g
Fat Calories: 260	Cholest: 90 mg	Fiber: 0 g	

Chardonnay Cheese Sauce

Chardonnay is one of several wines you can use in this sauce. Try Gewurztraminer, Sauvignon Blanc, Chablis or a Moselle. But only the Sherries, Muscatos or Marsalas will impart the same taste you enjoy in the glass. In most cases white wines are overwhelmed by the other ingredients. However, this sauce is a pretty simple one, so if you use a very mild cheese, you can actually taste the flavor of the wine.

INGREDIENTS:	$1/_2$	POUND SHREDDED SWISS, COLBY OR LONGHORN CHEDDAR
	$1/_2$	CUP WINE
	1	TABLESPOON BUTTER

METHOD: In a double boiler, melt the butter and add the cheese, stirring constantly until the cheese has melted. Whisk in the wine and when thoroughly blended, remove the sauce from the heat.

USE ON: Steamed vegetables, such as broccoli, cauliflower and carrots. Egg omelets and poached fish.

YIELD: $2\,^1/_4$ cups.

NUTRITIONAL FACTS:

Serving Size: 1/4 cup	Total Fat: 12 g	Sodium: 120 mg	Sugar: 0 g
Calories Per Serving: 170	Sat Fat: 8 g	Total Carbs: 1 g	Protein: 11 g
Fat Calories: 110	Cholest: 40 mg	Fiber: 0 g	

Italian Cheese Sauce

This is a simple yet tasty Italian style cheese sauce. It's a nice finishing sauce for braised meat, but also easily used on a variety of other foods.

Ingredients:	2	CUPS CHICKEN BROTH
	3	WHOLE EGGS, WELL BEATEN AND STRAINED
	$^1/_2$	CUP FRESHLY GRATED PARMESAN CHEESE
	$^1/_2$	CUP FRESHLY GRATED ROMANO CHEESE
		SALT AND PEPPER TO TASTE

Method: In a sauce pan, bring the broth to a boil. Reduce the heat to low, use a small amount of hot broth to blend with the eggs then, while whisking, slowly pour the eggs into the hot broth. When well blended, whisk in the cheeses and cook without boiling until the cheeses are melted and the sauce has thickened. Season to taste.

Option: If you are going to use this sauce on a braised meat (as a final step), add the meat and its juices to the sauce. Cook for an additional 1 to 2 minutes and serve.

Use On: Braised lamb cubes, veal medallions, boneless chicken pieces, non-leafy vegetables, baked potatoes, wine poached whole mushrooms.

Yield: 3 cups.

NUTRITIONAL FACTS:

Serving Size: 3 T	Total Fat: 3 g	Sodium: 210 mg	Sugar: 0 g
Calories Per Serving: 45	Sat Fat: 1.5 g	Total Carbs: 0 g	Protein: 4 g
Fat Calories: 25	Cholest: 45 mg	Fiber: 0 g	

Lemon Cheese Sauce

INGREDIENTS:	2	EGG YOLKS
	$1^1/_2$	TABLESPOONS LEMON JUICE
	$^1/_4$	CUP GRATED PARMESAN CHEESE
	PINCH	FRESHLY GRATED NUTMEG
	$^1/_4$	TEASPOON FRESHLY GROUND BLACK PEPPER
		SALT TO TASTE
	2	CUPS CHICKEN BROTH
	$^1/_4$	CUP WHITE WINE
	1	CLOVE GARLIC, BRUISED
	1	TABLESPOON CHOPPED PARSLEY FOR GARNISH

METHOD:

1. In a bowl, thoroughly mix the first six ingredients. Set aside.

2. In a sauce pan over medium heat, bring the chicken broth, wine and garlic to a boil. Add a little of the hot broth to the egg mixture then slowly, while whisking, add the egg mixture to the hot broth. Without boiling, cook the sauce for 2 additional minutes. Discard the garlic and serve.

OPTION: If you use this sauce with hot braised meats, you can put the meat, and any pan juices, into the sauce for a final moment of cooking.

USE ON: Braised meats such as lamb, veal or chicken, cold sliced lamb or veal. Poached or sauteed whole, halved or quartered mushrooms, steamed asparagus, broccoli, cauliflower or carrots.

YIELD: $2^2/_3$ cups.

NUTRITIONAL FACTS:			
Serving Size: 2 T	Total Fat: 1 g	Sodium: 95 mg	Sugar: 0 g
Calories Per Serving: 15	Sat Fat: 0 g	Total Carbs: 0 g	Protein: 1 g
Fat Calories: 10	Cholest: 20 mg	Fiber: 0 g	

WE TRIED THIS SAUCE ... AND

LOVED IT ( )
HATED IT ( )
MAYBE WE'LL TRY IT AGAIN ( )
WE'LL USE IT FOR UNWELCOME GUESTS ( )

CHEESE SAUCE

INGREDIENTS:

1	CUP SLICED MUSHROOMS
2	TABLESPOONS BUTTER
$^1/_4$	CUP FLOUR
$1\,^1/_2$	CUPS MILK
1	CUP SHREDDED CHEESE (COLBY, CHEDDAR, JACK, ETC.)
3	TABLESPOONS CHILI SAUCE
3	TABLESPOONS LEMON JUICE
$^1/_4$	TEASPOON SALT
PINCH	PAPRIKA

METHOD:

1. In a sauce pan, saute the mushrooms in the butter for 3 minutes. Remove the mushrooms and set aside.

2. Whisk the flour in the pan juices and cook for 2 minutes. Add the milk and bring to a scald. When the milk is hot, add the remaining ingredients and cook until the cheese has thoroughly melted and the sauce has thickened.

USE ON: Shrimp, crabmeat or canned and drained clams.

You can add one or more of the seafood items to the cheese sauce, to heat through and make a Seafood Rarebit. Serve it on toast or wide noodles.

YIELD: 3 cups.

NUTRITIONAL FACTS:

Serving Size: 3 T	Total Fat: 6 g	Sodium: 135 mg	Sugar: 1 g
Calories Per Serving: 80	Sat Fat: 3.5 g	Total Carbs: 4 g	Protein: 4 g
Fat Calories: 50	Cholest: 20 mg	Fiber: 0 g	

Chapter 24

Dressings And Sauces For Everything Without Its Own Chapter

For everyone who ever served in the military, this chapter is somewhat akin to Article 35 of the Uniform Code of Military Justice (UCMJ) which covers everything the writers and lawyers missed in the body of the code. It's a gottcha!

Well I've done the same thing with my book, if you can't find a recipe anywhere else, look here!

FRESH HORSERADISH SAUCE

If you've ever wanted to try a fresh horseradish sauce for your food, this is the one. Whether you grow your own horseradish or buy it, you'll like this preparation.

INGREDIENTS:	$^1/_3$	CUP FRESHLY PARED AND GROUND HORSERADISH
	1	CUP SOUR CREAM
		ADD SUGAR, SALT AND GROUND BLACK PEPPER TO TASTE

OPTIONS:	$^1/_2$	TEASPOON GROUND CARAWAY SEED.
	1	MEDIUM APPLE, PEELED AND SHREDDED.

METHOD: Mix the first 3 ingredients, or all five, in a small bowl. Pack the mixture in an airtight container and store in the refrigerator. It will keep for about one week.

USE ON: Prime rib, sandwiches, corned beef, pastrami, roast pork, or add to other sauces that need a lift.

YIELD: 1 $^1/_3$ to 2 cups.

NUTRITIONAL FACTS:

Serving Size: 2 Tsp	Total Fat: 1.5 g	Sodium: 0 mg	Sugar: 0 g
Calories Per Serving: 20	Sat Fat: 1 g	Total Carbs: 1 g	Protein: 0 g
Fat Calories: 15	Cholest: 5 mg	Fiber: 0 g	

HOT PEPPER SAUCE

It may be easier to buy this sauce than make it, but if you're up for a little excitement, this ought to do it. Also buy a pair of rubber gloves (you don't want to handle the peppers with bare hands!). A small baby food sized bottle will do fine for storing the sauce.

INGREDIENTS: 2 OR 3   OUNCES OF THE 1 TO 2 INCH SKINNY FRESH OR DRIED HOT RED PEPPERS (IF YOU GARDEN, USE YOUR OWN).
DISTILLED WHITE VINEGAR
SALT

METHOD: Stuff as many peppers as you can fit into a small, sterilized bottle. Fill the bottle with vinegar and a pinch or two of salt. Cap the bottle and store for 2 to 3 weeks before using.

When you first use the sauce, use small amounts until you gage it's strength. When you've emptied the bottle, refill it with vinegar, cap the bottle and store again for several weeks.

ALTERNATE: Try filling the bottle with hot vinegar, along with a little sugar, salt and any spice that appeals to you.

USE ON: Eggs, cooked meat or fried potatoes.

YIELD: $^1/_4$ cup and up.

NUTRITIONAL FACTS:			
Serving Size: Drops	Total Fat: 0 g	Sodium: 0 mg	Sugar: 0 g
Calories Per Serving: 0	Sat Fat: 0 g	Total Carbs: 0 g	Protein: 0 g
Fat Calories: 0	Cholest: 0 mg	Fiber: 0 g	

GREEN CHILI SAUCE

INGREDIENTS:	4	OUNCE CAN OF CHOPPED JALAPENO
	1	ONION, COARSELY CHOPPED
	1	CLOVE GARLIC
	2	TABLESPOON CILANTRO (CHINESE PARSLEY)
	1	TABLESPOON OLIVE OIL
	$^1/_2$	TEASPOON SALT

METHOD: Place all the ingredients in a blender and puree until fairly smooth. Chill in the refrigerator.

OPTION #1 ADD: 1 TOMATO, BLANCHED AND PEELED.

OPTION #2: Bring the sauce to a boil. Reduce the heat and simmer for 5 minutes, then chill.

USE ON: Tacos, burritos, tostadas.

YIELD: 1 $^1/_4$ cups.

NUTRITIONAL FACTS:			
Serving Size: 1 Tsp	Total Fat: 0 g	Sodium: 50 mg	Sugar: 0 g
Calories Per Serving: 0	Sat Fat: 0 g	Total Carbs: 0 g	Protein: 0 g
Fat Calories: 0	Cholest: 0 mg	Fiber: 0 g	

GREEN CHILI SAUCE II

I'm giving you two ways to prepare this sauce, cooked or uncooked. Your choice.

INGREDIENTS:	1	LARGE TOMATO, PEELED AND QUARTERED
	1	LARGE ANAHEIM CHILI PEPPER, SEEDED AND CHOPPED OR
	1	4 OUNCE CAN OF JALAPENO PEPPERS, RINSED, SEEDED AND CHOPPED
	1	SMALL ONION, CHOPPED
	1	TABLESPOON CHOPPED CILANTRO (AKA CHINESE PARSLEY) OR BROAD LEAF PARSLEY
	1	CLOVE GARLIC
	$^1/_2$	TEASPOON SALT
	1	TABLESPOON RED WINE VINEGAR

METHOD: Place all the ingredients into a blender and run at the puree setting until it's fairly smooth. Transfer the sauce to a sauce pan and bring to a boil. Reduce the heat and cook on low for 5 minutes.

ALTERNATE: Omit the garlic. Chop the tomato, onion, peppers and cilantro into small pieces, then add the salt and vinegar and mix well. Use uncooked as a chip dipping salsa.

USE ON: Refried beans, tacos, burritos and anything else that comes to mind.

YIELD: 2 cups.

NUTRITIONAL FACTS:

Serving Size: 2 T	Total Fat: 0 g	Sodium: 50 mg	Sugar: 1 g
Calories Per Serving: 0	Sat Fat: 0 g	Total Carbs: 1 g	Protein: 0 g
Fat Calories: 0	Cholest: 0 mg	Fiber: 0 g	

RED CHILI SAUCE

(A FIERY DUDE)

INGREDIENTS:	2	TEASPOONS CRUSHED RED PEPPER
	1	6 OUNCE CAN TOMATO PASTE
	2	CUPS WATER
	1	ONION, CHOPPED
	1	CLOVE GARLIC MINCED
	1	TEASPOON SALT
	$^1/_2$	TEASPOON SUGAR
	1	TABLESPOON OLIVE OIL

OPTION: You can exchange the tomato paste for 2 pounds of fresh tomatoes, blanched, peeled and quartered.

METHOD: Place all the ingredients into a blender and run at the puree setting until it's fairly smooth. Transfer the mixture to a sauce pan and bring to a boil. Reduce heat to medium and cook for 10 minutes.

USE ON: Scrambled eggs, egg omelettes. Or use as a barbecue sauce, as a low fat baked potato dressing, a chip dip or as a seafood cocktail sauce.

YIELD: $3\,^3/_4$ cups.

NUTRITIONAL FACTS:

Serving Size: 1 T	Total Fat: 0 g	Sodium: 45 mg	Sugar: 0 g
Calories Per Serving: 5	Sat Fat: 0 g	Total Carbs: 1 g	Protein: 0 g
Fat Calories: 0	Cholest: 0 mg	Fiber: 0 g	

CHAPTER 25

GLAZES FOR SWEETS, MEATS AND VEGETABLES

Glazes are used for a variety of foods and they are also difficult to define.

Basically they are a coating that is:

1)   thin

2)   smooth

3)   glassy

And they can be:

4)   colored

5)   opaque

6)   transparent

They add:

7)   color

8)   glamor

9)   sheen

Glazes are a chef's show stopper. They make your food look too pretty to eat. If that is how yours turns out, you did it right!

CHOCOLATE GLAZE

INGREDIENTS:

$1/_2$	CUP BUTTER
2	CUPS POWDERED SUGAR
2	OUNCES UNSWEETENED CHOCOLATE, MELTED AND COOLED
$1\,1/_2$	TEASPOONS VANILLA EXTRACT
$1/_4$	CUP VERY HOT WATER

METHOD: Melt the butter. Remove from the heat and add the sugar, chocolate and vanilla. Stir to blend. Dribble in the hot water while whisking, to get a smooth consistency. Spread immediately.

USE ON: Cake.

YIELD: $2\,1/_4$ cups.

NUTRITIONAL FACTS:

Serving Size: 1 T	Total Fat: 3.5 g	Sodium: 30 mg	Sugar: 7 g
Calories Per Serving: 60	Sat Fat: 2.5 g	Total Carbs: 8 g	Protein: 0 g
Fat Calories: 35	Cholest: 10 mg	Fiber: 0 g	

HONEY BUTTER GLAZE

INGREDIENTS:	$^1/_2$	CUP HONEY
	$^1/_2$	CUP WATER
	1	TABLESPOON BUTTER
	$^1/_4$	TEASPOON FRESHLY GRATED NUTMEG

OPTION: You can increase the butter up to $^1/_2$ cup.

METHOD: Place the first 3 ingredients into a small sauce pan and bring to a boil. Boil for 1 minute then remove from the heat and add nutmeg.

USE ON: Ham, pork roast, game birds, onion and carrots.

YIELD: 1 cup.

NUTRITIONAL FACTS:

Serving Size: 2 Tsp	Total Fat: 0 g	Sodium: 0 mg	Sugar: 5 g
Calories Per Serving: 20	Sat Fat: 0 g	Total Carbs: 5 g	Protein: 0 g
Fat Calories: 0	Cholest: 0 mg	Fiber: 0 g	

MUSTARD HORSERADISH GLAZE

Some glazes seem to belong to a period when more time was available for cooking. They are easy to do and it may require several applications to give your roast a proper glaze, but it's no more involved than basting.

INGREDIENTS:

$^1/_4$	CUP HONEY
$^1/_4$	CUP WATER
2	TABLESPOONS BUTTER
1	TABLESPOON PREPARED MUSTARD (YOUR CHOICE)
1	TABLESPOON GROUND HORSERADISH
PINCH	GROUND NUTMEG

METHOD: In a sauce pan, bring the honey, water and butter to a boil. Hold at the boil for 1 minute then add and thoroughly blend in the mustard and horseradish. Remove from the heat.

USE ON: Roast pork or ham.

YIELD: $^3/_4$ cup.

NUTRITIONAL FACTS:

Serving Size: 2 Tsp	Total Fat: 1 g	Sodium: 20 mg	Sugar: 3 g
Calories Per Serving: 25	Sat Fat: 0.5 g	Total Carbs: 4 g	Protein: 0 g
Fat Calories: 10	Cholest: 5 mg	Fiber: 0 g	

SUGAR GLAZE

If you love glazed donuts, you'll love this recipe. Put it on any cake, or if you're into donut making, try it on your donuts. No cooking, just mix and use.

INGREDIENTS:	1	CUP POWDERED SUGAR
	1	TABLESPOON MILK
	1	TEASPOON FLAVORING EXTRACT (YOUR CHOICE)

METHOD: Blend all the ingredients until you get a smooth texture.

USE ON: Cake, donuts or pie if the filling is not sweet.

YIELD: $^3/_4$ cup.

NUTRITIONAL FACTS:

Serving Size: 2 Tsp	Total Fat: 0 g	Sodium: 0 mg	Sugar: 8 g
Calories Per Serving: 35	Sat Fat: 0 g	Total Carbs: 9 g	Protein: 0 g
Fat Calories: 0	Cholest: 0 mg	Fiber: 0 g	

BOURBON GLAZE

When your taste buds hanker for a whiskey flavored glaze, this one can satisfy the hankering.

INGREDIENTS:	1	CUP BOURBON WHISKEY
	1	CUP BROWN SUGAR
	6	WHOLE CLOVES
	2	TABLESPOONS GRATED ORANGE PEEL

ALTERNATE: Replace up to 1/2 the bourbon with a dry wine.

METHOD: Combine all the ingredients in a small bowl. Use the sauce to baste your meat during the last half hour of roasting.

USE ON: Ham, pork roast.

YIELD: 1 $^1/_2$ cups.

NUTRITIONAL FACTS:

Serving Size: 2 Tsp	Total Fat: 0 g	Sodium: 0 mg	Sugar: 3 g
Calories Per Serving: 30	Sat Fat: 0 g	Total Carbs: 4 g	Protein: 0 g
Fat Calories: 0	Cholest: 0 mg	Fiber: 0 g	

CRANBERRY GLAZE

Cranberries and turkey seem to be a natural pairing. In years past, the winter holidays were the time of year when most Americans ate turkey because they weren't readily available the rest of the year. And when they were available, you bought them either fresh, or live. When I was a boy my family had turkey twice a year. The "twice", thirty days apart, were Thanksgiving and Christmas! Add to that, the additional days eating leftover turkey, made "twice a year" seem like an eternity. But, things have changed. Today turkey comes in parts and pieces not dreamed of by turkey lovers of yesteryear. It's also available year round and that gives us many opportunities to enjoy eating it more frequently. It also allows us to serve it in different ways. Next time try it glazed.

INGREDIENTS:	1	CUP JELLIED CRANBERRY
	$^1/_2$	CUP BROWN SUGAR
	2	TABLESPOONS LEMON (OR ORANGE) JUICE

METHOD: Thoroughly blend together all the ingredients. Use the glaze to baste your bird during the last 30 minutes of roasting.

USE ON: Whole roast turkey, or smaller parts such as breast, legs or turkey roll. Also try it on chicken or Cornish rock hens.

YIELD: 1 $^2/_3$ cups.

NUTRITIONAL FACTS:

Serving Size: 1 T	Total Fat:0 g	Sodium: 0 mg	Sugar: 3 g
Calories Per Serving: 25	Sat Fat: 0 g	Total Carbs: 7 g	Protein: 0 g
Fat Calories: 0	Cholest: 0 mg	Fiber: 0 g	

Aspic Glaze

I've never trusted aspics since they easily become "weepy". But a very large number of people love 'em. To me it is the binding agent of head cheese, and I'm still not sure that I like head cheese. I'll eat it, but always with apprehension. Now that you understand my prejudice, lets move on to the recipe. It is simplicity itself.

Your choice of liquid will compliment, contrast or enhance any meat with which it is used. You can choose any meat or vegetable stock and you can substitute some of the stock with wine.

Aspic is a basic preparation that is often recommended with a number of different sauces, as well as a transparent glaze over colored a glaze.

| INGREDIENTS: | 1 | TABLESPOON GELATIN |
| | 2 | CUPS FLAVORED AND/OR CLARIFIED LIQUID |

METHOD:

1. Dissolve the gelatin in $1/_2$ cup of hot liquid.

2. Add the remaining $1^1/_2$ cups of room temperature liquid to the gelatin. Cool until slightly thickened.

3. Cover the meat (room temperature or chilled) with a thin coating of the aspic and chill.

4. Add a second coating if desired. Chill again and serve.

USE ON: Cold sliced meat, cold buffet foods, open faced sandwiches and with other sauces.

YIELD: 2 cups.

NUTRITIONAL FACTS:			
Serving Size: 2 Tsp	Total Fat: 0 g	Sodium: 30 mg	Sugar: 0 g
Calories Per Serving: 0	Sat Fat: 0 g	Total Carbs: 0 g	Protein: 0 g
Fat Calories: 0	Cholest: 0 mg	Fiber: 0 g	

GELATIN MAYONNAISE

(MAYONNAISE COLLEE)

Your creative abilities shine with this glaze, if you are into gorgeous, coated foods. It covers aspics, cold fish, meats or poultry with an opaque mask. It's very simple and if you make it stiff enough, you'll be able to apply it with a pastry pipe. You can even add a drop of color for a pastel effect.

INGREDIENTS:

$^1/_4$	CUP ASPIC (SEE PRECEDING PAGE FOR RECIPE)
1	CUP MAYONNAISE

METHOD:

1. The aspic must be in liquid form. If it has jelled, warm it in tepid water until it is liquid again.

2. Place your food on a wire rack (if possible) over a large tray.

3. Have the mayonnaise at room temperature and whisk the liquid aspic into the mayonnaise very quickly.

4. Spread the mixture over your cold food with a spatula, as though frosting a cake. When the aspic is set, remove your food from the wire rack and arrange it on a platter or plate.

5. For fancy design work, pipe the remaining mixture through a frosting tube.

USE ON: Cold fish, cold meat or cold poultry. You can also spread it over a cold dish that already has a transparent aspic coating.

YIELD: $1\,^1/_4$ cups.

NUTRITIONAL FACTS:			
Serving Size: 1 T	Total Fat: 10 g	Sodium: 80 mg	Sugar: 0 g
Calories Per Serving: 90	Sat Fat: 1.5 g	Total Carbs: 0 g	Protein: 0 g
Fat Calories: 90	Cholest: 5 mg	Fiber: 0 g	

SAUCE CHAUD-FROID

This one sounds more difficult than it is. It is one of those multi-sauce combinations that French chefs love. You'll need a white sauce, an aspic in liquid form and stock or drippings from your meat. If that hasn't slowed you down, lets go for it.

INGREDIENTS:	2	CUPS WHITE SAUCE
	2	TABLESPOONS GELATIN
	3	TABLESPOONS STOCK (SAME AS THE MEAT YOU'LL COVER)

ALTERNATE: If you prefer a dark glaze, replace the white sauce with a brown sauce.

METHOD:

1. Stir the gelatin into the stock to soften and set aside. Bring your white sauce to a low simmering boil and add the gelatin/stock to the white sauce. Cook for several minutes until the gelatin is fully dissolved. Set aside to cool. Stir periodically to prevent a skin from forming on the top.

2. When cool, but not set, use a large spoon or ladle to pour the sauce evenly over your cold food (with a slow motion to get a smooth coating). Refrigerate. If you would like a second coating, repeat the process.

3. When the food is cold, glaze it with a clear aspic. A final touch is a decoration, made from food, such as a flower, with stem and leaves, even real ones. Dip the decoration into the clear aspic and place it on your food.

USE ON: Whole cooked chicken, ham, veal or fish.

YIELD: 2 $\frac{1}{4}$ cups.

NUTRITIONAL FACTS:			
Serving Size: 1 T	Total Fat: 1.5 g	Sodium: 20 mg	Sugar: 1 g
Calories Per Serving: 20	Sat Fat: 1 g	Total Carbs: 1 g	Protein: 1 g
Fat Calories: 15	Cholest: 5 mg	Fiber: 0 g	

HONEY MUSTARD GLAZE

INGREDIENTS:	1	TEASPOON ORANGE JUICE
	1	TEASPOON DRY MUSTARD
	1	TEASPOON EXTRA LIGHT OLIVE OIL
	2	TABLESPOONS ORANGE BLOSSOM HONEY (OTHER FLOWER HONEYS MAY BE USED)

METHOD: In a small sauce pan, blend the orange juice and mustard until the mustard is dissolved. Add the oil and honey and slowly heat the sauce to scalding. Remove from heat and use.

USE ON: Baked salmon or other pink fleshed fish.

YIELD: Less than $^1/_4$ cup.

NUTRITIONAL FACTS:

Serving Size: 1 T	Total Fat: 1.5 g	Sodium: 0 mg	Sugar: 10 g
Calories Per Serving: 50	Sat Fat: 0 g	Total Carbs: 10 g	Protein: 0 g
Fat Calories: 10	Cholest: 0 mg	Fiber: 0 g	

Apricot Glaze

This recipe uses fresh apricots, but it could also be made from dried apricots. To reconstitute them place $1/4$ pound dried apricots in a sauce pan, barely cover them with water and bring them to a boil. Cover and cook for 1 minute, remove from the heat, cool and allow them to sit over night. Puree the plumped apricots and then add an equal amount of sugar to match the pulp. Follow the cooking procedure as shown below.

Ingredients:	2	CUPS CHOPPED FRESH APRICOTS
	1	CUP SUGAR
	1	TABLESPOON WATER, APRICOT BRANDY OR APRICOT LIQUEUR

Method: Place all the ingredients into a sauce pan. Stirring constantly, cook them over medium heat until the mix comes to a boil. Cook for 5 minutes, then at this point either sieve or puree the sauce in a blender. Serve.

Use On: Cakes; as a topping or between layers, as a filling in little pocket pastries or cookies and on Baba au Rhum.

Yield: 2 cups.

NUTRITIONAL FACTS:			
Serving Size: 2 T	Total Fat: 0 g	Sodium: 0 mg	Sugar: 10 g
Calories Per Serving: 45	Sat Fat: 0 g	Total Carbs: 11 g	Protein: 0 g
Fat Calories: 0	Cholest: 0 mg	Fiber: 0 g	

"This page is blank by Design"

CHAPTER 26

DRESSINGS AND SAUCES SERVED OVER OR WITH

SALADS

Salad dressings are divided into two basic categories. Those made with oil and an acid, like vinegar, lemon or lime juice. These are generally known as Savory Sauces or Dressings. The second category consists of a base of mayonnaise, which is made from oil plus egg yolks, like Thousand Island, French, etc.

In the 40's, 50's and into the 60's, it was fairly easy to define a salad.

Basically it was a dish of lettuce, leafy greens, vegetables, cold meats, fish, shrimp or other foods singly or in combination with a dressing. That made the salad. This has not changed.

Salad dressings back then were fewer in number and most of them were centered around mayonnaise as the base. What passed for "French" dressing then was some orangy sugared-thinned mayonnaise. Also popular was Thousand Island Dressing, that is, mayonnaise liberally spiked with pickle relish. Or mayonnaise thinned with honey for use in the popular Waldorf salad and in slaw dressings. We also had vegetables or fruit blended with a flavored gelatin, with or without mayonnaise.

It's a little more complicated today, because we now have well over one hundred different commercial salad dressings to choose from and more coming. Especially with the never ending ability of cooks to create wonderful salads from the newly available varieties of greens, fruits, berries, vegetables and pasta.

Along with those new salads, come wonderful new dressings. Todays salad dressings seem to show up with the speed of light. Dressings made from creams and cheeses that are synthetic or real, yogurts, berries, seeds and herbs. Then there are "no fat" or "low fat" dressings. Add to that hot dressings that create wilted salads, and fruit salads, dressed or undressed. Just trying to stay abreast of the changes is enough to get you out of breath.

You might be surprised to learn that the variety of fresh fruits, vegetables and greens available to you today simply did not exist during the 40's and 50's.

To the new and novice cook, I'm giving you a starter inventory of salad dressings in this chapter. The list is a long way from the dressings that are available or what might be coming in the future, but it does give you a rudimentary and valuable basic group. Something that will serve you well for as long as you choose to cook.

The first three recipes are the basic dressings of the western world; vinegar and oil. If you tend to call your vinegar and oil mixture, "French Dressing", instead of Italian (or possibly even Spanish Dressing), be alert to the fact that this combination is widely known as "Vinaigrette".

Cooks alert: Oil and vinegar separate within seconds after the shaking stops. A little lemon juice slows down the separation.

Basic Italian And French Salad Dressing With

Helpful Measurements

If you are too timid to wing it, here is the following dressing with basic measurements. A point worth noting is that these measurements are approximate. The need for more or less of any ingredient is determined by your choice of salad ingredients. Some ingredients, like lettuce, need more oil than a vegetable, such as green beans. Conversely, asparagus may need more vinegar, whereas tomatoes and cucumbers need more salt.

INGREDIENTS:	3	PARTS OLIVE OIL
	1	PART RED WINE VINEGAR
	$^1/_2$	TEASPOON SALT

METHOD: Mix or shake and use.

OPTION: To get better emulsification use;

| | $^1/_2$ | PART VINEGAR AND |
| | $^1/_2$ | PART LEMON JUICE |

USE ON: Any salad ingredients.

NUTRITIONAL FACTS:			
Serving Size: 1 Tsp	Total Fat: 3.5 g	Sodium: 100 mg	Sugar: 0 g
Calories Per Serving: 30	Sat Fat: 0 g	Total Carbs: 0 g	Protein: 0 g
Fat Calories: 30	Cholest: 0 mg	Fiber: 0 g	

ITALIAN AND FRENCH BASIC SALAD DRESSING

There is no difference between these two dressings. In Italy, as in France, salad dressing is not an option, but a requirement. Dressing is a verb, an action to be taken, not a noun. And there is a procedural requirement. It's as simple as 1, 2, 3. The olive oil should barely coat the ingredients, the vinegar should be added in small splashes. Neither the olive oil, or vinegar should pool at the bottom of the bowl.

INGREDIENTS: OLIVE OIL
RED WINE VINEGAR
SALT

METHOD: 1. Rinse and dry the salad ingredients then cut or tear them into bite size pieces.

2. The rest is done in the mixing bowl, one ingredient at a time.

   a) Add olive oil and toss to coat all the ingredients.
   b) Add red wine vinegar, toss and serve.
   c) Add salt, toss and taste.

OPTION: To occasionally vary the taste, use one or more of the following:

Freshly ground black pepper

Shredded fresh basil

Chopped parsley

Garlic (cut in half, rub the bowl, discard)

Shallots, thinly sliced

Onion slices (use sweet varieties or rinse several times)

Croutons

Capers (drained and rinsed)

Anchovies

Tuna

Shrimp

Hard cooked egg, shredded, sliced or diced

Blue veined cheese, any variety

Dry mustard

Paprika

USE ON: Any single item or combination of; tomatoes, asparagus, artichokes, spinach, bell peppers, celery, escarole, arugula, endive, dandelion, string beans, cucumber, zucchini, swiss-chard and all lettuce varieties.

Cooked vegetables such as; cauliflower, broccoli, small potatoes, kidney beans, great northern beans and other bean varieties.

Roots such as; jerusalem artichokes, celeric, anise bulb, fennel bulb and carrots.

NUTRITIONAL FACTS:			
Serving Size: 1 Tsp	Total Fat: 2 g	Sodium: 100 mg	Sugar: 0 g
Calories Per Serving: 20	Sat Fat: 0 g	Total Carbs: 0 g	Protein: 0 g
Fat Calories: 20	Cholest: 0 mg	Fiber: 0 g	

VINEGAR AND OIL

(VINAIGRETTE)

This is one of several recipes you may know as a "Vinaigrette". There are a few differences between the recipes, but they are very slight. Then again, that's what makes recipes and their tastes so different.

There is an another distinction between this recipe and the preceding Italian/French recipes. That's the basic ratio of oil to vinegar (2 oil to 1 vinegar). This ratio tends to be used by many cooks when using balsamic vinegar. I believe it to be way out of line because it puts too much balsamic vinegar in the dressing.

Balsamic vinegar is an aged wine vinegar and is sold when aged 2 years to well over 100. The ageing process yields a condensed vinegar that retains all the taste qualities and natural sugar of the grapes. The result is a mellow, but sweet acid. It is my opinion that balsamic vinegar should not be used like a standard wine vinegar, but rather handled judiciously according to its' age and quality. Start with a teaspoon for the younger ones and just a few drops of the older ones. One final note on balsamic vinegar, its' age will determine its price.

INGREDIENTS:	6	TABLESPOONS OLIVE OIL
	3	TABLESPOONS VINEGAR (YOUR CHOICE)
	$^{1}/_{4}$	TEASPOON EACH OF SALT, (OMIT THE NEXT 3 ITEMS IF USING BALSAMIC VINEGAR) BLACK PEPPER, DRY MUSTARD AND PAPRIKA.

OPTION: Qualities such as the heaviness of your oil or the sharpness of your vinegar may call for an adjustment of the ratio. For a heavy oil, reverse the ratio. For a sharp vinegar, try a 3 oil to 1 vinegar or 4 oil to 1 vinegar ratio.

METHOD: Place all the ingredients into a jar, cover and shake the daylights out of it. Pour immediately over your salad, toss and serve.

USE ON: Green salads (any greens you'll eat).

YIELD: $^2/_3$ cup.

NUTRITIONAL FACTS:

Serving Size: 2 Tsp	Total Fat: 6 g	Sodium: 45 mg	Sugar: 0 g
Calories Per Serving: 60	Sat Fat: 1 g	Total Carbs: 0 g	Protein: 0 g
Fat Calories: 60	Cholest: 0 mg	Fiber: 0 g	

LEMON ORANGE DRESSING

This salad dressing is more likely to be used in the winter, as a holiday dressing, than at any other time of the year. It is very rich.

INGREDIENTS:	1	EGG, WELL BEATEN
	1	TABLESPOON MINCED FRESH LEMON PEEL (ZEST ONLY)
	1	TABLESPOON MINCED FRESH ORANGE PEEL (ZEST ONLY)
	2	TABLESPOONS JUICE (LEMON OR ORANGE)
	$1/_3$	CUP SUGAR
	1	CUP WHIPPING CREAM

ALTERNATE:	$1/_2$	TEASPOON DRIED LEMON PEEL
	$1/_2$	TEASPOON DRIED ORANGE PEEL

METHOD: Place all the ingredients, except the whipping cream, into a sauce pan and bring it slowly to the boiling point. Remove the sauce from the heat and let it cool.

YOUR CHOICE: Whip the cream and fold it into the mixture, or add the whipping cream as it comes from the carton.

USE ON: Fruit salads, celery/walnut salad, rhubarb salad, carrot salad.

YIELD: $1^1/_2$ cups.

NUTRITIONAL FACTS:

Serving Size: 2 Tsp	Total Fat: 2 g	Sodium: 0 mg	Sugar: 1 g
Calories Per Serving: 25	Sat Fat: 1.5 g	Total Carbs: 2 g	Protein: 0 g
Fat Calories: 20	Cholest: 15 mg	Fiber: 0 g	

SOUR CREAM DRESSING

This is a good all 'round dressing for many types of cold vegetables and salad.

INGREDIENTS:	1	CUP SOUR CREAM
	3	TABLESPOONS CIDER VINEGAR
	1	TEASPOON SALT
	1	TABLESPOON SUGAR
	PINCH	PAPRIKA

ALTERNATE: Replace some or all of the vinegar with lemon juice.

METHOD: Combine all the ingredients and blend well. Serve.

USE ON: Slaws and vegetables as well as carrot or celery salads.

YIELD: 1 1/4 cups.

NUTRITIONAL FACTS:

Serving Size: 1 T	Total Fat: 2.5 g	Sodium: 130 mg	Sugar: 1 g
Calories Per Serving: 30	Sat Fat: 1.5 g	Total Carbs: 1 g	Protein: 0 g
Fat Calories: 20	Cholest: 5 mg	Fiber: 0 g	

BLACK PEPPER DRESSING

This dressing has a variety of applications. It is primarily a green salad dressing, but that is only a starter. Use your imagination. If you like the taste, try it on other foods.

INGREDIENTS:	$1/_3$	CUP MAYONNAISE (LOW-FAT IF YOU WISH)
	2	TABLESPOONS HONEY
	1	TABLESPOON WHITE WINE VINEGAR
	1	TABLESPOON WATER
	$1/_2$	TEASPOON FRESHLY GROUND BLACK PEPPER
	$1/_4$	TEASPOON MINCED OR DRY GRANULATED GARLIC
	$1/_4$	TEASPOON SALT

ALTERNATE:

1. Omit the garlic when using on fresh fruit.

2. If you don't want fresh garlic in your salad, crush it, marinate it in the dressing for an hour or so, then discard before using.

3. Or, rub the salad bowl with the cut clove before mixing your salad, discard the garlic.

METHOD: Whisk to blend the ingredients.

USE ON: Spinach or leaf lettuce. but, don't stop there. Use it on fruit, such as strawberries, and on tomato salads.

YIELD: $2/_3$ cup.

NUTRITIONAL FACTS:			
Serving Size: 1 T	Total Fat: 2 g	Sodium: 115 mg	Sugar: 4 g
Calories Per Serving: 35	Sat Fat: 0 g	Total Carbs: 5 g	Protein: 0 g
Fat Calories: 20	Cholest: 5 mg	Fiber: 0 g	

HOT DRESSING

This dressing poured hot over greens gives you a wilted salad. It is an interesting change from cold, crisp salads. Don't alter the ingredient measurements since they are balanced. Altering them might give you an unpalatable oily dressing.

INGREDIENTS:	1	OR SEVERAL HARD COOKED EGGS SHREDDED OR SLICED AND SET ASIDE.
	4	SLICES BACON, COOKED CRISP, DRAINED AND CRUMBLED.
	2	TABLESPOONS BACON OIL, OR OLIVE OIL.
	$^1/_4$	CUP WINE VINEGAR
	1	TEASPOON SUGAR

METHOD: Heat the oil, vinegar and sugar to a boil. Remove from the heat and pour over the greens. Add the crumbled bacon and shredded egg. Toss and serve.

ALTERNATIVE: If you choose to use sliced egg to garnish the salad, place it on the greens before serving.

USE ON: Spinach, romaine, dandelion or other tart greens. Also use on shredded cabbage/apple mix.

YIELD: $^1/_3$ cup.

NUTRITIONAL FACTS:

Serving Size: 1 T	Total Fat: 4 g	Sodium: 40 mg	Sugar: 0 g
Calories Per Serving: 45	Sat Fat: 1 g	Total Carbs: 1 g	Protein: 1 g
Fat Calories: 35	Cholest: 20 mg	Fiber: 0 g	

CAESAR DRESSING

The Caesar Salad and its dressing has a quirky history. It was developed by Caesar Cardini during the days of prohibition. He was an Italian hotelier and owned the well known "Caesar's Place" restaurant in Tijuana. It was part genius, part inspiration and part good luck that led to this improvised salad developed on one hot, July 4th in 1924 when a double disaster seem to be in the making. The restaurants refrigeration system had broken down earlier in the day and no help was available to fix it. His dining room was filled with movie stars, aviators and gamblers. (The big Hollywood stars of the 20's often visited Tijuana to legally drink, play and gamble in elegant casino's, and many dined at Caesar's.) Doing what any creative chef would do, he improvised. Using what was available; romaine lettuce, egg, olive oil, vinegar, anchovy, garlic and Parmesan cheese and croutons. He moved around the dining room from table to table while deftly tossing the salad at each site. The end result was a pleased and happy group of diners.

The salad calls for romaine lettuce. Use it if you have it, but don't let that stop you from using spinach or other leafy greens. You can also dispense with the showmanship of adding and tossing each ingredient with the leafy greens at the table, unless you're impressing friends or someone special (then it becomes very important).

INGREDIENTS:	1	CUP FRENCH OR ITALIAN BREAD IN FINGER SIZED PIECES (PREPARE AS IN STEP ONE AND SET ASIDE)
	1	CLOVE GARLIC, HALVED
	$1/_2$	CUP OLIVE OIL
	3	TABLESPOONS WINE VINEGAR
		OR
	1	TABLESPOON BALSAMIC VINEGAR
	3	TABLESPOONS LEMON JUICE
	$1/_2$	TEASPOONS SALT
	$1/_4$	TEASPOON DRY MUSTARD
	$1/_2$	TEASPOON FRESHLY GRATED BLACK PEPPER, OR TO TASTE
	5	FILLETS OF ANCHOVY, CUT TO PREFERENCE,
		OR

2	TEASPOONS ANCHOVY PASTE
1	RAW EGG* (EGG WHITE OR EGG SUBSTITUTE IS ACCEPTABLE)
3	TABLESPOONS FRESHLY GRATED PARMESAN CHEESE

OPTION: * Coddle the egg by bringing a little water to a boil. Remove the pan from heat, place the unshelled egg in the water for 1 minute.

METHOD:
1. If the bread is fresh, saute it in 2 tablespoons of the olive oil until browned. If dried out, you can saute the cubes, or use them as they are.

2. If you are using garlic-flavored olive oil, disregard the garlic clove. If not, rub the bowl well with the garlic and discard.

3. Blend all the ingredients except the croutons and whisk well. Toss with your leafy greens, add the croutons and toss again, serve.

USE ON: Romaine lettuce, spinach, endive, or dandelion greens.

YIELD: $^3/_4$ cup.

NUTRITIONAL FACTS:

Serving Size: 1 T	Total Fat: 6 g	Sodium: 115 mg	Sugar: 0 g
Calories Per Serving: 60	Sat Fat: 1 g	Total Carbs: 1 g	Protein: 1 g
Fat Calories: 50	Cholest: 10 mg	Fiber: 0 g	

CUCUMBER DRESSING

This is not a dressing made with cucumber, but rather for cucumbers, and it is one of my favorites. You can use freshly sliced cucumbers, but my preference is to have them wilted first. That is; peeled, sliced, salted and allowed to rest in the refrigerator for several hours, then drained, squeezed and dressed.

INGREDIENTS:	1	CUP SOUR CREAM
	1	TEASPOON DRIED DILL WEED

OPTIONS: Substitutions for the dill weed are; caraway seed, dill seed, fresh minced basil, parsley, chervil, tarragon or fresh oregano leaves.

METHOD: Blend the sour cream and dill weed. Toss and serve.

USE ON: Peeled, sliced cucumbers. If your cucumbers are fresh from the garden, try scoring the skins instead of peeling them.

YIELD: 1 cup.

NUTRITIONAL FACTS:

Serving Size: 1 T	Total Fat: 3 g	Sodium: 10 mg	Sugar: 1 g
Calories Per Serving: 30	Sat Fat: 2 g	Total Carbs: 1 g	Protein: 0 g
Fat Calories: 30	Cholest: 5 mg	Fiber: 0 g	

CUCUMBER DRESSING II

Another personal favorite of mine is this cucumber dressing. It has a delightful sweet, sour quality. I find it to be equally good, whether served before, during or after the meal.

INGREDIENTS:	$^1/_4$	CUP DISTILLED WHITE VINEGAR
	1	TABLESPOON SUGAR
	1	TABLESPOON WATER
	$^1/_2$	TEASPOON SALT (USE ONLY IF YOU DO NOT WILT THE CUCUMBERS)
	PINCH	GROUND WHITE PEPPER
	1	TABLESPOON FRESHLY CHOPPED PARSLEY.

METHOD: Blend all the ingredients.

USE ON: Cucumbers.

YIELD: $^1/_3$ cup.

NUTRITIONAL FACTS:

Serving Size: 1 T	Total Fat: 0 g	Sodium: 65 mg	Sugar: 0 g
Calories Per Serving: 0	Sat Fat: 0 g	Total Carbs: 1 g	Protein: 0 g
Fat Calories: 0	Cholest: 0 mg	Fiber: 0 g	

BOILED DRESSING

This may be mis-named. While you do get it hot, it isn't really boiled. If you like sweet dressings, you'll enjoy this one.

If you're using an electric stove, it's a good idea to use a double boiler or a device that keeps your pan slightly off the burner. With a gas stove, keep the flame low.

INGREDIENTS:	2	EGGS
	6	TABLESPOONS SUGAR OR HONEY
	1	TEASPOON DRY MUSTARD
	$1/2$	TEASPOON SALT
	4	TABLESPOONS BUTTER
	1	TABLESPOON FLOUR
	$1/2$	CUP WATER
	$1/2$	CUP WHITE WINE VINEGAR

METHOD:

1. Beat the eggs, sugar, mustard and salt together until well blended and set aside.

2. Melt the butter in a small sauce pan and whisk in the flour until smooth. Cook for several minutes. add water and bring to a boil.

3. Remove the pan from the heat and slowly whisk the egg mixture into the hot ingredients. Return the pan to the stove and cook until slightly thickened and smooth. Remove from the heat and whisk in the vinegar. Allow the dressing to cool before using.

USE ON: Shredded cabbage or shredded carrots. This dressing can also be used on very sweet, raw or boiled onions (vidalias, walla wallas, etc.).

YIELD: $1 \, ^3/_4$ cups.

NUTRITIONAL FACTS:

Serving Size: 1 T	Total Fat: 2 g	Sodium: 60 mg	Sugar: 2 g
Calories Per Serving: 25	Sat Fat: 1 g	Total Carbs: 2 g	Protein: 0 g
Fat Calories: 15	Cholest: 20 mg	Fiber: 0 g	

ROQUEFORT DRESSING

While this recipe calls for Roquefort cheese, you can use Blue, Gorgonzola or Stilton. These cheeses have a taste difference and it will show up in your dressing.

When mixing, keep in mind that the crumbled texture is visually appealing and the little chunks and pieces make a better tasting dressing than if it is creamed.

INGREDIENTS:		
	$1/4$	CUP SOUR CREAM
	$1\,1/2$	CUPS MAYONNAISE
	1	TEASPOON GARLIC POWDER
	2	TABLESPOONS WHITE WINE VINEGAR OR DISTILLED VINEGAR
	2-3	DROPS TABASCO
		SALT TO TASTE
	12	OUNCES ROQUEFORT CHEESE, CRUMBLED

OPTION: Freshly Ground Black Pepper To Taste

METHOD: Whisk the first 6 ingredients together. Carefully fold in the crumbled cheese. Chill for several hours, or over night if possible before using.

USE ON: Mixed tossed greens salad, iceberg quarters, tomato wedges, sliced cucumbers.

YIELD: $3\,1/2$ cups.

NUTRITIONAL FACTS:			
Serving Size: 1 T	Total Fat: 7 g	Sodium: 160 mg	Sugar: 0 g
Calories Per Serving: 70	Sat Fat: 2 g	Total Carbs: 0 g	Protein: 2 g
Fat Calories: 70	Cholest: 10 mg	Fiber: 0 g	

MAYONNAISE DRESSING

(FOR POTATO SALAD, MACARONI SALAD OR COLD MEATS)

This dressing is my personal favorite for potato or macaroni salad. Remember to "KISS", (Keep It Simple Sweetie).

However should you choose to ignore my caveat, you can embellish the dressing to include one or more of the following; chopped onion or green onion, and/or variously colored bell peppers. You can also sweeten the dressing with a little sugar, or incorporate extra acid by adding, lemon juice, vinegar or prepared mustard. I don't think these items improve the basic dressing, but you might think so.

INGREDIENTS:		
	1	CUP MAYONNAISE
	$1/_2$	TEASPOON SALT
	$1/_4$	TEASPOON WHITE PEPPER
	1	CUP SLICED CELERY OR FINELY CHOPPED
	2	EGGS, HARD COOKED AND CHOPPED
	$1/_4$	CUP FRESH CHOPPED PARSLEY

OPTION: $1/_2$ the parsley and one sliced egg can be used as garnish for your salad.

METHOD: Combine all the ingredients.

USE ON: For macaroni salad, omit the eggs. Use on 4 cups cooked salad mac or Ditalini (that's 8 ounces of uncooked pasta). Add additional ingredients of your choice.

4 cups boiled and diced potatoes (about 5 to 6 medium) and 1 cup of chopped celery for potato salad.

26-18

Cold cubed meats: chicken, turkey, ham or veal.

YIELD: 2 $\frac{1}{2}$ cups.

NUTRITIONAL FACTS:

Serving Size: 1 T	Total Fat: 6 g	Sodium: 85 mg	Sugar: 0 g
Calories Per Serving: 60	Sat Fat: 1 g	Total Carbs: 0 g	Protein: 1 g
Fat Calories: 50	Cholest: 15 mg	Fiber: 0 g	

RANCH ROQUEFORT DRESSING

Substantially different than the other Roquefort dressing in this chapter. It has fewer ingredients and the Roquefort taste comes through more noticeably. You do have the option of using any blue-veined cheese. But if you choose a different cheese, change the name to include that cheese. The French Roquefort cheese producers get quite unpleasant about using the name Roquefort, if you are not using Roquefort. They have in fact sued many restaurants for doing that very thing.

INGREDIENTS:

1	CUP SOUR CREAM
1	CUP MAYONNAISE
4	OUNCES CRUMBLED ROQUEFORT CHEESE

MULTIPLIER: Double or triple as desired.

METHOD: Thoroughly blend the sour cream and mayonnaise. Stir in the crumbled cheese. Chill and use.

USE ON: Mixed salad greens of any variety. Cold asparagus spears or tomato slices. Greek type salad mixtures of cucumber, zucchini, tomato wedges and celery.

YIELD: 2 $^1/_2$ cups.

NUTRITIONAL FACTS:

Serving Size: 1 T	Total Fat: 7 g	Sodium: 90 mg	Sugar: 0 g
Calories Per Serving: 70	Sat Fat: 2 g	Total Carbs: 0 g	Protein: 1 g
Fat Calories: 60	Cholest: 10 mg	Fiber: 0 g	

CREAMY PARMESAN DRESSING

INGREDIENTS:

1/4	CUP FRESHLY GRATED PARMESAN CHEESE
1/2	CUP WHIPPING CREAM
1/2	CUP EXTRA LIGHT OLIVE OIL
1/4	TEASPOON CHERVIL
1/4	TEASPOON TARRAGON
1	TABLESPOON LEMON JUICE
1/4	TEASPOON BLACK PEPPER
1/2	TEASPOON SALT

METHOD: Place the cheese and whipping cream into a bowl and whisk them together thoroughly. Then whisk in the oil, a few teaspoonfuls at a time. Next, add and whisk in the remaining ingredients.

USE ON: Mixed greens salad, chef salads, hearts of lettuce or sliced tomatoes.

YIELD: 1 1/4 cups.

NUTRITIONAL FACTS:			
Serving Size: 1 T	Total Fat: 8 g	Sodium: 90 mg	Sugar: 0 g
Calories Per Serving: 80	Sat Fat: 2.5 g	Total Carbs: 0 g	Protein: 1 g
Fat Calories: 80	Cholest: 10 mg	Fiber: 0 g	

HONEYED SHERRY VINAIGRETTE

INGREDIENTS:	1	SCANT TABLESPOON HONEY
	3	TABLESPOONS SHERRY
	2	TABLESPOONS LEMON JUICE
	1	TABLESPOON WINE VINEGAR
	1	TABLESPOON EXTRA LIGHT OLIVE OIL
	PINCH	PAPRIKA (FOR ADDED ZIP USE CAYENNE PEPPER)

METHOD: Thoroughly blend all the ingredients.

USE ON: Cole slaw, melon/fruit salad, seafood salad.

YIELD: $^1/_2$ cup.

NUTRITIONAL FACTS:

Serving Size: 1 T	Total Fat: 1.5 g	Sodium: 0 mg	Sugar: 2 g
Calories Per Serving: 30	Sat Fat: 0 g	Total Carbs: 3 g	Protein: 0 g
Fat Calories: 15	Cholest: 0 mg	Fiber: 0 g	

HONEY-VINAIGRETTE

INGREDIENTS:

1	CLOVE GARLIC
$^1/_2$	TEASPOON DRY MUSTARD
$^1/_4$	TEASPOON SALT
3	TABLESPOONS TARRAGON VINEGAR, OR SWEET RED WINE VINEGAR
1	TABLESPOON LEMON JUICE
1	CUP EXTRA LIGHT OLIVE OIL

OPTION: Balsamic vinegar can be used, but..., with this reduced measurement; 1 tablespoon balsamic and 2 tablespoons water.

METHOD:

1. Crush the garlic clove on a cutting board. Sprinkle salt on the garlic, then mince the garlic and salt together until you have a paste.

2. Scrape the garlic and salt into a blender. Add the vinegar and lemon juice. Start the blender to mix the contents, then slowly add the oil. Run for 1 minute to emulsify.

USE ON: Salad greens, (all but iceberg), or a mixed salad of acidic fruits such as kiwi, orange segments, grapefruit segments, grapes and greens.

YIELD: 1 $^1/_4$ cups.

NUTRITIONAL FACTS:

Serving Size: 1 T	Total Fat: 12 g	Sodium: 30 mg	Sugar: 0 g
Calories Per Serving: 100	Sat Fat: 1.5 g	Total Carbs: 0 g	Protein: 0 g
Fat Calories: 100	Cholest: 0 mg	Fiber: 0 g	

"This page is blank by Design"

CHAPTER 27

SAUCES FOR CREPES AND OTHER PANCAKES

These thin European pancakes lend themselves well to all kinds of entrees, as well as desserts. In the United States, thanks to the diversity of our immigrant population, we can choose from a very large selection of Europe's best thin pancakes, filled and/or sauced. Choose from French, Swedish, German, Austrian, Hungarian, Russian or Jewish pancakes and have an absolutely delightful meal or dessert.

In this chapter you'll find a number of sauces that are designed to be served on the side, poured over, or under these crepes.

Recipes for crepes change very slightly from one country to another. They all use an egg to flour ratio of somewhere between 2 eggs to $^1/_4$ cup of flour, or 1 egg to 1 cup of flour. They all use milk to thin the batter, a little sugar to sweeten breakfast or dessert crepes (unsweetened for lunch or diner) and possibly a little flavoring such as vanilla, lemon, orange or anise.

Some French crepes have an egg to flour ratio of 2 eggs to $^1/_4$ cup of flour.

Hungarian crepes (Palacsinta) have an egg to flour ratio of 1 egg plus 1 yolk to $^1/_4$ cup of flour, or 1 egg to $^1/_2$ cup of flour.

Thin Swedish pancakes use one egg to $^1/_2$ cup of flour.

Russian Blini use 1 egg to 1 cup flour or 1 egg plus 1 yolk to $^1/_2$ cup flour (when using buckwheat flour).

Jewish blintzes may not use egg at all, opting instead for cottage cheese.

What all this means to you is that if you try to follow these ratios, without a recipe, you may be in trouble. While it is beyond the scope of this book to provide multiple recipes for non-sauce preparations, I've decided to give you one. So read on.

Since my mother is Hungarian and I eat Palacsinta, and to save you the trouble of hunting through several cookbooks for a thin pancake recipe. I'll give you my favorite:

INGREDIENTS:	2	CUPS FLOUR (SIFT OR REMOVE 1 TABLESPOON FLOUR FROM EACH UNSIFTED CUP)
	$^1/_2$	TEASPOON SALT
	4	EGGS*
	2	CUPS MILK
	1	CUP SODA WATER
	1	TABLESPOON SUGAR
		BUTTER, LARD OR EXTRA LIGHT OLIVE OIL

OPTION: Omit the sugar and increase the salt by $^1/_2$ teaspoon for lunch/dinner fillings.

*For more delicate cakes, you can separate the egg yolks from the whites and beat the whites until stiff. Fold them into the batter.

COOKS ALERT: Important: The size skillet you use determines the number of pancakes you'll get from this recipe. An 8" skillet will yield about 20 pancakes.

You may need to adjust your ingredients; because dry or wet weather affects the consistency of the batter, so adjust the liquid or the flour, when necessary, to get a thin batter. Use only large eggs.

METHOD:

1. Whisk, or use a blender, to blend all the ingredients. (When using a blender, put the flour in last). The rest is in the wrist.

2. Spread a little butter, with a small, natural bristle brush, over the surface of a hot skillet.

3. Pour the smallest amount of batter necessary into the skillet, (approximately $1/4$ cup) while you deftly swirl the pan to cover the entire bottom of the skillet.

4. Put the pan back on the heat and cook until the edges are lightly browned. Flip the crepe using a spatula (or your fingers) and cook for a moment longer. Stack them on a plate in a warm oven and keep them covered with a towel until you are ready to serve the crepes.

FILLINGS:

They're limited only by your imagination: Soft cheeses, ham, bacon, shrimp, lobster, crab, mushrooms, spinach, vegetables (the meat/seafood and vegetables can be in a thick sauce) fruit, preserves, jams, et cetera, et cetera.

My favorite fillings are: prune butter (Hungarian; Lekvar), sweetened, creamed and fruited soft cheese such as cottage cheese, pot cheese, hoop cheese, farmers, Ricotta, cream cheese and homemade cheeses.

NUTRITIONAL FACTS:			
Serving Size: 2 pancakes	Total Fat: 3 g	Sodium: 130 mg	Sugar: 3 g
Calories Per Serving: 120	Sat Fat: 1.5 g	Total Carbs: 17 g	Protein: 5 g
Fat Calories: 25	Cholest: 70 mg	Fiber: 1 g	

WE TRIED THIS SAUCE ... AND

LOVED IT ( )
HATED IT ( )
MAYBE WE'LL TRY IT AGAIN ( )
WE'LL USE IT FOR UNWELCOME GUESTS ( )

ORANGE SAUCE

This sauce has an interesting mix of orange and honey flavors. If you wish to dip the crepe into the sauce before folding it into quarters to serve, double the recipe.

INGREDIENTS:

¹/₂	CUP ORANGE JUICE
1	TABLESPOON GRATED ORANGE RIND
3	TABLESPOONS TRIPLE SEC OR CURACOA
¹/₂	CUP HONEY

METHOD: Combine all the ingredients and let the flavors meld. Heat when ready to use.

USE ON: Rolled or folded, but unfilled crepes.

YIELD: 1 ¹/₄ cups.

NUTRITIONAL FACTS:

Serving Size: 2 T	Total Fat: 0 g	Sodium: 0 mg	Sugar: 13 g
Calories Per Serving: 60	Sat Fat: 0 g	Total Carbs: 14 g	Protein: 0 g
Fat Calories: 0	Cholest: 0 mg	Fiber: 0 g	

COINTREAU SAUCE

This sauce can be used in two ways. You can serve it, as is, over French crepes. Or, if you wish to convert them to Crepes Suzette, you can further cook the crepes in the sauce for up to 5 minutes before folding them into quarters and serving. You might even gain a round of applause from your appreciative guests if you flame the crepes at the table. Showmanship never hurts!

To flame the crepes, place a ladle into boiling water for a moment. When the ladle is quite warm, empty the water from it with a quick shake or two and pour 1/4 cup brandy into the ladle. Ignite the brandy and immediately pour it over the crepes. When the flame dies, pour the sauce over the crepes and serve.

P.S. You can use any orange extracted liqueur instead of Cointreau, like Grand Marnier, Curacoa or Triple Sec.

INGREDIENTS:	$^1/_2$	CUP BUTTER
	$^1/_4$	CUP COINTREAU
	$^1/_2$	CUP ORANGE JUICE
	1	TABLESPOON GRATED LEMON RIND (ZEST ONLY)

METHOD: Mix all the ingredients in a sauce pan or skillet and bring to a boil. Cook for 1 minute, use.

USE ON: Any thin pancake.

YIELD: 1 $^1/_4$ cups.

NUTRITIONAL FACTS:			
Serving Size: 2 T	Total Fat: 9 g	Sodium: 95 mg	Sugar: 1 g
Calories Per Serving: 90	Sat Fat: 6 g	Total Carbs: 2 g	Protein: 0 g
Fat Calories: 80	Cholest: 25 mg	Fiber: 0 g	

Strawberry Sauce

This is not made from fresh strawberries, but from strawberry jam.

INGREDIENTS:	1	TABLESPOON CORN STARCH
	2	TABLESPOONS STRAWBERRY JAM
	$1/_2$	CUP WATER
	$1/_2$	CUP SWEET WINE
	2	TABLESPOONS SUGAR
	$1/_4$	TEASPOON SALT

METHOD:
1. Thoroughly mix the corn starch and jam and set aside.

2. Bring the remaining ingredients to a boil and stir in the jam mixture. Cook until the sauce thickens, then cool slightly before using.

USE ON: Thin pancakes, sponge, white or yellow cake or fruit pies.

YIELD: 1 $1/_2$ cups.

NUTRITIONAL FACTS:

Serving Size: 2 T	Total Fat: 0 g	Sodium: 60 mg	Sugar: 4 g
Calories Per Serving: 40	Sat Fat: 0 g	Total Carbs: 7 g	Protein: 0 g
Fat Calories: 0	Cholest: 0 mg	Fiber: 0 g	

PRUNE SAUCE

This is a spiked prune butter. You can make several variations on this sauce by exchanging the prunes for any one of a variety of dried fruits, like apricots, cherries, raisins, plums (not all dried plums are prunes) and figs.

INGREDIENTS:	2	CUPS PITTED PRUNES, COARSELY CHOPPED
	1	CUP WATER
	$^1/_4$	CUP SUGAR
	$^1/_4$	CUP RUM

METHOD:

1. Place the water, prunes and sugar into a sauce pan and bring the mixture to a boil. Reduce the heat and cook for 10 minutes.

2. Remove the mixture from the heat. Add the rum and allow to cool.

3. Transfer the mixture to a blender or food processor and blend until smooth.

USE ON: Thin pancakes or in the East European manner, on dumplings.

YIELD: 2 $^1/_4$ cups.

NUTRITIONAL FACTS:			
Serving Size: 2 T	Total Fat: 0 g	Sodium: 0 mg	Sugar: 7 g
Calories Per Serving: 60	Sat Fat: 0 g	Total Carbs: 12 g	Protein: 0 g
Fat Calories: 0	Cholest: 0 mg	Fiber: 1 g	

BLUEBERRY SAUCE

This is a very simple mixture of berries cooked in milk and thickened. It is a sauce in which almost any berry can be used. Feel free to use your choice of berry.

INGREDIENTS:

1	TABLESPOON CORN STARCH
2	CUPS MILK
2	CUPS BLUEBERRIES
$^1/_2$	CUP SUGAR
2	TABLESPOONS BUTTER (YOU COULD REPLACE THE BUTTER WITH RUM OR A FLAVORED BRANDY TO MATCH YOUR BERRY CHOICE)

METHOD: Mix the corn starch and the milk together in a sauce pan. Add the berries and sugar and bring to a boil. Reduce the heat and cook until the sauce has thickened. Remove from the heat and add the butter. Serve warm.

OPTION: In the above method, some of the berries will burst, but if you want to have a smooth sauce, put the sauce in a blender, or process it in the sauce pan with a hand held blender.

USE ON: Thin pancakes or in the East European manner, on dumplings.

YIELD: 3 $^1/_2$ cups.

NUTRITIONAL FACTS:			
Serving Size: 1/4 cup	Total Fat: 2.5 g	Sodium: 35 mg	Sugar: 7 g
Calories Per Serving: 70	Sat Fat: 1.5 g	Total Carbs: 10 g	Protein: 1 g
Fat Calories: 25	Cholest: 10 mg	Fiber: 1 g	

CHAPTER 28

FLAVORED BUTTERS

Flavored butters are a solid sauce at room temperature and when spread on hot foods, will melt and cover the food. From a culinary historical perspective, flavored butters have been around a very long time.

To fire up your creativity realize that almost anything can be blended with softened butter to provide a delightful and complimentary sauce for a dish you've just whipped up. Including, but not limited to meats that have been roasted, grilled or barbecued such as steaks, chops, burgers, broiled or poached fish, crepes, steamed vegetables and omelets.

ONION BUTTER

INGREDIENTS: $^1/_2$ CUP BUTTER
                  $^1/_4$ TEASPOON WORCESTERSHIRE
                  $^1/_4$ CUP GRATED ONION

METHOD: Cream the butter with the worcestershire sauce and set aside. Grate or chop the onion, then puree it in your blender. Thoroughly mix the onion and butter until smooth.

USE ON: As an addition to sandwich fillings, such as tuna or salmon patties and egg, chicken or ham salad. Use as an appetizer on toast rounds, or spread on half loaves of French bread and broil until golden.

YIELD: $^3/_4$ cup.

NUTRITIONAL FACTS:

Serving Size: 2 Tsp	Total Fat: 5 g	Sodium: 55 mg	Sugar: 0 g
Calories Per Serving: 50	Sat Fat: 3.5 g	Total Carbs: 0 g	Protein: 02 g
Fat Calories: 50	Cholest: 15 mg	Fiber: 0 g	

ANCHOVY BUTTER

INGREDIENTS:　　$^1/_2$　　CUP SOFT SWEET BUTTER
　　　　　　　　1　　TUBE (1.6 OZ) ANCHOVY PASTE

METHOD:　　Cream the butter and anchovy together.

USE ON:　　Broiled or barbecued steaks, chops and fish fillets.

YIELD:　　$^2/_3$ cup.

NUTRITIONAL FACTS:

Serving Size: 2 Tsp	Total Fat: 6 g	Sodium: 105 mg	Sugar: 0 g
Calories Per Serving: 60	Sat Fat: 3.5 g	Total Carbs: 0 g	Protein: 1 g
Fat Calories: 50	Cholest: 20 mg	Fiber: 0 g	

CAVIAR BUTTER

Not a hard item to find. Today most grocery stores carry American caviar and it is not as expensive as the Beluga Caviar. American caviar is somewhat larger than the Russian sturgeon roe, but since you'll be pureeing them it doesn't matter.

INGREDIENTS:	$^1/_2$	CUP BUTTER, CREAMED OR AT ROOM TEMPERATURE
	2	OUNCES CAVIAR

METHOD: Puree the caviar using a small cup-size processor, or press it through a large strainer using a rubber spatula. Cream the caviar and butter together. Use.

USE ON: Fish, baked, poached or broiled. Use sparingly.

YIELD: $^3/_4$ cup.

NUTRITIONAL FACTS:

Serving Size: 2 Tsp	Total Fat: 6 g	Sodium: 105 mg	Sugar: 0g
Calories Per Serving: 60	Sat Fat: 3.5 g	Total Carbs: 0 g	Protein: 1 g
Fat Calories: 50	Cholest: 35 mg	Fiber: 0 g	

TOMATO BUTTER

INGREDIENTS:	1	POUND BUTTER - AT ROOM TEMPERATURE
	4	TOMATOES, BLANCHED, PEELED, SEEDED AND MINCED
	$^{1}/_{2}$	TEASPOON FRESH, FINELY CHOPPED BASIL LEAVES

METHOD: Cream the butter, add the remaining ingredients and cream again.

USE ON: Spread over hamburger, and grilled or broiled beef cuts. Or seafood, such as shrimp or fish fillets, and eggs either poached, or shirred.

YIELD: 3 cups.

NUTRITIONAL FACTS:

Serving Size: 2 Tsp	Total Fat: 3.5 g	Sodium: 35 mg	Sugar: 0 g
Calories Per Serving: 30	Sat Fat: 2 g	Total Carbs: 0 g	Protein: 0 g
Fat Calories: 30	Cholest: 10 mg	Fiber: 0 g	

HERBAL AND SPICED BUTTERS

The object of an herbal butter is to add flavor to anything after the cooking is completed. For instance with sauteed or broiled meat an herbal butter is an excellent choice for added flavor, while spiced butters are generally used on freshly baked goods. Not all herbs or spices will work in this fashion, but if a combination sounds good to you, try it.

INGREDIENTS: $^1/_4$ CUP BUTTER
$^1/_2$ TO 1   TEASPOON OF ONE OF THE HERBS AND SPICES LISTED BELOW: LET YOUR TASTE BE YOUR GUIDE.

METHOD: Bring the butter to room temperature and add your chosen flavor. Cream until smooth and well blended. Simply spread it over your hot food.

CHOOSE FROM: ANISE, GROUND OR CRUSHED - Especially good on broiled pork, or as a baste.

CAYENNE - On any meat or egg dish.

DILL WEED - Use on fish, egg dishes and baked potatoes.

FENNEL, GROUND OR CRUSHED - Especially good on pork.

GARLIC PASTE - Use on broiled steak or chicken.

MUSTARD, GROUND - Burgers and beef cuts.

PAPRIKA - Chicken, veal, poached or broiled fish, baked potatoes.

PARSLEY, CHOPPED - Meats, fish, baked potatoes and assorted vegetables.

USE ON: Meats, Seafoods and vegetables.

CHOOSE FROM: ALMONDS - Ground or minced plus a little sugar.

CINNAMON - A touch of sugar would be a nice addition.

CLOVE, GROUND - You might want to add a touch of sugar or honey to this one.

28-6

LEMON ZEST, FRESHLY GRATED - Add a few drops of a favorite liqueur.

ORANGE ZEST, FRESHLY GRATED - Add a teaspoon of orange juice.

USE ON: Fresh from the oven sweet yeast dough products.

YIELD: $^1/_4$ cup.

NUTRITIONAL FACTS:			
Serving Size: 2 Tsp	Total Fat: 8 g	Sodium: 85 mg	Sugar: 0 g
Calories Per Serving: 70	Sat Fat: 5 g	Total Carbs: 0 g	Protein: 0 g
Fat Calories: 70	Cholest: 20 mg	Fiber: 0 g	

BASIL BUTTER

Two choices, two ways to use the butter. As a spread, use the Parmesan cheese and as an alternate add the cracked peppercorns. When you choose the flavored butter to saute vegetables or scramble eggs, omit the cheese.

INGREDIENTS:

$^1/_2$	CUP BUTTER
1	CLOVE GARLIC, MINCED
$^1/_4$	CUP MINCED FRESH BASIL LEAVES
1	TEASPOON CRACKED PEPPERCORNS
	OR
1	TABLESPOON FRESHLY GRATED PARMESAN CHEESE

METHOD: Let the butter warm to room temperature, then thoroughly blend all the ingredients. Let the butter stand, to meld the flavors before chilling.

USE ON: Freshly cooked pasta, as a vegetable saute, to flavor scrambled eggs, on broiled chicken, steak or fish, as a spread on crusty toast made from French or Italian bread.

YIELD: $^3/_4$ cup.

NUTRITIONAL FACTS:

Serving Size: 1 T	Total Fat: 11 g	Sodium: 120 mg	Sugar: 0 g
Calories Per Serving: 100	Sat Fat: 7 g	Total Carbs: 0 g	Protein: 0 g
Fat Calories: 100	Cholest: 30 mg	Fiber: 0 g	

PROVENCE BUTTER

As I have previously noted in this book. "Aioli Sauce" in some areas of France, is called a "Provence Butter". Well, so is this one. Sauce names travel, recipes don't. Here is an excellent example.

INGREDIENTS:	1	POUND BUTTER
	1	SHALLOT, MINCED
	2	CLOVES GARLIC, MINCED OR SMASHED TO A PASTE
	2	TABLESPOONS DEMI GLACE
	PINCH	FRESHLY GROUND BLACK PEPPER
	1	TABLESPOON CHOPPED PARSLEY
	$^1/_4$	CUP DEEP RED WINE (YOUR CHOICE)

METHOD: Thoroughly blend all the ingredients. (This butter can be frozen.)

USE ON: Steak and grilled fish.

YIELD: 2 $^1/_3$ cups.

NUTRITIONAL FACTS:			
Serving Size: 1 T	Total Fat: 10 g	Sodium: 105 mg	Sugar: 0 g
Calories Per Serving: 90	Sat Fat: 6 g	Total Carbs: 0 g	Protein: 0 g
Fat Calories: 90	Cholest: 25 mg	Fiber: 0 g	

"This page is blank by Design"

CHAPTER 29

SAUCES FOR HOT OR COLD VEGETABLE DISHES.

CHEESE SAUCE

You'll need a white sauce as a base for this one. It's a very simple sauce as well as a quick and easy one.

INGREDIENTS:	1	CUP WHITE SAUCE
	1	CUP GRATED CHEESE (USE ANY SOFT AND MILD ONE)
	$^1/_2$	TEASPOON SALT
	PINCH	PAPRIKA
	SMALL	PINCH CAYENNE

OPTION: $^1/_2$ TEASPOON DRY MUSTARD

METHOD: Bring the white sauce to a low boil and add all the remaining ingredients. Stir until the cheese has melted. Serve.

USE ON: Hot or cold cooked vegetables, corn chips to make nachos.

Also..., use for Baked Macaroni (mix with cooked elbow macaroni or sea shells, bake 30 minutes at 325° F).

YIELD: $1^1/_2$ cups.

NUTRITIONAL FACTS:

Serving Size: 3 T	Total Fat: 9 g	Sodium: 280 mg	Sugar: 2 g
Calories Per Serving: 110	Sat Fat: 6 g	Total Carbs: 3 g	Protein: 5 g
Fat Calories: 80	Cholest: 25 mg	Fiber: 0 g	

Brown Sauce For Vegetables

On the face of it, this doesn't even sound good, as brown is not a good color for vegetables. However, it is a good sauce.

You'll need some browned flour, the definition of which you'll find in the front of the book at "Cooks Information" under "Sauce Thickeners".

INGREDIENTS:	2	TABLESPOONS BUTTER
	$1/4$	CUP BROWNED FLOUR
	1	CUP BROTH (YOUR CHOICE)
	$1/4$	TEASPOON SALT

METHOD: Make a roux of the butter and flour. When ready whisk in the broth until the sauce is thickened.

USE ON: Green beans, cooked whole leaf spinach and any other vegetable when your taste buds would enjoy a nice additional flavor.

YIELD: $1 1/4$ cups.

NUTRITIONAL FACTS:

Serving Size: 2 T	Total Fat: 2.5 g	Sodium: 160 mg	Sugar: 0 g
Calories Per Serving: 35	Sat Fat: 1.5 g	Total Carbs: 2 g	Protein: 1 g
Fat Calories: 20	Cholest: 5 mg	Fiber: 0 g	

STRING BEAN SAUCE

This is a marvelous sauce for string beans when you are weary of butter, salt and pepper.

INGREDIENTS:	4	SLICES BACON
	2	TABLESPOONS RED WINE VINEGAR
	1	TEASPOON SUGAR
	$^1/_4$	TEASPOON DRY MUSTARD
		DROP OR 2 TABASCO SAUCE

METHOD:

1. Cut the bacon slices into pieces several inches long. Saute the pieces until done but not fully crisp. Remove the bacon from the skillet and set aside.

2. Add the remaining ingredients to the bacon grease and cook until the sugar is dissolved. Return the bacon to the sauce.

USE ON: Steamed green or yellow string beans.

YIELD: $^1/_3$ to $^1/_2$ cup.

NUTRITIONAL FACTS:

Serving Size: 1 T	Total Fat: 6 g	Sodium: 80 mg	Sugar: 0 g
Calories Per Serving: 60	Sat Fat: 2.5 g	Total Carbs: 1 g	Protein: 1 g
Fat Calories: 60	Cholest: 5 mg	Fiber: 0 g	

DILL SPLASH

The smell of freshly picked dill or even dried dill weed is one of the most inviting bouquets in a kitchen. You could easily learn to love this sauce.

INGREDIENTS:	$^1/_4$	CUP EXTRA LIGHT OLIVE OIL
	1	TABLESPOON LIME JUICE
	2	TEASPOONS DRIED DILL WEED
		OR
	2	TABLESPOONS CHOPPED FRESH DILL WEED

METHOD: Place all the ingredients into a small jar and shake well.

USE ON: Steamed lima beans, or butter beans.

YIELD: $^1/_3$ cup

NUTRITIONAL FACTS:

Serving Size: 1 T	Total Fat: 11 g	Sodium: 0 mg	Sugar: 0 g
Calories Per Serving: 100	Sat Fat: 1.5 g	Total Carbs: 1 g	Protein: 0 g
Fat Calories: 100	Cholest: 0 mg	Fiber: 0 g	

ONION CREAM SAUCE

The flavor of onion is a marvelous compliment to many vegetables, so if you like onions, you'll enjoy this sauce.

INGREDIENTS:	2	TABLESPOONS BUTTER
	$^1/_2$	CUP MINCED ONION
	1	CUP SOUR CREAM OR WHIPPING CREAM

METHOD: Saute the onions in butter until golden. Add the cream and cook long enough to heat through.

USE ON: String beans, cauliflower, brussel sprouts, broccoli.

YIELD: 1 $^1/_3$ cups.

NUTRITIONAL FACTS:

Serving Size: 1 T	Total Fat: 3 g	Sodium: 15 mg	Sugar: 1 g
Calories Per Serving: 30	Sat Fat: 2 g	Total Carbs: 1 g	Protein: 0 g
Fat Calories: 25	Cholest: 5 mg	Fiber: 0 g	

SUGAR SAUCE

Some vegetables are naturally sweet and they can be further enhanced by adding a small amount of sugar to them, as this sauce does.

INGREDIENTS:	$^1/_4$	CUP BUTTER
	1	TABLESPOON BROWN SUGAR
	1	TEASPOON DRY MUSTARD
	$^1/_4$	TEASPOON SALT
		DROP TABASCO SAUCE

MULTIPLIER: Double or triple the above ingredients.

METHOD: Melt the butter and at the foaming stage add the remaining ingredients. Cook until the sugar has dissolved.

USE ON: Steamed carrots, boiled or sauteed onions.

YIELD: $^1/_3$ cup.

NUTRITIONAL FACTS:

Serving Size: 1 T	Total Fat: 10 g	Sodium: 230 mg	Sugar: 2 g
Calories Per Serving: 100	Sat Fat: 6 g	Total Carbs: 2 g	Protein: 0 g
Fat Calories: 90	Cholest: 25 mg	Fiber: 0 g	

BREAD SAUCE

INGREDIENTS:

$^1/_2$	CUP BREAD CRUMBS
$^1/_2$	CUP WATER
1	TABLESPOON BUTTER
1	CUP MILK OR CREAM
6+/-	WHOLE SMALL HOT PEPPERS
	SALT AND PEPPER TO TASTE

METHOD:

1. Place all the ingredients except the milk into a sauce pan and bring it to a boil. Reduce the heat and cook for 5 minutes.

2. Add the milk and return the sauce to a boil. Reduce the heat and cook 5 minutes more. Discard the peppers and season to taste with salt and pepper.

USE ON: Fresh string beans.

YIELD: 1 $^2/_3$ cups.

NUTRITIONAL FACTS:

Serving Size: 2 T	Total Fat: 1.5 g	Sodium: 45 mg	Sugar: 1 g
Calories Per Serving: 30	Sat Fat: 1 g	Total Carbs: 3 g	Protein: 1 g
Fat Calories: 15	Cholest: 5 mg	Fiber: 0 g	

BREAD CRUMB SAUCE

(POLONAISE)

The word Polonaise as used here is a sauce and it is applicable to things Polish. It was also a term for a fashionable dance in the 19th Century Polish Court and a music form used by the composers Mozart, Beethoven, Schubert, all the Bach's and most notably, Chopin.

INGREDIENTS:	$1/3$	CUP BUTTER
	1	CUP BREAD CRUMBS FROM FRENCH OR ITALIAN BREAD
	2	TEASPOONS LEMON JUICE
	2	TABLESPOONS CHOPPED PARSLEY
	1	HARD COOKED EGG, SHREDDED

METHOD: Saute the bread crumbs in the butter until they begin to turn color. Remove them from the heat and stir in the remaining ingredients.

USE ON: Asparagus, string beans, cauliflower, brussel sprouts, quartered green cabbage.

YIELD: 1 cup.

NUTRITIONAL FACTS:			
Serving Size: 2 T	Total Fat: 9 g	Sodium: 180 mg	Sugar: 0 g
Calories Per Serving: 130	Sat Fat: 5 g	Total Carbs: 9 g	Protein: 2 g
Fat Calories: 80	Cholest: 45 mg	Fiber: 1 g	

CREAMED ONION SAUCE

In my book, "The Encyclopedia of Sauces for Your Pasta", I wrote a chapter of No Fat (or Low Fat) sauces, because I have several friends who asked me to create fat free recipes for their diets. Also a special friend asked for help in making her baked potatoes virtually fat free, but still tasty. So what I have here is an absolutely delightful topping for a fluffy baked potato with a crisp skin that has been properly oven baked.

At home, the bane of a crisp-skin oven-baked potato is the microwave oven. Many restaurants seem to compulsively wrap their baking potatoes in foil, which steams the potato and leaves the skin soft and pliant. The microwave and foil wrap have left at least one, and maybe two generations of Americans who have never had a gen-u-ine crispy-skin, hot from the oven, baked potato. Too bad! They are extraordinarily good. My favorite way to eat a crispy-skin baked potato is to scoop out the potato and slather the interior of the still hot skin with butter and eat it immediately. And I still do!

For this sauce use the sweetest onion you can buy and cook it in a pan with a tight fitting lid.

INGREDIENTS:	2	TEASPOONS LIGHT OLIVE OIL
	1	MEDIUM ONION, CHOPPED
	1 OR 2	CLOVE(S) GARLIC, SMASHED
	$^1/_2$	TEASPOON SALT
	PINCH	ALLSPICE
		DROP OR 2 OF YELLOW FOOD COLORING

METHOD:

1. Saute the onion and garlic in the olive oil for 3 minutes or until the onion is wilted. Remove the pan from the heat and add the salt, allspice and food coloring. Blend thoroughly, cover and set aside for 10 minutes.

2. Place the sauce in a blender and puree until creamy.

OPTION: For a non-fat sauce, replace the olive oil with 1/4 cup of white wine. Poach the onion and garlic in the wine in a covered pan for 10 minutes, then continue as above.

Use On: Hot, crispy-skinned oven-baked potatoes. Also marvelous on string beans and steamed carrots.

Yield: $^3/_4$ cup.

NUTRITIONAL FACTS:

Serving Size: 2 T	Total Fat: 1.5 g	Sodium: 210 mg	Sugar: 2 g
Calories Per Serving: 25	Sat Fat: 0 g	Total Carbs: 3 g	Protein: 0 g
Fat Calories: 15	Cholest: 0 mg	Fiber: 1 g	

COLD VEGETABLE DRESSING

It seems as though I always cook more vegetables than I can eat and the result is - - - leftovers. Finding ways to use them, other than tossing them into a salad, calls for an interesting and flavorful sauce and this dressing has come to my rescue more than once. It is the perfect accompaniment for cold vegetables.

INGREDIENTS:	$^1/_2$	CUP MAYONNAISE
	1	TABLESPOON CHOPPED FRESH BASIL
	2	TABLESPOONS EXTRA LIGHT OLIVE OIL
	1	TEASPOON VINEGAR
		SALT AND PEPPER TO TASTE

METHOD: Thoroughly blend all the ingredients, use.

USE ON: Cold cooked asparagus, string beans, cauliflower or broccoli.

YIELD: $^3/_4$ cup.

NUTRITIONAL FACTS:

Serving Size: 1 T	Total Fat: 12 g	Sodium: 65 mg	Sugar: 0 g
Calories Per Serving: 110	Sat Fat: 1.5 g	Total Carbs: 0 g	Protein: 0 g
Fat Calories: 110	Cholest: 5 mg	Fiber: 0 g	

PEANUT SAUCE

INGREDIENTS:		
	2	TABLESPOONS LIGHT OLIVE OIL
	2	SHALLOTS, MINCED
	1	CLOVE GARLIC, MINCED
	2	CUPS UNSALTED PEANUTS (IF YOU CAN'T FIND THEM IN A CAN, BUY WHOLE AND REMOVE THE HULLS)
	1	TABLESPOON BROWN SUGAR
	1	TABLESPOON LIME JUICE
	1	TEASPOON CAYENNE
	2	CUPS WATER

METHOD:

1. Saute the shallots and garlic in the olive oil for 3 minutes, then remove from the heat. Place the hot mixture and the remaining ingredients into a food processor or blender and puree the sauce until smooth.

2. Return the sauce to your skillet and cook for an additional 5 minutes while stirring constantly. Serve.

USE ON:

Vegetable medley (i.e., boiled small red skin potatoes, steamed and cut string beans, cooked or raw shredded cabbage, tomatoes, cucumber, hard-cooked eggs). The sauce should be served warm over these vegetables at room temperature.

The sauce needs to be room temperature when it is served over a Greek style salad, or a chicken salad with either greens or vegetables.

YIELD: 3 cups.

NUTRITIONAL FACTS:			
Serving Size: 2 T	Total Fat: 6 g	Sodium: 0 mg	Sugar: 1 g
Calories Per Serving: 70	Sat Fat: 1 g	Total Carbs: 3 g	Protein: 2 g
Fat Calories: 50	Cholest: 0 mg	Fiber: 1 g	

VEGETABLE SALAD HONEY DRESSING

INGREDIENTS:	$1/2$	CUP HONEY
	$1/3$	CUP EXTRA LIGHT OLIVE OIL
	$1/3$	CUP DISTILLED WHITE VINEGAR (CHARDONNAY WINE VINEGAR MAY BE USED)

OPTIONS: TRY THEM ALL, BUT ONLY ONE AT A TIME;

1	TEASPOON POPPY SEED.
6	MINCED AND DRAINED SEGMENTS OF MANDARIN ORANGES.
1	TEASPOON SESAME SEEDS.
PINCH	OF CAYENNE.

METHOD: Thoroughly blend all the ingredients.

USE ON: Shredded vegetables, carrots, cole slaw, zucchini, crookneck squash, snow peas or cucumbers .

YIELD: $1 1/4$ cups.

NUTRITIONAL FACTS:

Serving Size: 2 T	Total Fat: 7 g	Sodium: 0 mg	Sugar: 13 g
Calories Per Serving: 110	Sat Fat: 1 g	Total Carbs: 13 g	Protein: 0 g
Fat Calories: 60	Cholest: 0 mg	Fiber: 0 g	

CUCUMBER SAUCE

INGREDIENTS:	1	CUCUMBER, PARED AND FINELY CHOPPED
	1	CUP SOUR CREAM
	2	TABLESPOONS LEMON JUICE
	1	TABLESPOON MINCED PARSLEY

OPTION: Exchange mayonnaise or yogurt for the sour cream.

METHOD: Blend all the ingredients and chill before using.

USE ON: Cold vegetables such as; boiled potatoes, string beans, summer squash, or as a celery dip. Also on sliced cold veal, lamb or fish.

YIELD: 1 $^3/_4$ cups.

NUTRITIONAL FACTS:

Serving Size: 1 T	Total Fat: 1.5 g	Sodium: 0 mg	Sugar: 0 g
Calories Per Serving: 15	Sat Fat: 1 g	Total Carbs: 1 g	Protein: 0 g
Fat Calories: 10	Cholest: 5 mg	Fiber: 0 g	

"This page is blank by Design"

CHAPTER 30

RELISH TYPE SAUCES MADE TO BE USED AS DIPS

An interesting feature of a relish is that you can blenderize or process them to any degree of smoothness you want and it doesn't change the taste. In the case of a salsa dip, it allows the sauce to hang on to the chip, as opposed to your using the chip as a scoop. With foods you eat often, its nice to vary the presentation.

GUACAMOLE

Since avocado turns an unappetizing brown color very quickly and that is something you want to avoid, then this recipe is for you, because it lets the Guacamole retain its green color. There are those who maintain that citric acid is what allows the mix to keep its bright green color. Mexican friends tell me it is the avocado pit that does it. My experience is, that it's a combination of both the pit and the acid. And I wouldn't bet the farm on that experience either.

Ingredients:	1	RIPE AVOCADO
	1	TABLESPOONS LEMON OR LIME JUICE
	$^1/_2$	TEASPOON SALT
	$^1/_2$	TEASPOON BLACK PEPPER
	1	CLOVE GARLIC, GRATED OR PRESSED

Options:	2	TABLESPOONS CHOPPED BELL PEPPER.
	2	TABLESPOONS CHOPPED GREEN ONION.
	2	TABLESPOONS SEEDED DICED TOMATOES.

Method: Peel and mash the avocado, add the remaining ingredients and blend well. Return the avocado pit to the mixture.

Use On: Use as a dip for chips, (corn or potato). As a dressing on sandwiches, tomato wedges, omelets, tacos, burritos and tostadas.

Yield: 1 cup.

NUTRITIONAL FACTS:

Serving Size: 1/3 cup	Total Fat: 14 g	Sodium: 550 mg	Sugar: 1 g
Calories Per Serving: 140	Sat Fat: 2.5 g	Total Carbs: 9 g	Protein: 1 g
Fat Calories: 120	Cholest: 0 mg	Fiber: 6 g	

GUACAMOLE II

(WITH A ZIPPY BITE)

INGREDIENTS:	4	AVOCADOS, MASHED OR PUREED
	1	4 OUNCE CAN CHOPPED JALAPENO
	1	TEASPOON SALT, OR TO TASTE
	$1/4$	CUP FINELY CHOPPED ONION
	$1/4$	CUP LEMON JUICE
OPTIONS:	$1/2$	CUP SOUR CREAM.
	$1/2$	CUP BLANCHED, PEELED AND CHOPPED TOMATOES.
	$1/2$	TEASPOON TABASCO SAUCE EXCHANGED FOR THE JALAPENO.

METHOD: Combine all the ingredients and put them in the refrigerator for an hour or so to meld.

USE ON: Corn chips, or as a dressing for tomato wedges, omelets, tacos, burritos or tostadas.

YIELD: 4 cups.

NUTRITIONAL FACTS:

Serving Size: 1/3 cup	Total Fat: 11 g	Sodium: 390 mg	Sugar: 1 g
Calories Per Serving: 120	Sat Fat: 2 g	Total Carbs: 8 g	Protein: 1 g
Fat Calories: 100	Cholest: 0 mg	Fiber: 5 g	

FRESH TOMATO SALSA

A fresh tasting salsa without an ornery temperament. In almost every restaurant featuring Mexican food they serve an appetizer of salsa and corn chips. Far too many of them are hot enough to sear your taste buds. Now, I've never believed that eating an appetizer, designed to take the edge off my appetite, should simultaneously obliterate my ability to taste the entree. This salsa won't do that to you.

INGREDIENTS:	4	MEDIUM TOMATOES, BLANCHED, PEELED AND CHOPPED
	$1/2$	CUP CHOPPED ONION
	$1/2$	CUP CHOPPED CELERY
	$1/2$	CUP CHOPPED BELL PEPPER, ANAHEIM OR OTHER MILDLY HOT PEPPER
	3	TABLESPOONS RED WINE VINEGAR
	1	TEASPOON SALT
	PINCH	GROUND CORIANDER SEED

METHOD: Blend all the ingredients and leave them at room temperature for an hour or more, to let them meld.

USE ON: Corn chips or ridged potato chips.

YIELD: 5 cups.

NUTRITIONAL FACTS:			
Serving Size: 1/2 cup	Total Fat: 0.5 g	Sodium: 340 mg	Sugar: 3 g
Calories Per Serving: 30	Sat Fat: 0 g	Total Carbs: 7 g	Protein: 1 g
Fat Calories: 5	Cholest: 0 mg	Fiber: 1 g	

FRESH TOMATO SALSA TOO!

This recipe is from Mexican friends who occasionally featured a salsa when our monthly pinochle game was held at their house.

INGREDIENTS:	1	CLOVE GARLIC, MASHED
	$1/2$	TEASPOON SALT
	2	TABLESPOONS FRESH LIME JUICE
		OR
		WHITE WINE VINEGAR WHEN FRESH LIMES ARE HARD TO GET
	1	LB (APPROXIMATELY 8) ROMA, SALADETTE OR PLUM TOMATOES (SAME TOMATO, DIFFERENT NAMES), SEEDED AND DICED
	1	FRESH JALAPENO, SEEDED
		OR
	2	TABLESPOONS CANNED AND DICED (MILDER THAN THE FRESH)
	2	FRESH ANAHEIM CHILI PEPPERS OR OTHER MILDLY HOT GREEN PEPPER, SEEDED AND DICED
	1	MEDIUM SWEET ONION, CHOPPED
	3	TABLESPOONS CHOPPED PARSLEY OR CILANTRO

METHOD: On a cutting board, mash the garlic with the salt, scrape it up and place into your serving bowl. Whisk in the vinegar or lime juice and add the remaining ingredients. Toss to blend and let it meld for an hour or so at room temperature. Serve.

USE ON: Corn chip dip, on scrambled eggs or in omelets.

YIELD: 3 cups.

NUTRITIONAL FACTS:			
Serving Size: 1/2 cup	Total Fat: 0.5 g	Sodium: 260 mg	Sugar: 4 g
Calories Per Serving: 35	Sat Fat: 0 g	Total Carbs: 8 g	Protein: 1 g
Fat Calories: 5	Cholest: 0 mg	Fiber: 1 g	

TOMATO SALSA

Similar to the preceding salsa, but there are several differences. This one has a slight zip to it and uses canned tomatoes instead of fresh and a little jalapeno. If you cannot find the canned weights suggested, get as close as possible.

INGREDIENTS:	1	16 OUNCE CAN OF PEELED AND DICED TOMATOES
	1	4 OUNCE CAN PEELED, CHOPPED AND RINSED JALAPENO
	2	TABLESPOONS WINE VINEGAR
	1/2	CUP CHOPPED ONION
		TEASPOON SUGAR
		SALT TO TASTE

OPTION: Replace the canned jalapeno with chopped fresh anaheim chili pepper.

METHOD: Blend all the ingredients and let it meld for an hour or more at room temperature.

USE ON: Corn chips.

YIELD: 3 cups.

NUTRITIONAL FACTS:

Serving Size: 1/2 cup	Total Fat: 0 g	Sodium: 400 mg	Sugar: 4 g
Calories Per Serving: 30	Sat Fat: 0 g	Total Carbs: 7 g	Protein: 1 g
Fat Calories: 0	Cholest: 0 mg	Fiber: 2 g	

FRESH DIP

INGREDIENTS:	2	TOMATOES, PEELED AND CHOPPED
	1/4	CUP ONION
	1/2	CUP CHOPPED GREEN BELL PEPPER
	1/4	CUP CHOPPED RED BELL PEPPER
	1/2	CUP LEMON JUICE

METHOD: toss all the ingredients together and allow to meld for an hour or so at room temperature.

USE ON: Corn chips, pita bread, sesame crackers or toss with cooked medium sea shells or rotelle (twists) for a pasta salad.

YIELD: 3 cups.

NUTRITIONAL FACTS:

Serving Size: 1/2 cup	Total Fat: 0 g	Sodium: 0 mg	Sugar: 4 g
Calories Per Serving: 30	Sat Fat: 0 g	Total Carbs: 8 g	Protein: 1 g
Fat Calories: 0	Cholest: 0 mg	Fiber: 1 g	

CLAM DIP

INGREDIENTS:
1	$6^{1}/_{2}$ OUNCE CAN MINCED CLAMS
1	POUND CREAM CHEESE OR COTTAGE CHEESE
1	CLOVE GARLIC, MINCED
1	TABLESPOON LEMON JUICE

METHOD: Drain the clam juice into a blender. Add the lemon juice and garlic and puree until you get a smooth sauce. Transfer the mixture to a serving bowl and stir in the minced clams.

OPTION: Double up on the clams.

USE ON: Chips, cooked fish sticks, baked quartered potatoes.

YIELD: $2^{3}/_{4}$ cups.

NUTRITIONAL FACTS:			
Serving Size: 1/4 cup	Total Fat: 15 g	Sodium: 170 mg	Sugar: 1 g
Calories Per Serving: 170	Sat Fat: 7 g	Total Carbs: 3 g	Protein: 7 g
Fat Calories: 130	Cholest: 55 mg	Fiber: 0 g	

CHAPTER 31

SAUCES MADE FOR FRUIT

CITRUS AND MELON DRESSING

If you enjoy a fruit salad of citrus and melon, I think you're going to love this sauce. And if you wish, the citrus can be sectioned and the melons and pineapple can be chunked or balled.

INGREDIENTS:

1	CUP HONEY
PINCH	GROUND CARDAMOM
$^1/_2$	CUP WATER
$^1/_2$	TEASPOON SALT
12	FRESH MINT LEAVES
1	CUP BLUSH OR WHITE ZINFANDEL WINE
2	TABLESPOONS LEMON JUICE

METHOD:

1. Place the first 4 ingredients into a sauce pan and bring to a boil. Lower the heat and cook for 5 minutes. Remove from the heat, add the mint leaves and stir. Let the sauce cool. When cool, strain to remove any mint leaves and stir in the wine and lemon juice.

2. You can use this sauce immediately, or marinate your fruit in the sauce at room temperature for several hours before chilling to serve.

OPTION: Mince the mint leaves if you would like to leave them in the sauce.

USE ON: Pineapple, grapefruit, oranges, cantaloupe, honeydew, casaba canary, Santa Claus or other varieties of melon (but not watermelon).

YIELD: 2 $^2/_3$ cups.

NUTRITIONAL FACTS:

Serving Size: 1/4 cup	Total Fat: 0 g	Sodium: 100 mg	Sugar: 23 g
Calories Per Serving: 100	Sat Fat: 0 g	Total Carbs: 23 g	Protein: 0 g
Fat Calories: 0	Cholest: 0 mg	Fiber: 0 g	

RUM CUSTARD FRUIT SAUCE

When fruit that you love is in season, you're apt to buy a lot of it so that you can eat them to your heart's content. Don't you wish on occasion that you could add a "little something" just for a change? Well I've come to your rescue again. This sauce is that "little something". And it's easier to make than it is to say. While rum is the preferred choice of spirit in this sauce, feel free to exchange it for a liqueur such as Amaretto, Anisette or a fruit brandy, flavorful wines such as Marsala, Sherry, Port or a Muscato, or a good sour mash whiskey.

INGREDIENTS:

1 1/2	CUPS HALF-N-HALF
3	TABLESPOONS SUGAR
PINCH	SALT
2	EGGS PLUS 1 EGG YOLK
2	TABLESPOONS RUM

METHOD:

1. In a small bowl, thoroughly beat the eggs and egg yolk, then set aside.

2. In a small sauce pan, heat the half-and-half and the sugar and salt to scalding.

3. Remove the pan from the heat and pour a small amount of hot half-and-half into the eggs. Then whisk to blend.

4. Whisk the egg mixture into the hot half-and-half. Return the pan to the heat and cook until the sauce begins to thicken.

5. Remove the sauce from the heat add the rum. Cool and chill before using.

USE ON: Fresh fruit slices of: peaches, nectarines, strawberries, bananas or pineapple. Whole blackberries, boysenberries, seedless grapes or fruit cups.

YIELD: 2 1/2 cups.

NUTRITIONAL FACTS:

Serving Size: 3 T	Total Fat: 5 g	Sodium: 25 mg	Sugar: 3 g
Calories Per Serving: 70	Sat Fat: 2.5 g	Total Carbs: 4 g	Protein: 2 g
Fat Calories: 45	Cholest: 65 mg	Fiber: 0 g	

HOT CARAMEL SAUCE

This is an outstanding treat if you like caramel and apples. Instead of wrestling with a large caramel covered apple, serve it as I suggest. I'm sure you'll love it.

There is an easy way and a hard way to do this. The easy way is to melt 1/2 pound of caramels in one cup of half-and-half. Cook them over low heat, or in a double boiler until the caramels are completely melted. For a richer flavor use whipping cream, or for a less rich flavor, use milk. The hard way is to follow the recipe and make your own caramel syrup from scratch. It's almost like making chewy caramels, but you won't cook it to that stage.

INGREDIENTS:

2	CUPS SUGAR
$^1/_4$	TEASPOON SALT
2	CUPS WHITE CORN SYRUP
1	CUP BUTTER
2	CUPS MILK
1	CUP $^1/_2$ AND $^1/_2$

FLAVOR WITH 1 OF THE FOLLOWING:

1	TEASPOON VANILLA
2	TABLESPOONS RUM
3	TABLESPOONS MAPLE SYRUP
3	OUNCE PIECE OF UNSWEETENED CHOCOLATE

METHOD: Place the sugar, corn syrup and salt into a sauce pan over medium heat. Whisk to blend the ingredients while bringing the mixture slowly to a boil. Cook for about 5 minutes and add the butter. When the butter is melted and well blended, slowly whisk in the milk and the $^1/_2$ and $^1/_2$. Blend the mixture thoroughly and bring it back to a boil. Cook for 2 additional minutes. Remove it from the heat and add your choice of flavoring. Serve warm.

USE ON: Wedges of tart, crisp, cold apples. And it's great on ice cream.

YIELD: 7 cups.

NUTRITIONAL FACTS:			
Serving Size: 1/3 cup	Total Fat: 5 g	Sodium: 80 mg	Sugar: 15 g
Calories Per Serving: 120	Sat Fat: 3.5 g	Total Carbs: 19 g	Protein: 1 g
Fat Calories: 50	Cholest: 15 mg	Fiber: 0 g	

LEMON DIPPING SAUCE

Since most fruits are now available to us year round you may want to serve them with a slightly different twist. This sauce lets you do it.

INGREDIENTS:	1 1/2	TEASPOONS FRESHLY GRATED LEMON RIND
	1/3	CUP LEMON JUICE
	1 1/2	TABLESPOONS CORN STARCH
	1	CUP WATER
	1/2	CUP SUGAR
	PINCH	SALT

METHOD:

1. Grate the zest from the lemon and set aside.

2. Juice the lemon and dissolve the corn starch in the lemon juice and set aside.

3. Bring the water, sugar and salt to a boil and cook until the syrup is clear (about 3 minutes). Add lemon juice and the lemon zest to the boiling syrup and cook until slightly thickened. Cool before using.

USE ON: As a dipping sauce for a variety of melons (especially cantaloupe), apple wedges, orange segments.

YIELD: 1 2/3 cups.

NUTRITIONAL FACTS:			
Serving Size: 1/4 cup	Total Fat: 0 g	Sodium: 0 mg	Sugar: 10 g
Calories Per Serving: 150	Sat Fat: 0 g	Total Carbs: 13 g	Protein: 0 g
Fat Calories: 0	Cholest: 0 mg	Fiber: 0 g	

STRAWBERRY BALSAMIC SAUCE

At first glance this doesn't sound right at all, but it is. It's an excellent and easy sauce for sliced strawberries when you want to give the sugar some added "oomph".

INGREDIENTS:	$^1/_4$ to $^1/_3$	CUP SUGAR
	2	TABLESPOON BALSAMIC VINEGAR

METHOD: Blend both ingredients and allow to dissolve and meld, about 5 minutes.\

ALTERNATE: Toss the strawberries with the sugar about 1 hour before serving and let rest. Just before serving, add the balsamic vinegar and toss again.

USE ON: Thoroughly blend with 1 quart fresh sliced strawberries, fresh peach slices or fresh pear slices.

YIELD: $^1/_2$ cup.

NUTRITIONAL FACTS:

Serving Size: 2 Tsp	Total Fat: 0 g	Sodium: 0 mg	Sugar: 7 g
Calories Per Serving: 30	Sat Fat: 0 g	Total Carbs: 8 g	Protein: 0 g
Fat Calories: 0	Cholest: 0 mg	Fiber: 0 g	

WE TRIED THIS SAUCE ... AND

LOVED IT (   )
HATED IT (   )
MAYBE WE'LL TRY IT AGAIN (   )
WE'LL USE IT FOR UNWELCOME GUESTS (   )

STRAWBERRY CREAM SAUCE

This is a great all 'round summer sauce. I think you're going to like this one.

INGREDIENTS:

1	PINT STRAWBERRIES, STEMMED
2	TABLESPOONS TRIPLE SEC
2	TABLESPOONS WHIPPING CREAM
1/4	CUP SUGAR OR HONEY

METHOD: Place all the ingredients into a blender and puree until the sauce is smooth.

USE ON: Summer melons (except watermelon), pineapple chunks, ice cream, shortbread cakes, corn bread, pound cake slices.

YIELD: 1 1/2 cups.

NUTRITIONAL FACTS:

Serving Size: 1/4 cup	Total Fat: 1 g	Sodium: 0 mg	Sugar: 6 g
Calories Per Serving: 50	Sat Fat: 0.5 g	Total Carbs: 10 g	Protein: 0 g
Fat Calories: 10	Cholest: 5 mg	Fiber: 1 g	

ALMOND CREAM SAUCE

When you put this sauce on your fresh sliced fruit, it's going to look like a large spoonful of whipped cream, but with more flavor.

You can substitute the sour cream with a low fat dairy product.

INGREDIENTS:

$^1/_4$ CUP SLICED TOASTED ALMONDS
1 $^1/_2$ CUPS SOUR CREAM
$^1/_4$ CUP BROWN SUGAR
$^1/_4$ TEASPOON ALMOND EXTRACT

METHOD:

1. Toast the almonds in a dry skillet, either on your stove top or in the oven. Set them aside to cool.

2. Whisk the remaining ingredients together.

3. To serve, top your fresh fruit with a large dollop of the sauce and garnish with the toasted almonds.

USE ON: Fresh sliced strawberries, whole blackberries, fresh sliced peaches, or apricot halves.

YIELD: 1 $^3/_4$ cups.

NUTRITIONAL FACTS:

Serving Size: 2 T	Total Fat: 7 g	Sodium: 15 mg	Sugar: 3 g
Calories Per Serving: 80	Sat Fat: 3.5 g	Total Carbs: 4 g	Protein: 2 g
Fat Calories: 60	Cholest: 10 mg	Fiber: 0 g	

"This page is blank by Design"

CHAPTER 32

SAUCES MADE TO BE SERVED
OVER / UNDER OR WITH DESSERTS

BRANDY SAUCE

As with many holiday goodies, those with alcohol in them tend to require some aging to develop their maximum goodness. This one is no different. It should be aged for about a month, give or take a few days.

INGREDIENTS:	$^1/_2$	CUP BUTTER
	$1\,^1/_2$	CUPS POWDERED SUGAR
	1	EGG YOLK
	3	TABLESPOONS BRANDY OR RUM

METHOD:

1. Cream the butter and powdered sugar together. When light and fluffy, add the egg yolk and continue beating until the mixture is very light in color. Add the brandy and beat it into the sauce until it is smooth and creamy.

2. Pack the sauce into a small sterilized container and store in the refrigerator to age.

USE ON: Fruit cake, pound cake, steamed puddings.

YIELD: 2 cups.

NUTRITIONAL FACTS:			
Serving Size: 1 T	Total Fat: 4 g	Sodium: 40 mg	Sugar: 7 g
Calories Per Serving: 70	Sat Fat: 2.5 g	Total Carbs: 8 g	Protein: 0 g
Fat Calories: 35	Cholest: 20 mg	Fiber: 0 g	

WHIPPED LEMON CREAM SAUCE

INGREDIENTS:

1	CUP SUGAR
$^{1}/_{2}$	CUP WATER
3	EGG YOLKS, WELL BEATEN
1	CUP WHIPPING CREAM
$^{1}/_{2}$	CUP LEMON EXTRACT

METHOD:

1. Place the sugar and water into a sauce pan and bring to a boil. Boil for five minutes then remove from the heat. Set it aside.

2. In a medium sized bowl, beat the egg yolks until light. Pour the hot syrup into the egg in a thin, steady stream while constantly beating. When the mixture is smooth and light, set it aside and allow it to cool. Then stir the lemon extract into the mixture.

3. When ready to serve, whip the cream and fold it carefully into the mixture, serve.

USE ON: Puddings and steamed puddings.

YIELD: 3 cups.

NUTRITIONAL FACTS:

Serving Size: 2 T	Total Fat: 4 g	Sodium: 5 mg	Sugar: 6 g
Calories Per Serving: 60	Sat Fat: 2.5 g	Total Carbs: 7 g	Protein: 1 g
Fat Calories: 35	Cholest: 40 mg	Fiber: 0 g	

LEMON SAUCE

Lemon does such nice things to the foods we eat, and they are particularly enjoyable as a sauce for desserts. This is a fairly simple, old fashioned type of lemon sauce.

It is best to use a double boiler to make this sauce.

INGREDIENTS:		
	1	EGG YOLK, BEATEN
	$^1/_2$	CUP SUGAR
	1	TABLESPOON CORN STARCH
	PINCH	SALT
	1	CUP VERY HOT WATER
	2	TABLESPOONS BUTTER
	2	TABLESPOONS LEMON JUICE
	1	GRATED LEMON RIND (ZEST ONLY)

METHOD:

1. Beat the egg yolk and set aside.

2. Place the sugar, corn starch and salt into a small sauce pan. Pour hot water into the pan and set the pan on medium heat while whisking constantly, cook for 5 minutes. Add the butter, lemon juice and grated zest. Cook for 1 additional minute and remove from the heat.

3. Whisk $^1/_2$ cup of the lemon mixture with the egg yolk (to blend). Then add all the egg mixture to the remaining lemon sauce.

4. Return the sauce to the heat. Whisk to blend, while cooking, for 1 additional minute and remove from the heat. Cool before serving.

USE ON: Unfrosted cakes, gingerbread or puddings.

YIELD: 1 $^3/_4$ cups.

NUTRITIONAL FACTS:			
Serving Size: 2 T	Total Fat: 2 g	Sodium: 20 mg	Sugar: 5 g
Calories Per Serving: 45	Sat Fat: 1 g	Total Carbs: 6 g	Protein: 0 g
Fat Calories: 20	Cholest: 20 mg	Fiber: 0 g	

RUM SAUCE

This one is simplicity itself, quick and spirited, it has year long applications. If you don't tell anyone you've used a mix, you can, in a moment or two, show off your legendary culinary skills (acquired as result of using my book) during the Christmas season.

INGREDIENTS:	1	BOX INSTANT VANILLA PUDDING MIX
	$^1/_2$	CUP RUM (LIGHT OR DARK)

OPTION: Exchange half the rum for whipping cream.

METHOD: Blend the rum with the pudding package mix.

USE ON: Sparingly on bread pudding, plum pudding, rice pudding, cake that has slightly dried out and any other pudding you wish to enhance with a touch of spirits.

YIELD: 1 cup.

NUTRITIONAL FACTS:

Serving Size: 1 T	Total Fat: 0 g	Sodium: 100 mg	Sugar: 5 g
Calories Per Serving: 45	Sat Fat: 0 g	Total Carbs: 7 g	Protein: 0 g
Fat Calories: 0	Cholest: 0 mg	Fiber: 0 g	

Marmalade Sauce

Marmalades can be made from any citrus fruit. At the market, orange marmalade is the favorite choice and lime runs a distant second. Marmalades made from lemon or grapefruit, don't travel far from the kitchen they're made in. You'll rarely see them for sale.

INGREDIENTS:		
	2	TABLESPOONS MARMALADE
	1	TABLESPOON CORN STARCH
	$^1/_2$	CUP WATER
	$^1/_2$	CUP SWEET WINE
	$^1/_4$	TEASPOON SALT
	2	TABLESPOONS SUGAR

METHOD:

1. Mix the corn starch and marmalade and set aside.

2. Place the remaining ingredients into a sauce pan and bring them to a boil. Whisk in the marmalade mixture and cook for about 3 minutes. Cool to room temperature before using.

USE ON: Sponge cake, white cake yellow cake or fruit pie.

YIELD: 1 $^1/_4$ cups.

NUTRITIONAL FACTS:			
Serving Size: 2 T	Total Fat: 0 g	Sodium: 60 mg	Sugar: 2 g
Calories Per Serving: 35	Sat Fat: 0 g	Total Carbs: 6 g	Protein: 0 g
Fat Calories: 0	Cholest: 0 mg	Fiber: 0 g	

NUTMEG SAUCE

INGREDIENTS:

1	TABLESPOON CORN STARCH
3	TABLESPOONS SUGAR
$^{1}/_{4}$	TEASPOON SALT
$^{1}/_{2}$	CUP WATER
$^{1}/_{4}$	TEASPOON FRESHLY GROUND NUTMEG

OPTION: Exchange the nutmeg for 2 teaspoons lemon juice.

METHOD: Place the first 4 ingredients into a sauce pan and stir to thoroughly blend. Turn on the heat and bring the mixture to a boil. Cook for 1 minute or until the sugar is dissolved. Remove from the heat and whisk in the nutmeg. Allow to cool slightly, then use warm.

USE ON: Fruit filled turnovers, slices of apple and /or peach fruit pies or sweet ricotta filled ravioli.

If you exchange the nutmeg for the lemon juice, use the sauce on fruit turnovers or puddings.

YIELD: $^{3}/_{4}$ cup.

NUTRITIONAL FACTS:

Serving Size: 1 T	Total Fat: 0 g	Sodium: 55 mg	Sugar: 2 g
Calories Per Serving: 15	Sat Fat: 0 g	Total Carbs: 3 g	Protein: 0 g
Fat Calories: 0	Cholest: 0 mg	Fiber: 0 g	

CINNAMON SAUCE

This sauce, when served warm over fresh-from-the-oven apple pie, is hard to beat.

INGREDIENTS:	$^2/_3$	CUP WATER
	3	TABLESPOONS SUGAR
	PINCH	SALT
	$^1/_2$	SCANT TEASPOON GROUND CINNAMON
	1	TABLESPOON CORN STARCH

METHOD: Place all the ingredients, except the corn starch, into a sauce pan and whisk to blend. Turn on the heat and bring the sauce to a boil. Cook for 3 minutes. Whisk in the corn starch and cook until thickened. Use warm.

USE ON: Oven warm apple pie, apple turnovers, apple tarts, apple filled crepes und effen abble struddle!

YIELD: $^3/_4$ cup.

NUTRITIONAL FACTS:

Serving Size: 3 T	Total Fat: 0 g	Sodium: 0 mg	Sugar: 6 g
Calories Per Serving: 30	Sat Fat: 0 g	Total Carbs: 8 g	Protein: 0 g
Fat Calories: 0	Cholest: 0 mg	Fiber: 0 g	

CREME ANGLAISE

Creme Anglaise is the French term for English Cream. It is a versatile sauce for a variety of desserts, including fresh fruit bowls.

INGREDIENTS:
3	EGG YOLKS
3	TABLESPOONS SUGAR
1	TEASPOON SUGAR
1	CUP MILK

METHOD:

1. Thoroughly blend the egg yolks, sugar and vanilla together in a bowl and set aside.

2. Place the milk into a sauce pan and bring to a scald. Remove from the heat.

3. Whisk continuously while slowly pouring the scalded milk into the egg mixture. When thoroughly blended transfer the mixture back into the sauce pan.

4. Return the pan to the heat and cook over medium until sauce begins to thicken slightly. Remove the sauce from the heat and cool to room temperature to serve.

USE ON: Fresh fruit cups, cake, pie, ice cream and puddings.

YIELD: 1 $^3/_4$ cups

NUTRITIONAL FACTS:

Serving Size: 3 T	Total Fat: 3.5 g	Sodium: 20 mg	Sugar: 5 g
Calories Per Serving: 60	Sat Fat: 1.5 g	Total Carbs: 6 g	Protein: 2 g
Fat Calories: 30	Cholest: 95 mg	Fiber: 0 g	

HOMEMADE HOT FUDGE SAUCE

Back in the 40's when I was in junior high school, I worked as a soda jerk in my neighborhood pharmacy. Those were the days when neighborhood drug stores had luncheon counters and soda fountains. At that time I had two favorite sundaes, a "Tin Roof", (also the favorite of former Clevelander, Bob Hope), which was vanilla ice cream covered with chocolate syrup, generously sprinkled with Spanish peanuts, a dollop of whipped cream and topped with a maraschino cherry. My second favorite was, and still is, a hot fudge sundae. Two generous scoops of vanilla ice cream and slathered with warm velvety hot fudge sauce. I'm delighted to share with you, a very good, homemade hot fudge sauce.

INGREDIENTS: 1   14 OUNCE CAN OF SWEETENED CONDENSED MILK (DON'T USE EVAPORATED MILK)

$^1/_2$ CUP COCOA POWDER

3   TABLESPOONS MILK

1   TABLESPOON BUTTER

1   TEASPOON VANILLA

METHOD: Place the first 3 ingredients into a sauce pan and slowly bring the mixture to a scald. Remove the mixture from the heat and whisk in the butter and vanilla. Serve.

IMPORTANT: There are several methods used in making this sauce.

The 1st, my favorite, is as described above. If cooking on a gas stove, make the sauce in a pan above the direct heat, by using a diffuser. Use a wire separator/lifter for an electric stove. These devices will keep the pan from direct contact with the heat source and substantially slow down the potential for scorching.

The 2nd and quickest method is to microwave the first three ingredients on high for 1 minute then remove the mixture and stir. Return the sauce to the microwave to cook for 1 additional minute. Remove the mixture from the microwave and whisk in the butter and vanilla and serve.

The 3rd method is to use a double boiler. Bring the mixture to scald, remove it from the heat and whisk in the butter and vanilla and serve.

Use On: Ice cream and anything else you want to embellish with hot fudge.

Yield: 2 ¹/₂ cups.

NUTRITIONAL FACTS:

Serving Size: 1/4 cup	Total Fat: 5 g	Sodium: 115 mg	Sugar: 25 g
Calories Per Serving: 190	Sat Fat: 3.5 g	Total Carbs: 32 g	Protein: 5 g
Fat Calories: 50	Cholest: 20 mg	Fiber: 0 g	

CHOCOLATE SAUCE

Very, very, rich ice cream sauce. Use for anything you want to load with chocolate calories.

INGREDIENTS:

$1/2$	CUP CLARIFIED SWEET BUTTER
$1/2$	CUP WHIPPING CREAM
8	OUNCES BITTERSWEET CHOCOLATE, SHREDDED
$1/2$	TEASPOON VANILLA EXTRACT

METHOD: If you don't have any on hand, clarify the butter first:

1. Melt the butter over a low heat or in the microwave oven. Chill and when solid again, cut away the white solids and discard.

2. Heat the clarified butter in a double boiler, stir in the whipping cream and shredded chocolate and bring the mixture to a simmer. Cook until the chocolate has melted and the sauce is very smooth. Remove from the heat, stir in the vanilla and cool to room temperature.

OPTION: For a darker sauce, replace the whipping cream with an equal amount of clarified butter.

USE ON: Ice cream.

YIELD: 2 cups.

NUTRITIONAL FACTS:

Serving Size: 1/4 cup	Total Fat: 33 g	Sodium: 10 mg	Sugar: 1 g
Calories Per Serving: 310	Sat Fat: 20 g	Total Carbs: 9 g	Protein: 4 g
Fat Calories: 300	Cholest: 50 mg	Fiber: 5 g	

BABA AU RHUM SAUCE

Rum and brandies seem to find their way to many winter holiday foods between Thanksgiving and the New Year. This is a rum flavored sauce. It is drizzled over a rich cake and then allowed to rest for a while so the sauce can be fully absorbed by the cake.

INGREDIENTS:	1	CUP SUGAR
	1	CUP STRONG TEA
	3	TABLESPOONS RUM

OPTION: 2 teaspoons of rum extract can be exchanged for the rum. Add after the mixture has cooled.

METHOD: Make a syrup of the tea and sugar by boiling them for 5 minutes. Remove from the heat, add the rum and cool before drizzling over cake.

USE ON: A rich egg and butter yeast cake or a pound cake. Allow the syruped cake to stand for a hour or so, or let it age for one to seven days.

YIELD: 2 cups.

NUTRITIONAL FACTS:

Serving Size: 1 T	Total Fat: 0 g	Sodium: 0 mg	Sugar: 5 g
Calories Per Serving: 25	Sat Fat: 0 g	Total Carbs: 6 g	Protein: 0 g
Fat Calories: 0	Cholest: 0 mg	Fiber: 0 g	

FRESH PEACH SAUCE

The method for preparing this recipe gives you a very smooth sauce. If you would prefer a different texture, there are 2 steps to follow. First, very thinly slice (rather than chop) the peaches. Second, do not puree the sauce.

INGREDIENTS:	$^1/_4$	CUP (SCANT) SUGAR
	2	TEASPOONS CORN STARCH
	$^1/_2$	CUP WATER
	2	PEACHES, PARED AND CHOPPED
	$^1/_4$	TEASPOON ALMOND EXTRACT

METHOD: Blend the corn starch and water. Place all the ingredients except, the almond extract, into a sauce pan. Over a medium heat, bring the mixture to a boil and cook 1 minute. Remove from the heat and add the almond extract. While in the pan, puree the sauce with a hand held processor. Or transfer the sauce into a blender and puree. Serve warm.

USE ON: Pound cake, unfrosted white or yellow cake cake, muffins.

YIELD: 1 $^3/_4$ cups.

NUTRITIONAL FACTS:			
Serving Size: 3 T	Total Fat: 0 g	Sodium: 0 mg	Sugar: 6 g
Calories Per Serving: 30	Sat Fat: 0 g	Total Carbs: 8 g	Protein: 0 g
Fat Calories: 0	Cholest: 0 mg	Fiber: 0 g	

BOURBON SAUCE

While this recipe calls for bourbon, you could use any whiskey including Irish whiskey. In my opinion, bourbon is America's version of Irish whiskey. I'd be hard pressed to identify Irish whiskey next to bourbon in a side by side comparison. The name Bourbon comes from Bourbon County, Kentucky, the birth place of bourbon and distilled by the Irish Celtics who lived there. The distinguishing feature of bourbon is, that it is made from corn and by federal law bourbon must contain at least 51% corn whiskey.

INGREDIENTS:		
	$^3/_4$	CUP WATER
	2	TABLESPOONS SUGAR
	1	TABLESPOON CORN STARCH
	1	TABLESPOON BUTTER
	$^1/_4$	CUP BOURBON

METHOD: Place water, sugar, corn starch and butter into a sauce pan. Bring the mixture to a boil over medium heat whisking constantly. Cook for 1 minute then remove the sauce from the heat and add the bourbon.

OPTION: The above method will give you the most alcohol content along with the bourbon flavor. To decrease the alcohol content of the sauce, add the bourbon with the other ingredients so the alcohol can evaporate.

USE ON: Warm bread pudding, fruit filled muffins, pound cake or other unfrosted cake.

YIELD: 1 $^1/_4$ cups.

NUTRITIONAL FACTS:

Serving Size: 1 T	Total Fat: 0.5 g	Sodium: 5 mg	Sugar: 1 g
Calories Per Serving: 20	Sat Fat: 0 g	Total Carbs: 1 g	Protein: 0 g
Fat Calories: 5	Cholest: 0 mg	Fiber: 0 g	

ZABAGLIONE

Zabaglione is decidedly Italy's most famous custard pudding. It is light, velvety and frothy. It was a dessert made just for me, on many an occasion, by my grandmother, I loved her and I love this pudding. It is a dish you make for people you love. While it is quick and simple (only 3 ingredients) it does require intensive effort. It is usually hand-whipped over hot water and generally served warm, but it can also be served chilled. Save wear and tear on your whisking arm by going high tech, use a power driven whisk [not an egg beater]. It must be served immediately in either case, as it will not hold together. And you can use this pudding as a sauce on fresh fruit, fruit salad and small pieces of unfrosted cake, Or you can serve it as a pudding by multiplying the ingredients by the number of guests being served.

INGREDIENTS:	1	EGG YOLK
	1	TABLESPOON SUGAR
	2	TABLESPOONS MARSALA WINE

METHOD:

1. Place all the ingredients into a round bottom, stainless steel, or copper bowl and beat until they are well blended.

2. Place the bowl over boiling water and whisk the Zabaglione until it is thick and frothy, about 5 to 10 minutes. Serve immediately.

3. To chill, place your mixing bowl into a larger bowl that is filled with ice and water. Continue whisking until the pudding has chilled. Serve immediately.

OPTIONS: You can omit the Marsala in favor of a white wine. That allows you to flavor the Zabaglione with any of the following: vanilla, liqueur, grated orange or lemon zest.

USE ON: Slices of lemon or orange cake, lemon or orange muffins, fresh orange segments or fruit salads. As a pudding serve the Zabaglione in wine glasses, garnished with orange or lemon zest and accompanied with lady fingers.

YIELD: Single serving (about $^3/_4$'s of a cup).

NUTRITIONAL FACTS:

Serving Size: 1/3 cup	Total Fat: 8 g	Sodium: 280 mg	Sugar: 12 g
Calories Per Serving: 170	Sat Fat: 2.5 g	Total Carbs: 13 g	Protein: 4 g
Fat Calories: 70	Cholest: 315 mg	Fiber: 0 g	

"This page is blank by Design"

Chapter 33

Dry Mixes And Wet Sauces

This is my do-it-yourself chapter. The formula's in this chapter are similar versions of products you often buy to use at home. Save a little money and make your own.

CHILI POWDER

As with any home made spice blend you have the option of adjusting the mix to suit your taste. If this one is too fiery for you, start with half of the ingredients and adjust with the second half to suit your palette.

INGREDIENTS:

$\frac{1}{4}$	CUP GROUND CHILI PEPPER (CAYENNE IS GOOD)
2	TABLESPOONS GROUND CUMIN
1	TEASPOON GARLIC POWDER
$\frac{1}{4}$	TEASPOON GROUND OREGANO
1	TEASPOON SALT

METHOD: Blend all the ingredients well. Store in a tightly closed container.

USE ON: Chili con carne, barbecued beans, barbecue sauces,sprinkle on eggs.

YIELD: $\frac{1}{3}$ cup mix.

NUTRITIONAL FACTS:

Serving Size: 1/4 tsp	Total Fat: 0 g	Sodium: 0 mg	Sugar: 0 g
Calories Per Serving: 0	Sat Fat: 0 g	Total Carbs: 0 g	Protein: 0 g
Fat Calories: 0	Cholest: 0 mg	Fiber: 0 g	

BAKING POWDER MIX

In my kitchen, baking powder dies of old age before I get part way through the can. This recipe allows me to make it up fresh when I need it.

INGREDIENTS:	1	TABLESPOON CREAM OF TARTAR
	$1\,^1/_2$	TEASPOONS BAKING SODA
	$1\,^1/_2$	TEASPOONS CORN STARCH

METHOD: Sift all the ingredients several times to ensure a good mix. Store in a container with a tight fitting lid.

USE ON: Use 1 teaspoon of the mix to each teaspoon of baking powder called for in your recipe.

YIELD: 2 tablespoons mix.

NUTRITIONAL FACTS:

Serving Size: 1 Tsp	Total Fat: 0 g	Sodium: 820 mg	Sugar: 0 g
Calories Per Serving: 10	Sat Fat: 0 g	Total Carbs: 2 g	Protein: 0 g
Fat Calories: 0	Cholest: 0 mg	Fiber: 0 g	

DRY SALAD DRESSING MIX

Make this yourself and save money. The mix will keep for years. Add it to a mixture of extra light olive oil, vinegar and lemon juice.

INGREDIENTS:	4	TEASPOONS SALT
	1	TEASPOON GRANULATED GARLIC (NOT POWDER)
	2	TEASPOONS DRIED MINCED ONION
	1	TEASPOON FRESHLY GROUND BLACK PEPPER
	1	TEASPOON SUGAR
	1	TEASPOON PAPRIKA

METHOD: Thoroughly blend all the ingredients. Seal in a plastic or glass container and store until needed.

USE: Start with 1 teaspoon dry mix to: $1/_2$ cup of olive oil, $1/_4$ cup vinegar and 1 tablespoon lemon juice. Adjust to your taste.

YIELD: 3 tablespoons mix.

NUTRITIONAL FACTS:

Serving Size: 1 Tsp	Total Fat: 2.5 g	Sodium: 230 mg	Sugar: 0 g
Calories Per Serving: 25	Sat Fat: 0 g	Total Carbs: 0 g	Protein: 0 g
Fat Calories: 20	Cholest: 0 mg	Fiber: 0 g	

SEAFOOD DRY MIX

INGREDIENTS:	$1/4$	CUP SALT
	3	TABLESPOONS WHOLE MUSTARD SEED
	2	TABLESPOONS WHOLE BLACK PEPPERCORNS
	1	TABLESPOON CRUSHED RED PEPPER
	6	BAY LEAVES
	2	TEASPOONS CELERY SEEDS
	2	TEASPOONS CORIANDER SEEDS
	2	TEASPOONS GROUND GINGER
	1	TEASPOON GROUND MACE
	1	TEASPOON DRY LEMON PEEL

METHOD: Place all the ingredients into a blender. Run at grind speed until the mixture is evenly ground. Store in an air tight container.

USE ON: Add a tablespoon of seasoning to your water when cooking shrimp and other shellfish.

YIELD: $3/4$ cup mix.

NUTRITIONAL FACTS:

Serving Size: 1 T	Total Fat: 0 g	Sodium: 35 mg	Sugar: 0 g
Calories Per Serving: 0	Sat Fat: 0 g	Total Carbs: 0 g	Protein: 0 g
Fat Calories: 0	Cholest: 0 mg	Fiber: 0 g	

WORCESTERSHIRE SAUCE

Unless you use a lot of this sauce, it's probably not worth the effort. But I've included it to give you the option of making your own

INGREDIENTS:

2	CUPS DISTILLED WHITE VINEGAR
$1/_2$	CUP MOLASSES
$1/_3$	CUP LEMON JUICE
	CHEESE CLOTH
1	ONION, COARSELY CHOPPED
3	TABLESPOONS OF WHOLE MUSTARD SEED
$1/_2$	TEASPOON CRUSHED RED PEPPER
2	GARLIC CLOVES, HALVED
12	WHOLE BLACK PEPPERCORNS
1	TEASPOON SIZED PIECE OF FRESH GINGER ROOT
1	ROLL OF CINNAMON BARK, BROKEN IN HALF
12	WHOLE CLOVES
$1/_2$	TEASPOON CARDAMOM SEED
3	TABLESPOONS SALT
$1/_2$	TEASPOON CURRY POWDER
1	TEASPOON ANCHOVY PASTE OR 1 MASHED FILLET
$1/_2$	CUP WATER
$1/_2$	CUP SUGAR

METHOD:

1. Place the vinegar, molasses and lemon juice into a sauce pan and bring the mixture to a boil.

2. In the meantime, place the second set of ingredients into a square of double thickness cheese cloth and tie it securely. When the liquids come to a boil, place the spice bag into the pan along with the salt,

anchovy, curry powder and water. Return the liquid to a boil. Reduce the heat to simmer and partially cover the pan. Cook for 1 hour.

3.   Near the end of the hour, caramelize the sugar by melting it in a stainless steel pan. Stirring constantly, cook the sugar until it turns dark amber in color. Remove the caramelized sugar from the heat and very slowly blend in about a cup of liquid from the spice mixture.

4.   When you have a thorough blending, empty the remaining caramelized mixture into the pan containing your spices and bring it to a boil. Remove from the heat and cool to room temperature. Transfer the contents to a bowl or jar, cover and refrigerate for 2 weeks. Shake the mixture occasionally. Discard the spice bag and strain the sauce.

Use On: Steaks, hamburgers or as recipes call for worcestershire.

Yield: 1 $\frac{1}{2}$ cups.

NUTRITIONAL FACTS:			
Serving Size: 1 Tsp	Total Fat: 0 g	Sodium: 90 mg	Sugar: 1 g
Calories Per Serving: 0	Sat Fat: 0 g	Total Carbs: 1 g	Protein: 0 g
Fat Calories: 0	Cholest: 0 mg	Fiber: 0 g	

NEARLY TABASCO SAUCE

Once, while in Louisiana I visited Avery Island, the home of Tabasco Sauce. I don't remember much about it, and it has absolutely nothing to do with this home made version of Tabasco Sauce. I just thought you'd like to know that I do get out of the kitchen once in a while.

INGREDIENTS:	1	OUNCE OF ANY DRIED HOT RED PEPPER
	1 ¹/₂	TEASPOONS SALT
	1	CUP DISTILLED WHITE VINEGAR
		SEVERAL DROPS OF RED FOOD COLORING

METHOD: Crush or grind the pepper. Transfer it to a sauce pan and add the salt and vinegar. Bring the mixture to a boil and remove it from the heat. Cool and add red food coloring. Pour it into a small container and store for one week. Strain and use.

SUGGESTION: Grind the pepper and salt in a blender, or in the sauce pan after heating, with a hand held blender/processor.

USE ON: As a table sauce. Add it to eggs or other sauces or as your recipes suggest.

YIELD: 1 cup.

NUTRITIONAL FACTS:

Serving Size: 1/4 Tsp	Total Fat: 0 g	Sodium: 15 mg	Sugar: 0 g
Calories Per Serving: 0	Sat Fat: 0 g	Total Carbs: 0 g	Protein: 0 g
Fat Calories: 0	Cholest: 0 mg	Fiber: 0 g	

Nearly Rice-A-Roni

Rice-a-Roni, the well known San Francisco seasoned rice mix is a product of the Golden Grain Company. I believe the original Rice-a-Roni was its' creators attempt to package the taste of at least one of Milan's famous risottos. What we have here is neither. But from a taste standpoint, what we have here ain't bad!

INGREDIENTS:		
	2	TEASPOONS SALT
	2	TEASPOONS DRY MUSTARD
	1 $^1/_2$	TEASPOONS DRY PARSLEY
	1	TEASPOON DRIED BASIL LEAF
	1	TEASPOON WHITE PEPPER
	$^3/_4$	TEASPOON GROUND GINGER
	$^1/_2$	TEASPOON GROUND BLACK PEPPER
	$^1/_2$	TEASPOON GRANULATED GARLIC (NOT POWDER)
	$^1/_2$	TEASPOON ONION POWDER

METHOD: Thoroughly blend all the ingredients.

USE ON THIS RECIPE:

	3	TABLESPOON OLIVE OIL
	1	CUP RICE
	$^1/_2$	CUP FILINI PASTA, OR
	1	CUP BROKEN VERMICELLI OR SPAGHETTINI
	3	CUPS WATER OR CHICKEN BROTH
	2	TABLESPOONS ABOVE MIX

Heat the oil, saute the rice and pasta until brown. Add the liquid and the mix. Cover and simmer for 20 minutes.

YIELD: 3 $^1/_2$ tablespoons mix.

NUTRITIONAL FACTS:			
Serving Size: 2 T	Total Fat: 1 g	Sodium: 5820 mg	Sugar: 0 g
Calories Per Serving: 50	Sat Fat: 0 g	Total Carbs: 9 g	Protein: 3 g
Fat Calories: 10	Cholest: 0 mg	Fiber: 2 g	

JAMACIAN JERK SAUCE

If you like "hot", this recipe will deliver. You may never be able to taste whatever it is you're eating with this sauce on it, but what-the-hey, The Fraternal Order of Fire Eaters will love you for your daring-do!

INGREDIENTS:	8	JALAPENO PEPPERS, MINCED (FRESH OR CANNED)
	1	BUNCH GREEN ONIONS, CHOPPED
	12	CLOVES GARLIC, CHOPPED
	1	TABLESPOON CAYENNE
	3	TABLESPOONS BLACK PEPPER
	1	TABLESPOON WHITE PEPPER
	1	TABLESPOON CELERY SALT
	1	TABLESPOON THYME
	3	TABLESPOONS CHOPPED FRESH BASIL, OR
	1	TABLESPOON DRY BASIL
	$1\,^{1}/_{2}$	TEASPOONS PAPRIKA
	$^{1}/_{2}$	CUP WORCESTERSHIRE
	$^{1}/_{2}$	CUP RED WINE VINEGAR
	$^{1}/_{4}$	CUP LOUISIANA STYLE HOT SAUCE

METHOD: Place all the ingredients into a sauce pan, partially cover and cook on medium heat for 20 minutes. Strain and use.

OPTION: For a sauce with more body, puree the jalapeno peppers and the green onion before cooking, then use without straining.

USE ON: Steaks, fish, eggs, a dash or two in a pot of beans.

YIELD: 2 cups.

NUTRITIONAL FACTS:			
Serving Size: 2 T	Total Fat: 0 g	Sodium: 400 mg	Sugar: 0 g
Calories Per Serving: 15	Sat Fat: 0 g	Total Carbs: 3 g	Protein: 1 g
Fat Calories: 0	Cholest: 0 mg	Fiber: 1 g	

JAMACIAN JERK DRY MIX

Not as hot as the preceding Jerk Sauce, but none the less, still quite warm.

INGREDIENTS:	1	TABLESPOON ONION POWDER
	1	TABLESPOON GARLIC POWDER
	1	TABLESPOON SUGAR
	2	TEASPOONS DRIED AND RUBBED THYME
	2	TEASPOONS SALT
	2	TEASPOONS GROUND ALLSPICE
	1/2	TEASPOON GROUND NUTMEG
	1/2	TEASPOON GROUND CINNAMON
	1	TEASPOON BLACK PEPPER
	1	TEASPOON GROUND WHITE PEPPER
	1	TEASPOON GROUND CAYENNE PEPPER

METHOD: Blend all the ingredients. Store any unused mix in a jar.

OPTION: You can make a paste of this mix by adding the following ingredients and then blenderize or process to liquefy. Store in the refrigerator.

	1/3	CUP WINE VINEGAR
	2	TABLESPOON LIGHT OLIVE OIL
	12	JALAPENO PEPPERS, SEEDED
	1	BUNCH CHOPPED GREEN ONIONS

USE ON: Rub on chicken or pork cuts prior to barbecuing, spit roasting or broiling.

YIELD: 1/3 cup.

NUTRITIONAL FACTS:

Serving Size: 1 Tsp	Total Fat: 0 g	Sodium: 460 mg	Sugar: 1 g
Calories Per Serving: 15	Sat Fat: 0 g	Total Carbs: 3 g	Protein: 0 g
Fat Calories: 0	Cholest: 0 mg	Fiber: 0 g	

"This page is blank by Design"

General Alphabetized Index

(   ) Indentifies a second name for a sauce

Additional copies of this book "The Encyclopedia of Sauces for Your Food" are available nationwide at book, gift and gourmet food stores. And selected wineries along the west coast.

Or, you may order directly from the publisher by phone, FAX or mail.

By phone, call toll free: 1-(888) 372-8237 with your Visa, Mastercard or

American Express Card.

By FAX, call 1-(916) 488-1863 with your Visa, Mastercard or American Express Card.

By mail, send your personal check, money order or credit card information to:

Marcus Kimberly Publishing, 2701 Watt Avenue, Sacramento, CA 95821